LAST NIGHT ON EARTH

Bill T. Jones, 1995 (RUVEN AFANADOR)

LAST NIGHT ON EARTH

◆

BILL T. JONES

with Peggy Gillespie

PANTHEON BOOKS
NEW YORK

Grateful acknowledgment is made to the following for permission to reprint previously published and unpublished material:
R. Justice Allen: "Somethin' to Think About" by R. Justice Allen. Reprinted by permission of R. Justice Allen. ▪ *Intellectual*
Properties Management: Excerpt from "I Have a Dream" by Martin Luther King, Jr., copyright © 1963 by Martin Luther
King, Jr., and The King Estate. Reprinted by permission of Intellectual Properties Management, Atlanta, Georgia, as Manager
for the King Estate. ▪ *Heidi Latsky:* Excerpt from monologue in *Last Supper at Uncle Tom's Cabin/The Promised Land* by Heidi
Latsky. Reprinted by permission of Heidi Latsky. ▪ *Hal Leonard Corporation:* Excerpt from "Long Road" by Bessie Smith,
copyright © 1931 (renewed), 1974 by Frank Music Corp. All rights reserved. Excerpt from "Shipwreck Blues" by Bessie
Smith, copyright © 1931 (renewed), 1974 by Frank Music Corp. All rights reserved. Excerpt from "Let the Good Times Roll,"
words and music by Sam Theard and Fleecie Moore, copyright © 1946 by Cherio Corp., copyright renewed Rytvoc, Inc.
All rights reserved. Reprinted by permission of Hal Leonard Corporation. ▪ *Rondor Music International, Inc.:* Excerpt from
"Going Back to Iuka" by Don Nix, copyright © 1971 by Irving Music, Inc. and Deerwood Music (BMI). All rights reserved.
International copyright secured. Reprinted by permission of Rondor Music International, Inc. ▪ *TRO-The Richmond*
Organization: Excerpt from "San Francisco Bay Blues," words and music by Jesse Fuller, TRO copyright © 1958 (renewed),
1963 (renewed) Hollis Music, Inc., New York, NY. Reprinted by permission of TRO-The Richmond Organization. ▪ *Warner*
Bros. Publications Inc.: Excerpt from "Touch Me," words and music by The Doors, copyright © 1968, 1969 by Doors Music Co.
Excerpt from "Pirate Jenny" by Kurt Weill, Bertolt Brecht, March Blitzstein (from: "Three Penny Opera"), copyright © 1928
by Universal Edition (renewed). All rights for U.S. and Canada administered by WB Music Corp. (ASCAP). All rights
reserved. Made in U.S.A. Reprinted by permission of Warner Bros. Publications Inc., Miami, FL 33014.

Library of Congress Cataloging-in-Publication Data
Jones, Bill T.
Last night on earth / Bill T. Jones with Peggy Gillespie.
p.   cm.
ISBN 0-679-43926-9
1. Jones, Bill T.   2. Choreographers—United States—Biography.
3. Dancers—United States—Biography.
I. Gillespie, Peggy.   II. Title.
GV1785.J55A3   1995
792.8´2´092—dc20
[B]   95–2962
CIP

BOOK DESIGN BY FEARN CUTLER

Manufactured in the United States of America
First Edition
2 4 6 8 9 7 5 3 1

The names and identifying characteristics of some individuals in this book
have been changed to protect their privacy and to address legal concerns.

THIS BOOK IS DEDICATED TO
BJORN AMELAN, MY HELPMATE

CONTENTS

FOREWORD

———•◆•———

I have named this book *Last Night on Earth* after a solo dance work of mine in which, through movement and text, I perform a number of voices that I have lived with all my life. Though this book relies on storytelling and strives to be a personal historical document, events are reported as I lived them and now, sometimes many years later, remember them. During my performance of *Last Night on Earth*, I contradict myself, remember the past, and project the future at will. In this "performance in text," I intend to do the same.

That this book came to be is still somewhat of a mystery to me. It certainly would not have happened without Peggy Gillespie. In the summer of 1992, she approached me about the possibility of writing an article on me, or including me in a book she was writing about creativity. In order to gain more insight, Peggy participated in a three-week dance residency workshop conducted by my company at Skidmore College. Evenings, we engaged in relaxed, tape-recorded conversations. From this experience, Peggy shaped an article for the *Boston Globe Magazine*.

When transcripts of our conversations reached the desk of editor Jenna Laslocky, she suggested that I author my own book. Recognizing our temperamental compatibility, Peggy and I continued the interview process to generate the book's substance. We reworked this spoken material—sometimes extensively, sometimes hardly at all—into text. I thank Peggy for her skillful interviewing and her sensitive and thoughtful manipulation of the transcripts and I acknowledge Jenna's enthusiasm and devotion to the material, her masterful blend of focused passion and tactful prodding.

I also thank Bjorn Amelan, my companion, who taught himself to type, adding yet another duty to his list of responsibilities—guide, scout, manager, critic, and friend. To Arthur Aviles, who has demonstrated greatness through love, thank you! To Jodi Krizer, Shawn Ruff, the Bill T. Jones/Arnie Zane Dance Company, Gregory Baine, Elizabeth Sobol and Gillian Newson of IMG Artists, and Bob Levine, I extend my heartfelt thanks. For their never-wavering love, I acknowledge Estella and Rhodessa Jones and Lois Welk. My gratitude to Edith and Lon Zane for becoming my family. And to Gretchen Bender, to Frank, Elaine, Maya, and Saskia Viner for providing continuous encouragement.

In addition to all these people, Peggy thanks her friend, photographer Gigi Kaeser, for working with her during the first years of this project—and for her encouragement and help throughout. Peggy appreciates Gregory Gillespie for his invaluable day-by-day support, making it possible for her to "tour" with me and my company around the world. And she thanks her daughter, Julianna, whose dancing spirit was a constant inspiration.

LAST NIGHT ON EARTH

AS IF MARCHING

We dance as if we are marching. As if we are stepping from mountaintop to mountaintop, afraid to fall yet not giving a good Goddamn if we do. We have been told that we are creatures full of song, creatures full of stories, and the stories are ancient ones. And they are brand-new—as new as what happened to me today and how I feel at this moment. When I open my arms, I am the most beautiful bird. A bird that is in fact a jet plane. This bird is capable of sorrow in the most lyric flight. This bird is capable of holding a knife and slashing your motherfucking throat.

This dance that I do, these people that I come from are one. This dance has been chastened by time and a certain benign neglect. Like a tree with its bark defiled, roots cramped, it grows. It grows in spite of the fact that the soil is poor. And has always been poor. In spite of the fact that the water is not there. And is unclean when it is. This tree, this dance, knows nothing other than to grow.

This dance calls out to us. It calls out, "Where have you been since the last time I saw you on the hill the day I was taken away? You called out to me then. I want to hear you call out to me again." It calls out to me, "Where are you? I want you. Come back to me. I want you to come back to me. Why won't you come back to me?"

This dance calls out. It calls out like the mother who knows she is never going to see her baby again. And her breasts hurt because they are full. It calls out like the father who wants to protect that mother. But he cannot protect that mother because there is a road to be built, and that road is more important than protecting that mother, that child.

It calls out, this dancing.

．　　　　．　　　　．

MAYBE IT WAS before we got a television. Maybe it was on one of those evenings when someone hadn't paid the bill and the electricity had been cut off. Or perhaps it was simply in a relaxed moment at the end of a long day, when my father was inclined to entertain.

He'd have on a flannel shirt, one of those polyester sports jackets he loved so well, and the fedora that he insisted upon wearing even indoors. He'd get comfortable, settle back at the kitchen table or on the couch in the living room, hike his pants up at the knee, and we would gravitate toward him. I don't remember him ever taking any of us up on his lap—there were so many children I don't think he could have done so without a squabble. He'd sip from his Ballantine or Iron City Ale and talk, sometimes about FDR and the Depression, sometimes about the Bible. Most often, though, he'd tell stories.

My father's tales never relied on the easy tag or the scary "boo." No, they unfolded with our being taken into his confidence. "Let me tell you somethin'," or "I remember a night . . ." And there was one that began, "You know that place where the two roads come together near the bridge."

He'd mention a place in Georgia where the trees had grown so thick as to make the night black as pitch. "No, you probably don't remember," he'd continue. "Well, this one night, my brother Slim and me been to a dance over in Valdosta but we left too late to catch the truck back home so we had to walk. And we saw this thing. At first I thought it was like a puddle, just somethin' black layin' on the ground. Then I thought it looked like a big old coon layin' there, then it looked like a dog, then it looked like a man. Maybe drunk or maybe dead. As we got closer to it, I saw it had a long tail. Now you know, we thought about goin' all the way back where we'd come from but it was real late and our daddy was sure gonna tear us up if we didn't get home. So we *had* to get past that thing. Boy, talk about scared! And, just as we was about to get by, this thing stood up on its hind legs. It was movin' like a man, and then it was movin' like a dog, and it was makin' sounds like I ain't never heard. I was as close as I is to you and I seen it had

4

yellow eyes. We started runnin', my brother and me. Slim was taller, but I was faster. I loved my brother, but right then I didn't care what happened to him. I ran so fast I thought my lungs was gonna bust. You all see them picture shows about them wolf men and stuff. Now you might not think there's nothin' to them, but I know they real. I seen one with my own eyes. I seen one."

He'd look at us, smile that smile, lean back in his chair, take a big sip off his beer, and leave us wondering. I'd be glad we didn't live down South where things that were part man and part animal lay in waiting by the sides of the road looking like puddles. And I felt strangely lucky to have a father who'd actually seen a wolf man—few other people in the world could claim the same. And, of course, his story made me wonder what would have happened had I been the one on that dark country road.

But if some of my father's stories were haunting, others were mythical and redeeming, and one of them seemed especially so. It was the one about the mermaid in the circus show down in Charleston. "This mermaid was a little bitty thing, not much bigger than"—and he'd point at one of the smaller kids—"but she looked like a woman. She had long, pretty, golden hair, and the bottom half of her didn't look like no fish, but then she didn't look like no normal woman neither. She was cryin'. It would have broke your heart to see that little thing sittin' up there in front of everybody just weepin'. She was cryin' and cryin', and it began to rain like nobody had never seen. Finally somebody figured that it was gonna stay rainin' until this little mermaid was let go back in the ocean. Then it began to flood and at last they let her go, and as soon as they put her into the ocean, it stopped rainin'. Just like that."

Somewhere among the roadside werewolves and carnival mermaids, in the swirling cloud of conjecture ("telling lies," as the family called it) and quiet-time entertainment lies my family's actual history. And most particularly, the origins of the Joneses in the United States.

My father told us that his father, Ike Jones, was an Indian and that he came from the Andes. He said that villages were being burned and people were running for their lives, and to save his sons, Ike's father—my great-grandfather—built a raft, strapped his boys to it, and set to sea. It took three weeks before they washed ashore in California. There's a gap in the story before it picks up again with Ike Jones, now a miraculously grown man taking an epic walk through the South.

"One afternoon he comes to a small village in Georgia and sees the prettiest little yellow-skinned girl. She looks like an Indian. 'What's your name?' he asks her.

" 'Flossie Jones,' she says and drops her eyes.

" 'Flossie Jones,' he says, 'I'm gonna marry you.'

"When her daddy comes out, Ike says, 'I want to marry this gal,' and her daddy says, 'Okay, since you both have the same last name, you can get married.' "

How did Ike get to Georgia if he had started in the Andes and landed in California? We kids struggled with that one for years. None of the grownups knew geography and we couldn't push them too hard either, so we spent a lot of time looking at geography books and maps. Eventually, we settled on the idea that Andes sounded a lot like Indies, that maybe the war my father spoke of was some sort of uprising or unrest, perhaps in Haiti or one of the other Caribbean islands, and that it wasn't in California but Florida that he came ashore with his brother and father.

I never met my grandfather Ike. I believe he had died before I was born. I wrote to my father's mother, my grandma Flossie, several times as a child but I don't remember ever receiving a reply and didn't meet her until I was twenty-five. I felt their absence in my life, and shortly before he died, I asked my father what had happened. He seemed surprised at the question, but after a pause, he looked me in the eyes and said, "It was 'cause of money." He searched my face for comprehension. There was none, so he continued. "When I was nineteen, I gave my mother my money to keep." Then, my father, who in his later years was fragile, prone to unpredictable shows of emotion, struggled in a way I had never seen before. His eyes became tearful and his voice broke as he told me that she'd given his money to his brother. And he said it again, "She gave away *my* money." Where this money came from we never knew for sure. My sister Rhodessa seems to think that it may have been a substantial sum gotten from both the government and liquor traffickers during Prohibition.

IT WAS MY FATHER who told the story of his courtship with my mother in the early forties in Valdosta, Georgia. Anna Edwards—or Big Mama, as we knew her—took in laundry, and Gus Jones used to take his shirts to her. Once he had met her daughter, the young Estella, he'd say, "Make sure you let Estella do my shirts."

My mother, Estella, was probably eighteen or so at the time, and no doubt she was quite impressed by Gus Jones. He was a star runner on the turpentine plantation, a man of stamina and strength who spent his days running along straight lines through acres of pine trees, slicing into their bark and tapping them. In a starched cowboy shirt and Stetson hat, with his thin mustache and coffee-colored skin, Gus Jones must have been a handsome man.

"Your mama was somethin' to look at back then," my father would say when he told us about dancing at the juke on Friday nights.

Big-boned, dark-skinned, Estella could stop the whole joint when she "stood back in her hocks." (To stand back in your hocks, plant your feet apart, squarely on the floor. Jam your fists right where your buttocks join into your back, thrust your hips forward and move them "real slow." Stare right into the eyes of the person you are dancing with.)

In these stories dance became a land

Gus and Estella Jones, circa 1948

to me—an exotic place where my parents were young and sexy. A time when their limbs were not weighed down with responsibility and they were there for each other. We were never allowed to see this place, this time, but we imagined it as they told us about the moves—about "Pickin'-the-Cherries," where your fingers plucked the open air as your hips and legs did other things, about "Throwin'-It-Out-the-Window," where you'd clap your hands and stick your ass way out toward your partner, then swing it back in, and about other moves, too: "Slippin'-on-the-Banana-Peel," "Buck'n-Wing," and, of course, the "Cakewalk."

"And your daddy was somethin', too. Back then they all called him 'Red,'" my mother would add in a sort of wistful voice. "Why, we'd come walkin' into the place, and he'd step on somebody's feet. Lord, don't let them say nothin' or else, him in his liquor, barely able to stand up, would yell at them, 'Cut your damn feet off and put 'em in your damn pocket if you don't want me steppin' on 'em.' He was bad. . . ."

Sometimes, after telling this story, Gus, perhaps a bit drunk, would grab Estella around the neck and start kissing her and moving against her. "Gus, leave me alone! Not in front of these children."

ESTELLA HAD TOLD this handsome man, Gus Jones, that her first husband had a terrible temper and there'd be hell to pay if he got out of jail, where he was doing time—many said for murder. "Tell me one thing," Gus replied. "Is he made out of metal or is he made out of meat? Because if he's made out of metal, then I can't do nothin' with him. But if he's made out of meat, I can. I got a gun and I got a knife and I ain't scared of no man who's made out of meat like me."

I guess that did it—that's when Estella recognized that Gus was the one who had come to save her, her mother, her sisters, and her four young kids— Harris, Janie May, Roosevelt, and Richard, who was called Boot because as a baby he always tasted his booties. It was decided that Estella would divorce Richard Evans and marry Gus. He was strong and beautiful and she was his. He could protect her.

Now Gus and Big Mama had their differences, but during those early times, he did all the right things. He knew exactly how to flirt with her to win her favor, to bring some fresh fish, or to listen patiently to her litany of ailments. The first thing he did after he married my mother was let her move Big Mama in with them. He even went so far as to take Big Mama along when he moved his new bride and her four children to Bunnell, Florida, where Iry, Azel, Flossie, Rhodessa, Vileana, and I were born. (I think my father came to regret this. In later years he took to calling Big Mama a hellion and remembering how she would wake up in the morning angry, fussing like my mother did, cursing people out, saying how disrespectful people were, calling Estella a no-good heifer, and throwing washtubs up against the side of the building.)

◆ ◆ ◆

IF MY FATHER'S STORIES were evening entertainment, my mother's and Big Mama's stories had their roots in slavery and sharecropping and were full of the weight and obligations that black women carry.

Big Mama's mother had been a healing woman, born a slave or born to slaves sometime in the 1860s. My mother recalls her grandma Matt Lee's skirts sweeping the ground as she—then a little girl known as "Priss" —scurried in front collecting cigarette and cigar butts off the ground that Matt Lee would crumble and smoke in her pipe. And Estella remembers the time the overseer took her mother, Big Mama, out to the barn, made her lean over a bale of hay and had my mother, her two sisters, and her brother, Uncle Cap'n, kneel down and watch as he whipped her with a huge leather strap for leaving the field to tend to her daughter's difficult labor. Uncle Cap'n, then eight years old, stood up to stop the man from hitting his mother. The blow broke his hand and he lived the rest of his days with a twisted finger.

There were many conflicting stories told about my mother's father, Tom Walden, and why he had disappeared. According to one, two white girls had said they'd seen him peeking through their bedroom window one night and he'd had to run before the mob caught up with him. But once, after a fight, my father told us kids that Estella's father and Big Mama used to fight all the time and he had just run off. "Estella came by her fussing nature naturally. Her mama drove her own husband away," he said. Then, in a more conspiratorial tone, he added, "I never told your mama this, but a friend of mine claims he saw her daddy, Tom Walden, goin' to the swamp with a Clorox bottle. He probably thought it was moonshine and was too drunk to tell the difference. Nobody ever saw that man again."

My mother used to say, "If I'd had my daddy, I would read better than I do now. White people ran my daddy away."

◆　　◆　　◆

ONE OF BIG MAMA's story-songs was, "Mama killed me, Daddy ate me, who's gonna hang me on the Christmas tree?":

There was a woman married to a angry man. They were raggedy poor. The woman was real scared of this man. When he left for work one morning, the angry man said to his wife, "When I come back, you better have somethin' for me to eat or I'm gonna beat you." When he came home, there was no food, so he beat his wife. This went on for many days. The poor woman was so scared she didn't know what to do. All day long she was alone in the house with her baby. All she could do was wring her hands, look up at the ceiling, and pray for the Lord to give her an answer.

Baby didn't eat all day. Baby began to cry, "Mama, I need somethin' to eat." And you know there is nothing so pitiful in the world as to hear your child hungry when you can't feed it. The little thing was crying out louder and louder, "Mama, I'm hungry."

Poor woman was about to start screaming and pulling her hair out. The little child was holding on to her, crying, "Mama, Mama, give me somethin' to eat."

All of a sudden the woman saw the big old steamer trunk in the corner and got real calm. She went over, opened it, and said, "Honey, come over here, you want somethin' to eat?"

The little thing started walking across the room and stopped. Mama seemed so strange, so quiet. She said, "Come on, sweetheart, come over here to Mama."

The little thing said, "What? What you want, Mama?"

Mama said, "I want you to look here in the trunk. I have some corn bread in there for you."

The little thing ran over to the trunk, looked in. "Where? Where, Mama?"

Mama stood there with one hand on the lid. "Stretch, honey. You got to look way in there."

Little thing was so hungry, it was up on its toes with its bare neck stretched way over in that trunk. Little thing said, "Mama, I don't see nothin'."

"You got to stretch a little bit more, baby. Just a little bit more."

And then, WHAM!!!! We would all jump because Big Mama had stomped on the floor or slapped the top of the table before continuing the story.

She slammed that trunk and cut off that child's head. She stripped the baby, skinned it, cooked it up real nice, just like you would a possum or a coon. She put gravy on it. That night when her husband came home, she served him a big plate of it. She saw him laughing for the first time in a long while. "Mmmm . . . ," he said. "This is good." He ate a big bellyful and said, "Where's Baby?"

"Never you mind," she said. "I sent it over to Mama."

They went to bed, he pulled her real close. Later that night when they were fast asleep, the house filled up with light. The husband shot straight up in bed. He heard a voice. He jumped out of the bed. The voice was coming out of the steamer trunk. A child's voice. It was crying and singing.

At this point Big Mama would pause, pull closer to us, and in a childlike voice sing, "Mama killed me, Daddy ate me, who's gonna hang me on the Christmas Tree?"

We understood men beating women. We understood what it was like to only have corn bread in the house until Mama provided something else. We'd seen wildness in our mother in moments when the responsibilities of motherhood were almost more than she could bear. This story-song tapped the whole reservoir of doubts and concerns we had about the contract between parents and children.

But it also reassured us. We knew Gus had been a hobo in his youth. We knew that there had been a time when one of my older brothers had thrown his arms around my father's leg and been dragged down the street trying to keep him from leaving us. Sometimes we felt that this time with my mother and with us kids was just one extended stay—especially when he sat on the porch tapping his foot and staring off into the distance, remembering how he had jumped trains, had been in this place and that. But we also knew he would never beat us—never raise his hand against my mother. And while Estella's anger, meanness, and fear were apparent, we also felt we belonged to her, that we were part of her. We knew that she would never throw us away.

◆   ◆   ◆

ONE NIGHT when I was very small, we kids were supposed to have been asleep but were raising hell instead. Our cramped sleeping quarters, filled with screeching laughter, were a tangle of bedsheets, yellowing flannel night-clothes, freshly bathed naked buttocks, arms and skinny legs catapulting from bed to bed. The air was filled with feathers from a mangled pillow. Without warning, our mother exploded into our midst like a storm trooper. She was everywhere at once, first going after the older kids, who should have known better, and giving me, who was too young to have really participated, ample time to panic. I was out of the house and down the road in no time.

I remember it now as if from a distance. I see a little black boy in a white nightshirt running through the dark and a big woman in a white dress running after him. I was heading straight down the road, straight for the light coming from the juke joint. My mother caught me. Of course. She was much younger and lighter at that time. I can't remember what happened then, but the next day, I showed her the scab that I had gotten on my knee when I fell. She looked past me and in an offhanded way said, "You got that 'cause you ran from me. Don't you ever run from your mama. I ain't no bear."

◆   ◆   ◆

GUS USED TO cry out in his sleep, frightened, childlike, as if trapped and battling some imaginary assailant. My mother would tell us, "Oh, that's just the people he killed." Those dreams of his always frightened me, made me feel helpless and sad.

My father shot Estella's brother-in-law, Pat. There had been fighting between Pat and my mother's sister, and she would flee to my parents' cabin whenever it got especially bad. One day, Pat came after her and Gus said to him, "Don't you never set foot in this house again because if I see you here, I'm gonna have to kill you."

Returning home from work a few days later, my father found Estella, her sister, and the children running around the yard screaming because Pat was there. Gus got his shotgun. Very calmly he walked out onto the porch. Pat was standing in the yard and Gus blew him in half. At least that's how the story goes.

My father said he felt sorry the minute he did it. He went back into the house, put down the gun, and took himself to the police station, where he confessed what he had done to the white police. But "Gus Jones was a good boy. He'd never caused nobody trouble before and that Pat was a drunk and a troublemaker." My father may have spent the night in jail, but the next day the sheriff probably said, "Oh, go on home, Gus. Don't worry about it, we'll take care of everything." No trial, no lawyers, no courtroom, no parole. Just "colored" business.

In my mind, my father could never be a murderer. If he had killed Pat, it was a reasonable, necessary act done with disinterest. In his stories of chain gangs, crap shoots, and showdowns, Gus Jones was like John Wayne or Wyatt Earp, but he didn't particularly like blood by the time I knew him. "Boy, you may not believe it, but when I was young I could cut a man's head off and then step on his chest to make the blood squirt out, and now it hurts me to see two dogs fight," he once told me. Nonetheless I'd seen him "move like a ghost," as my brother said, into a proximity with some young hothead who was up in my mother's face insulting her, threatening harm, and floor him elegantly with a piece of iron.

At the migrant camps where we lived, Gus was the law. If he couldn't handle a Friday night brawl between two drunken "bulls," the state trooper or Shorty, the town cop, would have to be called in, and nobody wanted those white men around.

STORIES, STEPS, AND STOMPS

— ◆ —

In 1955, there were only black people. In 1955, there were only black women with hair like gossamer, who sprinkled themselves with cheap perfume, "Evening in Paris," and were seduced, had babies, and were beaten by their men. In 1955, there were little boys who were wondering what to do with their penises. In 1955, there were little boys peeking through knotholes trying to see what grown-ups do. And in this world there were only black people with callused hands, working people who didn't speak in complete sentences, who would just as soon slice each other with knives as kiss.

In 1955, we were taking a break from traveling. It was a beautiful afternoon to rest. The big people, tired and hungry, had gotten out of the cars and walked over to the water pump. I was arguing with my sister and slapped her. My father rarely hit his children but neither would he tolerate wanton aggression. He snatched me, pulled down my pants, and tanned me good. The abruptness and severity of his movements left me gasping with humiliation, anger, and pain. He tossed me back into the backseat, not having to say "Sit there," while the other kids tumbled out to play in the gravel around the well-worn tires of the station wagon.

You know how it is when you are a child and you cry from such a deep place. You cry and you cannot find your breath. When the tears finally let up, I stayed in the car, sulking.

Coming out of my petulance, I peeked out of the car window, I saw all of the big people coming back to the caravan. I saw them like gods and goddesses. Like hillsides. Like Mount Everest. The sun was setting behind them on this day in 1955. The sun shone in the space between my mother and father's heads and I became happy. So happy that I tumbled out to join the other children in the dirt and started to dance.

In 1955, the world was nothing but black shadows against the setting sun.

IN THE LATE FORTIES and early fifties, harvesting fruit and vegetables along the East Coast was stable work, and there were many families who went on the season each year. In 1948, four years before I was born, my father became a contractor for migrant workers. He got backing of some sort—I don't know where—and bought a car and a twelve-wheeler truck with a flatbed that served as a makeshift bus for transporting workers on the road north and for hauling potatoes once there. Later, when the business picked up, he bought a secondhand Greyhound bus that was always breaking down, a pickup, and a station wagon.

In the early summer, my family and the workers and their families would hook up in a caravan and head north. The young men roughed the ride in the trucks while the rest of us rode in cars or on the bus. My parents sat up front in the station wagon. We kids were squeezed in the backseat. We never stopped at restaurants—we couldn't afford them. Instead, my mother opened cans of pork and beans, spread their contents on Wonder bread, and passed the sandwiches back to us. If we were good, she would give us a taste of the canned, unshelled peanuts in salt water that she and my father ate.

After countless hours, days, weeks of being on the road, we'd pull into Bellanger's Camp in the small town of Wayland in upstate New York and settle into a converted tractor barn for the late-summer and fall months. I remember standing outside this tractor barn one morning when I was four, perhaps five. I could feel the heat reflected off the cinder block wall. And then I "saw" myself standing there. I watched a car go by. A blond white woman wearing glasses was driving. Her pale green dress was caught in the door. In that moment, I understood that this was my life at its beginning— that I was here, now, in something that had been going on for a long time, and that would continue after me. Something about the woman, the car, the

(from the left) Steve, Azel, Rhodessa, Bill, Gus, Flossie, Carolyn (behind Flossie), Vileana, and cousin Robinelle

sun, the early morning, and me out there alone made me realize, "I am here now. I am here just for a while now."

◆   ◆   ◆

AFTER SEVEN YEARS contracting for his migrant crew, my father decided to settle up North—"to become a Black Yankee," as he liked to say. (There may not have been all that much of a choice about leaving Florida, anyway. There had been some sort of trouble—maybe something involving one of my older brothers. I seem to remember a tumultuous atmosphere not untainted with fear as my parents prepared us to leave town overnight.)

The year-round opportunities for field work up North were rich. Strawberries in June. Beans, peaches, blueberries, and cherries in the summer. Grapes and the very lucrative potato crop in the late summer and early fall. Indoor work grating potatoes in the winter. Tying grapes in the early spring. And we'd be free of Jim Crow.

The first place we settled was in the converted tractor barn at Bellanger's Camp. I still remember the barn as I experienced it as a child. It seemed huge—an improvement over some of the places we'd lived in, among them an old abandoned A-frame house in nearby Naples, where a brown bear had once interrupted our sleep.

At Bellanger's, there was a vast common room with a kitchen area, a makeshift counter along one side, tables and the jukebox along the other. Off this room, there was a narrow hall that separated the men's living area—the "bull pen"—from the large room and few smaller ones where my family lived. Gus had told Estella that if he was going to keep men coming to work, he had to have some women around. These women lived in rooms close to ours so my parents could protect them. Beyond their rooms were the married people's quarters.

The walls along this hallway were made of pine, and some of the knots had been poked out. It was through these knotholes that I was able to glimpse into the mysterious forbidden places—the bull pen and, once, into the married people's rooms.

I was quite young—little more than a toddler. It was a lazy Saturday morning, a beautiful, mellow sun was pouring into the hallway. We kids had just finished our breakfast and were about to embark on whatever diversions we could find when one of the older kids—I suspect it was one of the boys—came slyly skipping into the dining area and whispered something to one of my sisters. Her eyes stretched wide, she covered her mouth with her hand and let out a provocative "Oh, Woooo-wee. You nasty! . . . Where they at?" Suddenly everybody understood and rushed en masse down the hall, crouching, tiptoeing, running, tumbling, giggling—all while I, one of the youngest, did my best to divine what was going on. I'm sure, because there was only one knothole, everyone had to jockey for an opportunity to peek, and by the time I, last in the pecking order, reached it, the others had lost interest and were sidling down the long hall and out into the midmorning sun. Alone, I looked in on an abstract landscape of blankets and sheets. A man, fully clothed in a khaki work uniform, lay next to a sleeping woman.

I LOVED the orchards. Peaches. Cherries. Plums. They offered a world where an eight-year-old boy, on his way to find a discreet spot to pee, could meet enchantment imagining fairy godmothers, wood spirits, and gnomes. There were no demons, no dark things in the orchards.

Each field we worked had its own character, its own laws, perils, or charms. The vineyards were often located near Keuka and Canandaigua lakes. They were pleasurable, even romantic, with cool breezes blowing off the water and lush green trellises offering succulent fruit. In the hottest part of the summer, the raspberry patches were especially cruel, as the blistering, windless air drew moisture from scorched shoulders and foreheads, and singed the scrubby, treacherously prickled bushes. But the potato fields, enormous expanses of tilled earth and lush low vegetation, were where we spent most of our time from August to late October.

To prepare the fields for harvest, a man on a tractor would dig up the potatoes, after spraying what must have been defoliant. Then we children would go through, clearing away the fallen leaves and stalks, readying the rows for the grown folks, who would follow, gathering the potatoes.

Having cleared away the dead vegetation, our next responsibility was to gather as many burlap bags as we could carry from the big pile that the farmer had dumped in the middle of the field, and bring them to our parents and the other workers. Estella would send us ahead to save her the best row—the longest one, which would fill the most bags.

My mother, in her old calico print dress, bandanna, baggy men's jeans, and a pair of slides (old shoes with their backs broken down), was always accompanied by a child—in her belly, at her breast, or playing at her feet. When pregnant, she'd walk the rows with a pad in her hand, keeping track of how many bags each picker had filled. At other times, she'd pick potatoes while her newest baby, whichever one of us it was, lay in a cardboard box under a tree way down at the end of the field, sucking on a "sugar tit" (lard and sugar wrapped in cotton), until feeding time came.

Husbands and wives or teams of two men or two women would often start at opposite ends of rows half a mile long, and work toward meeting each other. There were rocks hidden in the dirt and people developed their own systems for dealing with them. Some fashioned elaborate knee pads from burlap bags. Some kept the bags under their legs like pillows, sliding them along just ahead of them. Others stood and bent over at the waist, but their backs suffered instead of their knees. My mother, one haunch to the ground and a bushel basket between her legs, moved quickly down her rows, separating potatoes from rocks, putting the potatoes in her basket, and, in one smooth unbroken gesture, picking up the basket, placing it in front of her, and swinging her body forward. Two bushel baskets filled a bag.

There were laws in the North to prohibit children from working the fields, so someone was always on the lookout for the "Labor Man's" black car. They'd call out and we would run to the end of the field, sit beneath the trees, and pretend to just be hanging out.

Being the son of Estella Jones, a woman who always finished her row first, who always had more bags filled than anyone else, I'm still ashamed to admit how I hated the work. But I could stand the potato fields if my sister Rhodessa was there. She would recite Sara Teasdale, tell me stories, talk about movies, philosophy, or architecture. From the field, the world seemed a great glowing place, and our imagined futures became more real than our present circumstances.

At lunchtime, while a few of the most diligent workers, like my mother, ate where they were, most left the field. Money would be collected. "I want some Royal Crown Cola," "I want an Orange Crush," "Bring me back a quarter pound of bologna, some bread, mustard, and pickles," and someone would make a run to the store. But after the break, work would begin again.

Loading the flatbed truck that took the potatoes to the warehouse was a rite one grew into, a privilege granted to the strongest young men, the magnificent young men. Their chests were bare and their heads wrapped in silk bandannas to protect their processed "dos" from the dust. One man would walk beside the truck as it was carefully and very slowly maneuvered between the rows. This man sang and told stories while, with a mechanical gesture, he heaved one-hundred-pound bags of potatoes to the man on the flatbed, who piled the bags higher and higher. The slicker the team, the higher they piled the bags without their spilling back to the ground—a terrible, embarrassing mishap that caused all the workers in the field to stop their work and waste precious daylight working minutes rebagging.

After the potatoes were brought in, they were sorted. In the basement of the gigantic warehouse, beneath utility lights strung from beam to beam, black men with scarves wrapped around their faces to protect them from the dust and the stench of rot went through mounds and mounds of stinking spuds. The better ones were resacked and stacked up to be sold. The rotten ones were discarded.

You were paid ten or fifteen cents for a full bag of potatoes. Maybe you picked fifty bags on Wednesday, sixty on Thursday, and, because you weren't feeling too well, only twenty-five on Friday. Twenty-six dollars a week in pay. As contractors, my parents provided the workers with room but not board. All comestibles were deducted from the wages. And with three sausage sandwiches for supper at twenty-five cents each and cheap wine at a dollar a bottle, this added up. These expenses would all be accounted for on a slip of paper written in the barely legible handwriting of my mother or the prim pen of my oldest brother, Harris, our unofficial bookkeeper.

"I don't remember havin' this bottle of wine," someone would say.

"Well, you did," my mother would answer. "You was too drunk to remember." And the arguing would commence.

◆ ◆ ◆

(from left) Flossie, Steve, Vileana holding baby Alleen (Louise's daughter), Gus, Elizabeth, Rhodessa, and Bill

IN THE CROWDED dormitories full of workers and in the rock-and-broken-glass-strewn tractor yard, we children played our games. One of our favorites was "Aunt Liza's Dead." Like all games in those days, it had rules that were divined, passed on from player to player, generation to generation.

Through some diplomatic process essential to this play of control and daring—the pulling of straws or flipping of coins—we selected our first "it." Perhaps Flossie. Flossie, the oldest girl of my parents' marriage. Flossie, the "pretty one" with the lovely soprano voice who was always the lady, even in her torn and faded dress.

The circle gathered around her included Rhodessa, honey-colored, the "yellow gal," so pale she actually had freckles like white folks. Rhodessa, who was always giving her things away, who was quick to cry but protective, too—especially protective of her younger brother, Billy. When she sat beside him, she'd take his small earlobe and, absentmindedly, tenderly mold it between her thumb and forefinger as if it were a bit of clay or a piece of chewing gum. And there was Vileana, or—as we wickedly called her—"Two Ton Tony." Plump little girl, one of the smartest, beset by demons who never allowed her to get enough of anything. Then there was Billy, nose always running, afraid of everything and embarrassed because people said he looked like his grandmother and his mother rather than like a man. Little Billy, able to cut a jig, to declare "that polecat done paid off" at the sight of a dead skunk—anything for a laugh. And Steve, bowlegged and skinny, with a strangely beautiful face—fragile, a little frightened, with one eyelid that drooped to give him a sleepy, slightly expectant expression. Last there was baby Gus, with his thumb always stuck in his mouth. A thumb that they had tried to tie behind his back. A thumb they had covered with hot pepper and vinegar. A thumb that defiantly found its way back into that sacred orifice.

"Aunt Liza's dead," Flossie would half-sing, half-chant.

"How'd she die?" we would challenge her back.

"Oh, she died like this," Flossie would sing and she would suddenly become Jayne Mansfield, offering her imagined, luscious breasts and big white-woman behind. We'd all go, "Wooooooo . . ." and repeat, "Oh, she died like this," in a chorus of little ragged Jayne Mansfields.

Then Flossie would call out again, "Aunt Liza's dead."

"How'd she die?"

"Oh, she died like this." And Flossie would become the Marilyn Monroe from the *Playboy* pinup calendar that we were not supposed to have seen but had. We would all sing, "Aunt Liza's dead. Oh, she died like this." We were all little make-believe Marilyn Monroes in a circle in the rock-and-broken-glass-strewn courtyard in front of the tractor barn at Bellanger's Camp.

After leading us through more and more outrageous contortions of our bodies and vocal antics of increasing complexity and absurdity, Flossie would say, "Aunt Liza's living."

We'd say—and we just loved this part—"Where's she at?" For, at this moment, we metamorphosed into Bessie Smith, Ruth Brown, or some big-voiced bluesy, barrelhouse singer—the kind we had no business even knowing about, given that Mama was a fervently practicing Christian.

"Aunt Liza's living."

"Where's she at?"

"She's gonna move to the country."

"She's gonna move out of town."

We pointed over our shoulders in a knowing, worldly way to show where "out of town" was located. We'd then thrust out our hips and sing with all the lasciviousness we could muster, "She's gonna shake that shimmy 'til the sun goes down," each word emphasized with a single swing of the hips before we went for broke, shaking and rolling until we'd collapse to the ground, laughing and congratulating ourselves. Then another "it" would be chosen and the dance would recommence.

We knew we had to be careful, though, because if you went too far, there would be an "Ooooh . . . I'm gonna tell Mama—you're so nasty." You would beg not to be told on because of the interrogation that would surely follow. "Where you learn that?" And we did know some things. We had experimented with each other's bodies, "mooched" and rubbed up against each other, but beyond this, we really had no idea what "doing it" was.

◆   ◆   ◆

My mother's hands are indisputably feminine. I can see the shadow of them in my own. Their veins coarse beneath the skin, their color that of the earth she was so comfortable handling, that of a road somewhere in Senegal. In those hands that for years I knew so intimately, those hands that knew how to pat dry and calm a colicky baby, whip a sprig of okra to make it grow, twist a young girl's wild tresses into orderly plaits, in those hands I found absolute care, absolute acceptance.

On one hand—I think her left—my mother wore a silver ring. At that time, in that place, jewelry was used in very subtle ways. Yes, sometimes someone would flash a smile and you would see an outrageous gold-covered tooth, so perfect for the exquisite blackness of their smiles and their frowns, so perfect for their laughing faces reflected in the jukebox light.

But my mother's left hand was the possessor of the most beautiful silver ring. This ring was one of the wonders of the world in our house. On it was engraved the entire Lord's Prayer. *Our Father who art in Heaven, Hallowed be Thy Name. Thy Kingdom come, Thy will be done, on earth as it is in Heaven. Give us this day our daily bread. And forgive us our trespasses as we forgive those who trespass against us. And lead us not into temptation but deliver us from evil. For Thine is the kingdom, the power, and the glory forever. Amen.*

WHEN I WAS ABOUT to enter kindergarten, my mother and father decided that it was important that I learn the ABC's. They bought me a new little school desk and I quaked with the awareness that, of so many of us kids, they would choose to give me this perfect new object—a smooth single unit, a small wooden chair and a desktop with block and script letters of the alphabet running across it. I could lift the desktop to find crayons, pencils, and maybe even a little chalkboard.

It was delicious to have my mother to myself, beside me, over me, sitting in her adult chair. *A, B, C.* It was easy. *D, E, F.* That was a little more difficult. But altogether, *ABCDEFG*, it could almost be sung. But then it became hard—*H, I, J*—*Jones. K, J, K.*

WHACK!

I hadn't even seen the strap, but it was there. *ABCDEFGH* . . . whack! *ABCDE* . . . *F* . . . whack! *ABCD* . . . *ABCDE*—whack! "How you gonna amount to anythin' in the world if I don't beat it into you? You gonna need an education and it's my place to see that you get one." Whack! *ABCDEFG* . . . whack! "You ain't no fool."

ABCDEFGHIJ—*Jones. That's me. ABCDEFGHI.* It was endless—this lesson. Somehow we made it through all twenty-six letters, then Estella, obviously exhausted, left the room. I sat there stunned, staring at the perfect desk, and I tried to do the ABC's on my own. I don't think I got much further than *F* or *G*. We never picked up with this lesson again.

IT HAD TO HAPPEN. I'd seen the older ones go through it and now it was going to happen to me. My first day of school. I'd hardly ever been up so close to white people before and now I was riding on a school bus with fifty of them.

They looked different. Little Terry O'Donnell had hair that was as blond and shiny as that spun fiberglass angel hair we decorated the Christmas tree with. No one blushed where I came from but these little people, when they were excited, tired, or sad, turned red around the ears and nose. They smelled different, too—had a kind of milky scent on their breath. And they were all soft. Even at age five, my own body seemed hard next to Terry's. But these bodies didn't shock me.

I'd seen white people before. Mr. Bellanger, for one. A pale stocky man with glasses, he would pull into our yard, with its trucks and broken-down automobiles, jump out of his late-model pickup, and walk into the place as if he owned it—which he did. And Mrs. Buell, the school nurse, who had come to register me. She had a huge bosom and a sort of Victorian air about her suggested by the lace collar that ran around her tremendous cleavage, her very, very sensible shoes and swollen ankles pouring over their tops. And the Frederick's of Hollywood catalogue, with its mysterious representations of women in spike heels, bikini lace panties, flip and beehive hairdos, gigantic pointed breasts, and vacantly inviting expressions. And, of course, the white people who appeared on the recently acquired television.

On my first day of school, the bus picked me up. I was trembling at having to leave my family for the first time. I met a pudgy blond boy who lived down the road. He said hello. I just stared at him. "What's the matter, cat got your tongue?" he asked.

"No."

"See what I got," he said and showed me a pale lavender handkerchief with little green leaves and embroidered flowers. Lacy. Strange for a boy. I liked it. "Look what I'm taking to the teacher," he boasted. "I've got a hanky for the teacher." It was delicate, these words coming from such a potato-like little boy. He became my friend, John.

I don't remember much about the rest of the day except the constant, gnawing fear that I would never see my home again. When recess came, they loaded us back on the bus with the same driver, and he headed out of town. I knew where my house was but he took a road unfamiliar to me. This was it. I knew it. This was the end. I'd never see Bellanger's Camp again. I stood at the front of the bus, gripped both metal handrails, and screamed. The next thing I remember I was in the backseat of the bus in the bus garage, being awakened by one of my brothers, maybe Harris or Iry, who'd come for me after working in the fields. I must have cried myself to sleep and the driver must have carried me to the backseat. I always thought how tender it was of the bus driver to gently carry me to the back of the bus and lay me on the seat, although looking back it doesn't really seem so.

Later that year a similar terror overtook me. There was one afternoon when no one was going to be home when the school bus dropped me off. It had all been discussed. I was to climb into the backseat of the Buick, where a blanket had been laid, and wait there. I was not, however, prepared for the reality of this careful plan. As the big yellow bus drove off, I looked at my home. The tractor barn was immense. The yard in front endless. I knew I was to go to the car and lie down, but I, jolted by the incomprehensible spectacle of this deserted place, went wild. Whimpering, I charged the front door as if by pure will everything would be as I remembered it had been that morning. Of course, it was not. Desperation turned to panic and panic to hysteria. I screamed and ran back outside. Jeered at by dust devils and a callous, objective sun, gasping, barely able to breathe, the screen door banging in the wind, I dashed to the waiting Buick, desperately pulled open its back door, and dove into the waiting blanket. Someone must later have come, awakened me, and carried me inside.

This feeling of being alone, knowing someone will be coming back but isn't there yet, needing them, still comes back to me in my dreams.

I came up with my own tactics for coping with school. I became furiously attached to my teacher, Mrs. Zimmer. I'd love to come near her, lean

27

against her under any pretext. I discovered early on that almost any offering—a crayon drawing, a dried leaf—would earn a smile and a "That's wonderful, Billy." Such encouragement was seldom heard at home. I must have gone ten times a day to show her what I had made, or point out my latest scrape or cut, and would then go back to my chair satisfied.

I felt safe when I took my hands, cupped them, and intertwined my fingers so as to make a small opening. I would peek between my thumbs and "zoom" around the room framing everybody's face as if with a movie camera. One day Mrs. Zimmer said, "We don't do that here." She said it nicely enough, but firmly. I stopped.

IT WAS TIME to go home. Vroom! Vroom! All of us five-year-olds were gathered together in a not so orderly line, observing our teacher's raised finger and sputtered "Ssh" as we waited our turn to go out to the buses. Dimple-cheeked, curly-haired Terry was standing in front of me. I was shoved snugly against his tiny corduroy-clad behind. Warmth came over me, starting in my chest, moving down my legs. At that moment I didn't want to be anywhere else but pressed up against him. When the door was opened, he made a sound like a jet plane and said, "Come on," giving me a smile as we ran out to board the bus.

Vroom! Vroom!

◆　　◆　　◆

ON EASTER, my parents usually took us to a church in Rochester. My mother, parched for the sound of a black preacher and a black organ player, hungry for the pageantry that only happens in black churches, would be excited in a way we could barely comprehend. We'd pile into the car, into the aura of her anticipation, but our excitement was restricted by the superstitions that governed any journey. We'd never turn around once we started a trip, because we'd call bad luck upon ourselves, so heaven forbid that any of us forget anything. Likewise, we were not to be too happy, because we'd come back crying.

At the church we were much impressed by the women, the "sisters of the church." They came in every shade of skin, every size of body, and they wore huge hats, outrageous hats. Their dresses presented amazing combinations of color, their accessories—the shape and style of the earrings, the gloves, the shoes—thought out to the most minute detail. The small girls, their hair braided so tightly as to make their eyes slant, in frothy pastel dresses, little fold-over socks with lacy trim, and black patent leather shoes, would run out of the church, and down the street into the early spring light.

Most of the time, though, our parents sent us to the white church over in Atlanta, about four miles away. My mother said she wasn't interested in white preachers, so Sunday mornings, we rose early, got dressed, and were dropped off.

There was an annual Christmas pageant at the church. One year, I was one of the Three Wise Men, and my teenage sisters, looking ever so glamorous in their Supremes-style wigs, sang "Elijah Rock." With no accompaniment but their fingers snapping to keep time, their youthful hips and shoulders swaying in a way that couldn't have been sanctified but was holy all the same, they sang. Flossie's voice would climb the scale, up, up, up, and just when you thought she couldn't go any higher, she'd loop before hitting that highest note, careening back to catch the downbeat with Rhodessa and Vileana.

Elijah Rock, shout, shout, shout,
Elijah Rock, coming up Lord,
Elijah Rock, shout, shout, shout,
Elijah Rock, coming up Lord.

People talked about them for weeks.

Sometimes we'd walk home after church. I'd start off feeling proud, walking down the road in my hand-me-down suit with its little fake bow tie, shirt too tight around the collar, turquoise jacket hiding the fact that my pants were too big. My schoolmates drove by and sheepishly stared out the back windows of their cars as their parents pretended not to see us. One Sunday, a bunch of young locals slowed up. "You niggers want a ride?" one of them called out to us. We knew who they were—I went to school with one of their younger brothers. Azel, the oldest one of us, just stared straight down the road and kept walking, so we copied him. No one spoke for minutes after they drove away.

◆　　◆　　◆

MY FATHER HAD a rapport with key white people. I remember hearing him say "Yes, sir"—noticing what it meant—when Mr. Bellanger drove up and jumped out of his truck. My father would move differently, drop his voice, seem somehow less definite in his gestures.

My mother dealt with white people too, but in another way. The rules were all different for black women. Estella wasn't like other women. She knew it. We all knew it. She broke the rules.

"Just because my face is black, don't mean I'm no fool," she'd say to the gas man when he came to collect on an unpaid bill. If there was trouble at school she'd put on her Sunday best—an enormous leopard print coat and a hat with a brim three feet in diameter—and go see the principal. She weighed well over two hundred pounds by this time, and her way of walking recalled a ship swaying side to side—she'd lurch down the halls of the school. There was a quality to my mother—and I think it's something I can summon too—which suggested barely controlled violence. It was as if she could go off at any moment. There, in the principal's office, the secretaries held their breath. Estella didn't hold back. She was not there to make peace but to find out exactly how the school was messing with her and her children. She was there to confront, to fight. Looking back, I imagine she may have been frightened—that's often what I am feeling when I behave in a similar way.

IMAGINE CLOTHESLINES cutting irregular angles to one another, catching the wind, swinging like a ship's riggings, and everywhere dresses, slips, work shirts, skirts, blouses, and enormous trousers billowing like so many obese men and women in the April wind. It was not laundry day. The ragman had come with his Goodwill store on wheels—huge bags of clothing smelling of mothballs, which he'd unpack and pin to the clotheslines around the yard. You could buy yourself a pair of work pants, a head scarf, or maybe a winter coat.

My parents liked the ragman. There was something about him that they respected—perhaps it was his sincerity and his effortless expression of equality with black folk. There was a moment, a lull in their conversation one day when the ragman looked past my mother and father and saw me standing there. He said, "That boy is going to be a preacher, isn't he?" My parents turned and looked over at me, flattered by his words. For them this prophecy explained my habit of sitting alone in a room—just sitting—something they regarded with no small suspicion.

Any form of distinction in my family was a precious thing. I took this man's words as a kind of challenge. In the world that was mine at the time, there were no black lawyers, no black doctors, no black teachers. But preachers—they were the thinkers, the philosophers, the artists. What the ragman said came as encouragement that I was allowed to be different.

◆　◆　◆

THERE WEREN'T MANY colored people around Wayland in the late fifties—at least not year-round. The Joneses, the Williamses, the Browns, and that was it. Little houses here, a small farm over there, and then—twenty miles away—the Crossroads, where a loose community of colored folk clustered around PeeWee's juke joint.

People would come home from the fields late on a Friday afternoon.

They'd be tired, their backs aching, their hands cut, but "Lord be Praised," it was the weekend. Friday night was theirs. A young single woman like my stepsister Midget would ask me to go to the pump and bring her some water so she might wash away the dust.

Then she might slip into her dress, maybe her "Carmen Jones." I loved watching her shimmy her ample hips and buttocks into this black mesh over taffeta dress with a flare of crinoline at the hem. Next she'd sprinkle the magic of glitter in her hair, line her lips with plum-colored lipstick, and brighten her cheeks with a dab of rouge. Drastic lines of eye pencil on the eyebrows and on each eyelid would complete her makeup. As she left, she'd inevitably stop at the door, rush back, open the cobalt blue bottle of "Evening in Paris," dab a bit behind each ear. Now she was ready. To my eyes, she floated out of the room.

The men fell into two categories. The slickest dudes sported a "process"—hair artificially straightened and blackened like patent leather. My brothers, wearing zoot suits, expensive two-toned leather shoes, silk handkerchiefs in their pockets, and gold key chains, had been slick dudes. But those days were behind them. Almost all the men at Bellanger's fell into the second category—cleaned-up field workers in freshly starched and ironed shirts opened at the throat and rolled up at the cuffs, pressed khaki pants, and beaten-up leather shoes that had been brightly polished—shoes that seemed to be waiting for the reflected light from the jukebox, waiting to be scuffed on the dance floor. Everybody felt fine, ready to go.

On Friday nights when we lived at Bellanger's Camp, these women and men would gather in the common room. My mother would cook up barbecue chicken and spare ribs, collard, turnip, and mustard greens, chitlins, black-eyed peas, trays of biscuits and corn bread, and serve it all up with iced tea, lemonade, maybe sugared water, and, of course, beer, wine, and whisky. People seemed to love sweet wines. Tocquay, port, dark port, white port. Everything was in jugs.

Estella usually sent us off to bed just when things were getting hot—when the sweating room began to jump with the jukebox's insistent pulsing in the people's thighs, hips, shoulders, hands. But I remember a particular night, when Vess's Mary had shown up. It looked as if someone had pounded her face with their fists, but her body was fantastic. My father said she was so black you could draw a white line on her with charcoal. She was standing in the carnival light of the jukebox, wearing a Frederick's of Hollywood hot-pink sequined dress. Her ass jutted out in the room, clearly for the benefit of a table of men watching. She caressed the machine nonchalantly, slipped in a quarter—for a dime you got one selection, for a quarter you got three—made her first pick, and in a detached way began to make love to the jukebox. The entire room was watching that huge pink-sequined behind undulating to the sounds of Bobby Blue Bland and B. B. King. She swiveled around and began to do "the Scratch." Placing her hands to her face, she moved her fingers, clawlike, ever so slowly down the contours of her fabulous body as if tormented, determined to shred the pink sequins and the flesh beneath them.

I was crouched down, peeking from the door of our family room, past the large silhouette of Estella, who stood just as captivated by the vision. I must have made an inadvertent sound or movement, just loud enough to snap her out of her revery. She spun around, grabbed my skinny shoulders through my flannel pajamas, turned me about swiftly, administering a staccato of whacks to my behind, and sent me back to bed.

But I had seen dancing.

MILLER ROAD

———— ◆ ————

I dream that I am back at Miller Road. I go there with my lover and I show him around the house. It is empty but not abandoned. We smell fire. Calmly, we walk through the rooms trying to find it. We climb the stairs to Azel's room.

Azel's room was always special. In a family where everything had to be shared, it was his own—given to him when Iry left for the military. It was here that I furtively rifled through Azel's papers and found the novel he was writing, and that I first saw pictures of naked women in the many magazines he kept stuffed under his bed. It was here that I found a copy of Das Kapital *and* Come Back Africa!. *And here, too, that Azel first explained to me and my younger brothers the meaning of words like clitoris, arousal, vagina.*

Next to Azel's room is the girls' room. It is the largest room upstairs, with the most windows and the most light. Poorly laid linoleum with golden specks covers the floor. This is where "Candy and the Sweets" rehearsed. This is where, when they would tolerate me, I had the privilege of listening to my sisters' fantasies, confessions, and exploits, their dreams about lovers real or imagined. This, too, is the room where the tears flowed as a fifteen-year-old girl's flat belly began to swell, telling a story that should not have been told until ten years later.

Across the landing is my parents' room. I see it in the late-afternoon light. The big bed made up of four mattresses stacked on top of one another is covered with a puce and sky blue chenille bedspread embroidered with two aloofly communicating peacocks whose heads converge in its sunken center. On the right-hand side of the bed is my mother's chamber pot, which I or a younger sibling would empty every morning. At this side of the bed, near the window, she used to kneel, fold her hands together, and bow her head in the least talked about, most assiduously observed ritual in the house.

The light changes in the room. This is where my father lived with my mother. Dressed only in his loose and ever-present long johns, he would move purposefully about, tending to his papers or some business with his guns. From this room, we heard our parents' voices rumbling like two troubled gods inside a mountain as they discussed things which would affect us all. This is the room where they struggled with disappointment—using their hands, heads, religion, and the supernatural. Peeking through the doorway, we could see them both in bed—or sometimes standing before their candles as they tried to change our luck.

On the back wall, opposite the window where my mother prayed, is another door, leading to a cramped, gabled attic room. It is here that Steve, Gus, and Billy—the three little boys—slept in a single bed, all secretly loving the familiarity of skinny bodies and rounded bellies. Billy slept here with Gus tucked securely under his arm. Gus slept with his small callussed thumb jammed in his puckering mouth. Steve, at the foot of the bed, was relegated to the contentiousness of Gus and Bill's legs. This is the room where little men were made, where we wet the bed, fought, and imagined the future. There was a pitch blackness here that smothered the breath when the lights were turned out. This room was destroyed in the great fire, and for the longest time after we rebuilt it, it smelled of burnt tar and wood.

It was from here that we heard Estella downstairs every morning banging the pots and pans about and protesting her life. And it was from this room that the first light of day would invite us out through the window onto the shed roof, wee-wees in hand, to relieve ourselves in what were to us huge fountains of urine cascading down from our tarred parapet to the shaggy weeds and debris below at the back corner of the house.

I have heard Maya Angelou disagree with the saying "You can never go home again." She says that most of us can never leave home, that home is a place we take with us—for better or worse—wherever we go. And so it is with Miller Road. It is in the language of dreams, in the dubious evidence of photographs and a fragment of memory whispered or guffawed at a family gathering. In the thirty years since I left it, I've seldom returned to Miller Road. I've had many other *homes. I've seen things born. I've held people in my arms as they've died. Yet Miller Road never leaves me.*

IN 1959, after ten years of building up the business, things were going so well for my father that he bought a house on Miller Road, five miles or so from Bellanger's Camp. One of the first wood frame houses in Steuben County, it had been built back in the 1880s and had fallen into disrepair, its once orange paint a peeling autumn shade of rust. It was a solitary, sad-looking house crowded in by trees. To furnish it, we bought, bartered for, and took an assortment of donated furniture. There were giant Victorian secretaries and sideboards, an authentic cherry Chippendale bookcase, enormous oak tables with lion claw legs, and ornate brass beds that we painted blue and pink. Hanging off a cherry cabinet, inadvertently ripping the molding and decorative details off, scratching our names into the surfaces of tables, we kids tore, broke, dented everything.

My father also bought my mother a car—a spanking new sky blue and white 1959 Ford Country Squire wagon. It was like something we'd see on television, and on the first afternoon we had to take our shoes off before we got into it.

I remember coming home to Miller Road after school one fall day and being surprised to find my father and a large group of helpers pulling down an old barn in order to build a cinder block dormitory for the workers. More surprising still was the fact that in a clearing he had already poured a cement foundation for what would be our new house—it was to be one of those modern homes like the ones we'd seen in *Life* magazine.

A year or so later the plans for the house were stymied. Family lore attributed this to the changing economics, or to a loan that fell through. After the weeds had already begun to grow through cracks in the foundation, Rhodessa and I would walk out onto this abandoned construction site and speak of the future and of architecture. Rhodessa talked to me about Frank Lloyd Wright and houses that came out of the earth, out of the hillside, or hung over falling water. I meanwhile conjured from the overgrown foundation a superhouse of the future—a house that was miles long and equipped with its own transportation system, a house big enough that my parents and my brothers and sisters, now immensely wealthy and successful, could all live together.

At night when the lights were shut off in the house on Miller Road, the woods surrounding it were haunted by wolf men and monsters. My brothers and I didn't dare drink at supper for fear of one of those horrifying nighttime journeys to the outhouse. In the dark I felt that I couldn't see, that I couldn't breathe. I dreaded what it hid. Sometimes in the quiet darkness, I would hear a sound, like bells, deafening, maddening. Later, I realized it was actually the sound of blood coursing through my veins.

That I was such an easily frightened child was understood in the family. "He's too sensitive." "A sissy boy." "Billy's afraid of snakes." I had nightmares. They remember having to come shake me free of those moments when they said, "Witches are riding him," times when I dreamt that I was screaming for help but all that passed my lips was a strangled shriek.

I'd be shuttled out of the room whenever those horror movies featuring enormous iguanas came on television. Somehow, though, I managed to see The Blob. It left me paralyzed and bewildered, truly horrified at the idea of a thing that could come from nowhere and by the end of the film be everywhere, sliding out of the shadows and into the sanctity of a doctor's office to eat people. But when I acted this saga out for my classmates, reduced the Blob to movement, I found something to love about it. As I hung on to chairs and tables and slurped about the classroom, the kids squealed with laughter and disbelief.

AT HOME my religious training came with the recitation of grace before meals and my mother's ritual prayers.

On Christmas Eve, we three youngest boys were sent to bed earlier than usual. We'd lie in our room listening for reindeer while downstairs, all night long, Estella and my sisters cooked and wrapped gifts. It always seemed to be just after we'd finally fallen asleep that Estella would waken us with a dark song:

Oh, one more time,
Oh, one more time,
Oh Lord, I'm glad to be in the number one more time.
Oh, one more time.

We'd be brought downstairs and find her already kneeling in her night-dress, moving as though in a trance. There was a Christmas tree—we'd already seen it, perhaps helped decorate it, but it had been further decorated during the night and now there were gifts beneath it. My mother would with a wordless gesture indicate that we were to kneel down in any nook, cranny, or chair, bow our heads, and listen to her. "Don't you even go near the tree until it's time."

"Lord, I reach my hands to Thee," she'd begin. "No other friend I know. If Thou should turn Thy face from me, Lord, where shall I go? Please Lord, please Cryin' Savior, remember this house this mornin', remember my children this mornin'. Give them the strength to grow up to be men and women. Remember my helpmate this mornin' and give him the strength because he needs You, Lord. Please Lord, please Cryin' Savior, remember the soldiers across the waters, remember the sick in the hospitals, Lord, please Cryin' Savior, I want You to come into this house this mornin'. I want You to touch everybody in this room this mornin'. I want You to touch this woman carryin' a child, my Lord. I want You to touch my daughter-in-law and teach her how to be a woman and not just a dress. I want You to teach my sons how to be men, how to walk upright, and take care of other women's daughters. Please Lord, please Cryin' Savior, I want You to walk in this house today and remove all evil. I want You to remove all distraction. I want You to remove all wickedness. I want You to strengthen my companion, because, You know, Lord, he needs it. I want You to strengthen me. Remember my mother, Lord, may I walk in her footsteps. Please Lord, please Cryin' Savior, when my bed has become like a public road, and my face has become like a lookin' glass, when others turn their faces from me, Lord, where should I go?"

By this time she'd be holding on to the couch, almost lifting it, and screaming. You didn't dare touch her. You didn't dare even go near her. She was crying and begging the Lord until she was spent. Then she would draw herself up and, in a hoarse whisper, say, "Okay, sister, hand out the gifts now," and one of the older girls would begin to divvy up the packages and bags to everyone gathered there.

THE RITUAL of my mother's bath organized our household. Which of us would draw the water? Which of us would stoke the fire in the woodstove to heat it? And which of us would carry the water to the basin in the bathroom?

Her soap was delicate. Ivory. So light, it floated on top of the water. I can imagine her washing beneath those pendulous breasts, all around the smooth mound of flesh that was her stomach and in between those thighs that held the mystery of mysteries. Remarkable that I have lived forty-two years and never glimpsed my mother's "pocket," as we called it as children.

Washing her feet was a privilege one graduated to and a responsibility for years. In the evenings, when we were sitting around after supper, or perhaps while she watched *What's My Line?* on television or picked her way through the Bible, her lips moving slowly as she sounded out the words, I would get a pan of warm water so that she could soak her feet. I would pat them dry, pick her toes, remove dried skin, clip her nails, place compresses over the corns, and shave her bunions.

She would become so relaxed that she'd almost forget that I was there and accept me into her intimate circle, along with my father, an older sister or brother—Janie Mae or Harris—or perhaps a visiting grown-up. Sitting there, I was allowed to hear things—whose children were hungry, what man couldn't trust his wife or what wife couldn't trust her husband, who was sleeping with a white woman or man, who had been a prostitute, who was pregnant, how Vess's Mary, jukebox goddess, met her end at the hands of a violent man.

Afterwards, I would wrap my arms around my mother's neck, feel those heavy breasts press against my skinny hard chest, and inhale her scent—part Ivory soap, part tobacco, part Vaseline, and part what I took to be her own secret smell.

There was the obligatory peck on the cheek, a kiss that confirmed our obeisance. At the end of her day, my mother didn't have the energy for affection and, as the fear of rejection was my blackest fear, I didn't dare let the kiss last too long before heading to bed.

"My mama understood me," my father used to explain. "When I was just a little boy runnin' round the house with the other chilluns, she'd take just one look at me and know what was wrong. She'd call me into the house, give me a teaspoonful of rum or whiskey—whatever there was—and send me back outdoors. I just come by it naturally."

Gus often drank while sitting in the living room telling stories, but there were times when he went to the bar in nearby Naples. Good-looking, easy at making toasts and telling jokes, he could entertain the whole place.

Mama, outraged by these occasions, would pack us into the car and head into town. "Your daddy's down there drinkin' up everythin' we got." This was never quite true—he always handed the paychecks to Estella to manage. "I got all these hungry chilluns and I know he's in that bar grinnin' in those white people's faces and messin' with those whores. I know they all talkin' 'bout me behind my back."

She'd careen into the small village of Naples, pull the station wagon full of tense children up somewhere near the bar in question but never directly in front of it, slam the door, and stride off. We all knew better than to run off anywhere. It wouldn't be long before we'd see them coming. She'd be shoving him ahead of her. He'd be obviously twisted, his hands jammed deep into the pockets of his trousers, his fedora askew. We would overhear their conversation.

"I shoulda listened to my mother. My mama told me you was no good. How'd I get myself messed up with you and all these damn kids?"

"Woman, I'm a man. It ain't none of your business what I want to do with my life."

"It is my damn business. As long as I got your damn little heifers and bastards to feed and dress, I ain't gonna have you drinkin' up all we got. Gus, give me that money you got. I know you got money in your pocket."

"I done give you everythin' I got."

"Why you got your hands jammed in your pockets, then? You hidin' somethin', ain't you? Ain't you?" At that moment, she would rip his pockets, sending whatever small change, keys, pocketknife, bottle opener were in there spilling onto the sidewalk.

This—not the fact that she had just interrupted a lighthearted revel between him and his friends, not that she had probably insulted and cursed everyone in the place and told them, "Kiss my black ass," and not that she had shoved him bodily out of the place—was the greatest humiliation, the greatest show of disrespect. Furious, he would get into the car and they would continue to fight as she drove us all back home.

IT WAS THE most beautiful Saturday morning. The sun's warmth was unexpected so early in February. And my mother, feeling particularly good, had decided to give each of us three little boys our individual baths herself, instead of letting one of the older girls do it—an unusual and cherished occurrence.

Her hands seemed very big, sure, and comforting as she bathed me between her knees in the tin tub. She was talking and laughing with my stepsister. In the glow of sunlight and soap bubbles, I didn't notice Vileana—Two Ton Tony—sidle up to Mama and, smiling, whisper something in her ear.

Nothing prepared me for the sharp crack of the wet washcloth striking my soapy back. The sunlight and warm water became a vortex of confusion. The only certainty was an iron grip and rage. This was the ritual whipping that marked each of our birthdays—the acknowledgment of another year added to our lives. We often begged her to give us our whippings the night before our birthdays so we needn't be shocked awake or otherwise surprised by them on the actual day of our births, but I had forgotten. It was a testament to my mother's power that even though I stood there trembling and naked, I had respect for her act. I understood this beating as a kind of elemental dispensation of justice, a way to help me grow. She was simply obliged to administer it as a responsibility of her station.

This woman, my mother, exists outside any philosophical realm that I might construct, outside any set of rules that I might adhere to. Like the sun, the moon, she *was*, and in some ways, she always will be. Going her own way, walking her own road, makes her exquisite and terrifying.

There were few days between the time I was born and the time I left home at eighteen that I didn't wake to the sound of her downstairs "fussing," banging pots and pans, complaining how inadequate we all were, disrespectful, lazy, and would never amount to anything, how if it wasn't for us kids she wouldn't be messed up with that man, Jones. This meanness was as accepted as the muddy roads in spring, as accepted as the water pump that was broken for over a year, as accepted as walking out in the snow with a pair of old socks on our hands because there were no mittens.

And as the road becomes a paradise of late May flowers, its once muddy surface yielding a dazzling collection of quartz crystals and smooth stones, she would smile, take her handkerchief, dab it on her tongue, and smudge the dirt off my face, grab me by the head, and pull me to her for a motherly examination or an affectionate embrace. She would laugh at a joke I made, beam with pride at something the rag merchant had said about me. In these moments, she was a blessing that graced our lives.

◆　　◆　　◆

WHITE KIDS. Fifties kids. They were our classmates and our friends. We learned to speak like them, to think like them, to share their values. I could—in fact, *had* to—go into their "white drag," although they could never come into mine.

We'd watch *Leave It to Beaver* and wonder. My mother wore men's trousers, a work dress over them, men's shoes, and a handkerchief tied around her head, and what was underneath her trousers, underneath her dress, we couldn't even begin to imagine. The older girls claimed that her stomach was swollen because the last baby just stayed inside her unborn. She herself chuckled, saying she was being punished because when she was young and skinny as a reed she used to laugh at fat women. Even today, I am not so far away from the touch, the feel of that big stomach.

Surely, Estella was not June Cleaver and I loved her as she was. And yet I also loved the politeness shared by white parents and children when they addressed one another. I loved those neat little bunk beds that my friends had at their houses. I loved the tray of cookies placed by their mothers on their well-organized desks while they did their homework. I loved the model cars, airplanes, and even the stamp collections. And I was not alone.

"Daddy's going to make a lot of money and we're going to have that 'light bread' every day and not those biscuits Mama makes," Rhodessa would say hopefully.

I envied my friends when they said so casually, "I went with Mom and Dad to the movies this weekend." Or when they went to restaurants with their parents. Casually. With us, no family outing was casual.

When I was fourteen, my friend Russ invited me to spend the night at his house. He lived with his parents and his sixteen-year-old sister, Cathy, in what seemed to me an extremely large and elegant house commanding several acres, including a pond that we skated on in the winter. My mother liked Russ, too—he was probably the first white friend ever allowed into our house. But when I asked my mother's permission to accept the invitation, she turned grave and in an unusual, almost resigned voice, she said, "Yeah, you can go. But listen here, boy. When you go to bed, lock your door. And don't you dare go walkin' 'round those people's house. There's a white girl there and before you know it that girl will be screamin' that you done messed with her. Now you almost a man and you gonna do what yo gonna do, but, son, if they put you in jail, I can't help you."

．　　　．　　　．

THE MIGRANTS continued to pass through Wayland long after we had settled there. By law their children were required to go to school, even if only for two months. But, as their grade levels were different, and it seemed they spoke another language, they were put in special classes.

I found these kids a source of concern, shame, and longing. They were very ragged. Their noses ran. Their shoes were ill-fitting and without laces. They spoke loudly. They ran down the halls. They fought with my friends, the kids I'd gone to school with since kindergarten, who wanted to talk intimately with me about "those others."

Bill, age ten

Out on the playground during recess one fall afternoon, the trees were a riot of auburn, orange, red, green, and yellow. The air was so crisp it hurt and made you run wild, tackle the kid nearest to you, and roll about in the grass. A migrant boy accidentally stepped out of one of his shoes. Two kids from my class—a little girl, a sweet strawberry blonde, and a little square-jawed, lumbering boy—grabbed this child's shoe and were tossing it back and forth between them. They were singing "Monkey in the Middle." Did they call him nigger, too? Perhaps. I'm not sure. Spittle had collected in the corner of the little girl's mouth from the ferocious abandon of her taunting.

At first I was paralyzed by what I saw. Then I got angry, ran over to Mrs. Cheshire, the most elegant teacher in the whole grade school. I could barely choke out what was happening. She made them return the shoe. The strawberry blonde and the lumbering boy threw it at the small migrant and glared at me.

Years later, I wrote a story called "Monkey in the Middle" for a class assignment. I mentioned how this boy needed that shoe to cover his "ashen foot." The teacher was impressed with my use of the word ashen and stopped the class to say, "Do any of you know what ashen means?" While I didn't know where I'd gotten the word, I felt proud and savored a vindictive pleasure. I hadn't named the perpetrators of this game in my story. My classmates, having long forgotten the event, wondered who they were.

"Are you saying that we did this?"

"Yes," I answered.

"Well, who was it?"

I willfully separated myself from them, choosing to reveal the mystery of the names in my own good time. Storytelling would never be the same for me after this.

◆　　◆　　◆

MANY OF the things that happened at Miller Road come to me now like dreams. There was, for example, the afternoon when I, aged ten or eleven, was home alone with my younger brothers, Steve and Gus. We were listening to the radio when suddenly President Kennedy came on to talk about Cuba.

We three all knew what nuclear war was—in school we regularly practiced duck-and-cover drills, evacuating our classrooms to sit in rows along the long darkened hallways and bury our heads between our knees. We heard planes fly overhead and it didn't occur to us to do anything but solemnly climb the stairs to our room. We lay close together across one of our beds. Not saying a word, we watched the shadows on the linoleum bedroom floor lengthen in the late-afternoon sun and waited for the end to come in an apocalyptic flash.

FOR A WHILE we had a woodstove in the kitchen at Miller Road. My older brother Azel was splitting logs for it and I was helping him by carrying the wood to the pile. As he chopped, he talked about molecules and about the idea of genius. He talked about Michaelangelo—his ease and brilliance in drawing, painting, sculpture, architecture, his diligence and commitment to the Sistine Chapel. And he spoke of Leonardo da Vinci, his unrelenting curiosity and imagination, his Godlike talent for conceiving weapons of war and for depicting the most delicate, ephemeral beauty of a smile. Leonardo, out of a passionate curiosity to understand, to know, would sneak into morgues at night to dissect and sketch bodies. Azel told me that this was what genius was. "At this very moment," he said, "you could be breathing in molecules from the dust of a buried genius."

Rome. Florence. The Sistine Chapel. From the perspective of that woodpile, these places seemed light-years away. Azel brought them within my imagination's reach. I was sure to visit them someday.

◆　　◆　　◆

WE USED TO have talent contests in our living room. We'd sit on the floor or on makeshift benches. An upturned wastebasket served as a stool or a drum. If my parents were watching, they'd have the places of honor in big over-stuffed chairs or on the couch, covered if not with plastic, then with the pale green chenille bedspread or early-sixties floral sheets, to "save them."

The floor was white linoleum, speckled with gold, bubbly in places, ripped up in others. The record player, a Zenith that my brother Iry had bought for us before joining the army, had seen better days. It, the center of our dance education, stood over in the corner of the room next to the television. Someone would put on Chubby Checkers, the Shirelles, maybe even Sarah Vaughn or Ray Charles, and we would take turns stepping out to the middle of the floor.

We adapted what we had seen, what we imagined from someone who'd been beamed into our shabby living room. We'd watch the *Mickey Mouse Club*, and *Jackie Gleason* with the June Taylor dancers. (They were particular favorites of mine. When the camera took its bird's-eye view to reveal a group of women suddenly become stars, flowers, birds, my breath stopped. I knew nothing then about Busby Berkeley's precedence.) And *American Bandstand*, with its handsome gods and goddesses enacting their cryptic rites, was a wonder too. We were spellbound by the selection of the song of the week and the best dancer in the television studio, when the camera swept across the teenage faces, looking for the one who had that necessary combination of charisma, style, and familiarity. And of course there was that long-awaited night when James Brown appeared on the *Ed Sullivan Show*. To see him cry out "Please, Please," to see him "screaming like a woman," as my older brothers would say in admiration, cutting the steps that only he could cut, falling to his knees, leaping up, and doing it all over again with even more passion, behaving the way we behaved, set us all to hollering. We couldn't believe it. We saw what was possible.

Spinning, dropping to our knees, flipping up from the floor with no hands—the moves we made were James Brown's, Jackie Wilson's, and Mary Wells's—whom we called the "female Jackie Wilson." We were doing the Dear Lady, and the Peppermint Twist, and the mincing, swishing dance called the Sissy that Azel had brought back to us from Rochester, which, barely fifty miles away, was the cultural mecca of our region.

My nieces and nephews—my older sister Janie's kids, who lived there —thought we were simple, gullible, and crude, and took our easygoing ways and open manner as an affront. Our versions of the twist, the Jerk, the Monkey, with their exuberance and improvisation, smelled strongly of "country." They would throw up their hands in mock disgust when trying to communicate the intricacies of rhythm or gesture that were essential for big-city social dancing. Nonetheless, we danced.

Perhaps my earliest public performance came at an amusement park in the town of Canandaigua. It had been our dream to go there some weekend, and after church one Sunday, Iry Lee loaded all of us kids into the Country Squire and drove us to the park through the lush northwestern New York landscape, with its steep hills, terraced vineyards, and winding lanes.

With Iry's encouragement we sampled every ride—the clamor of the bumper cars, the precarious thrill of the Ferris wheel, and the terror that was the roller-coaster. When Steve got off the Whip, he puked up a bright pink mound of cotton candy, candied apple, and ice cream. Azel went twice through the Scary House, claiming that there was a live gorilla running loose inside.

When it was time to leave, stoked with sugar, soda, and adrenaline, we wandered into the penny arcade, with its pinball machines and brightly lit jukebox. Someone slipped his remaining quarter into the machine and scanned the listing for songs we knew. We began to dance. Our eclectic appropriation of dance styles, steps from television, city relatives, and movies was matched only by the daring and eccentricity of our improvisation as we challenged one another, laughed, derided, and put on a show for the sizable audience that began to gather. The audience—composed of white families, a sprinkling of Puerto Ricans, maybe a few other blacks—found this free show every bit as entertaining as any ride on the midway or any sideshow attraction. Someone added more quarters to the jukebox and selected "White Silver Sands," one of our favorite tunes. I took the floor with one of my sisters and we danced to the edgy tone of the saxophone. I think I even surprised my brothers and sisters with my cutting up, my grimaces, my too worldly use of hips and pelvis. Everyone in the place was mesmerized. People clapped, offered to put even more money in the jukebox, but in an uncharacteristic show of restraint we walked away, leaving them wanting more.

Back in the living room at home, we had singing contests, too. We'd belt out anything that had emotion in it—from black spirituals, railroad songs, Irish ditties, Italian ballads, and nursery rhymes to "Climb Every Mountain," "On Top of Old Smokey," and "Swanee River." Our favorites were rhythm and blues songs, gleaned from one of the 45's in our collection and new tunes we'd heard on the radio.

We dreamed. Motown was the way to go. We'd make a million dollars, live in glorious mansions in Hollywood, and be chauffeured around in expensive cars. My parents understood this dream. "You all want to cut up? You oughta get people to pay you for it," my father said by way of encouragement.

My three sisters, Rhodessa, Flossie, and Vileana, decided to form a group called Candy and the Sweets, and I, the oldest of the three youngest boys, was allowed to join them. Our parents supported our endeavor by taking us to Buffalo—ninety miles away—to audition for talent scouts. For this occasion, Mama bought the girls the most sophisticated party dresses she could imagine and afford, along with matching pumps, new stockings, and corsages. For me, she bought a powder blue dinner jacket, with a new white shirt and black pants. I buffed my best shoes to a deep luster.

We got out of school early the day of the auditions in order to make the trip into Buffalo by seven. Our classmates and teachers had wished us luck and we felt very important. When we arrived at the theater, the stage manager gave us our own dressing room. We dressed in nervous silence. My mother sat out in the hall. My father was probably out in the parking lot smoking a cigarette.

We were called into the studio, and I saw television cameras for the first time. There, in front of them, we were told to stand in a single area lit by one spotlight. A woman and two men scrutinized us from the shadows.

I don't remember our performance, but I suspect that our nervous a capella squeaking and fervent wailing underwhelmed the judges sufficiently. They politely encouraged us to keep on working before saying, "We'll be in touch."

Everyone was exhausted, but during the long ride back home I felt a strange sense of satisfaction as I, half-eaten candy bar in hand, dropped off to sleep against Rhodessa. That evening marked the end of my tour with the group, but Candy and the Sweets continued without me. The girls, all under age at the time, would make frequent weekend trips into Rochester, where they sang illegally at a bar. And once they appeared in Syracuse on the same bill with Gary U.S. Bonds ("I danced 'til a quarter to three"). The girls sang one of their favorites—"Put on your high-heel sneakers / wear your wig hat on your head." They always came home triumphant, telling me they'd brought down the house. But these weekend sojourns resulted in at least one pregnancy and several life-altering heartbreaks. Young women strutting and fretting their hour on stage were suddenly young mothers remembering the night when. . . .

BALANCING THE WORLD

———•◆•———

"THEM PO' RICANS and Mexicans will work for nothin', that's why folks don't want to pay us right no more," Gus Jones explained, as we felt things changing in the 1960s. The only people he could hire to come north were people looking for a way out of the South, people running from the law, people with problems. He would pay for their transportation, room, and board, only to find that many of them simply disappeared during the night, going off to the big cities to find other, more lucrative prospects. And of course there were the machines—potato harvesters, cherry pickers—designed to do what human hands had always done. So, just as Camelot took up residence at the White House, things had begun to slide for some of the rest of us.

It was at these times that my parents would make secret journeys to a root worker and come home with herbs, candles, and Saint John the Conqueror root. They'd shut themselves in their room at night and read prayers and light the candles and incense. In the mornings, we'd find strange-smelling little satchels tucked under their pillows, but otherwise we weren't allowed to know what they were doing—just "workin' roots."

Sometimes, my parents would read passages in the Bible backwards for a certain number of days, to try to change our luck. My father, who was a Mason and wore the ring to prove it, understood mysteries hidden in the sixth and seventh Books of Moses. "Ah, Billy, there's knowledge in those Books of Moses. If you ain't careful, they'll backfire on you and destroy yourself and hurt other people." My parents were careful.

When I was fourteen or so, Azel, my hero, introduced me to the idea that the Bible was legend, myth. There was no God—Darwin and his theory of evolution explained everything. At school I was fed late-fifties, early-sixties science. I marveled at people going to outer space, lasers, the technology that was in the news. Yet I still had faith in the mysteries my parents taught us, still believed in the superstitions that were the guiding forces in our home. *Never balance your crossed arms on top of your head or your mother will die. Never touch a person's feet with a broom or they'll go to jail.*

I was recently given a hard black statuette. She's carved from a single piece of charred wood. (I say it's a she, although it's not especially clear.) She's got great, penetrating eyes and a fearsome expression. I have placed her by the window near my back door and joke with friends that she's the guardian of the house. I light candles around her and feel good that she's there.

AROUND THIS time, this already tough time, the house on Miller Road burned.

It was a Wednesday night, a school night, and late for us three little boys to be up watching television with Azel. The weekly western was just finishing. The man and horse and dog were walking into the sunset as the credits rolled. Everybody else was in bed except for Denise—one of a pair of sisters my mother had taken in when the state troopers removed them from their negligent aunt's care. (Margaret was the other sister.)

Denise was a handsome young woman—petite, a rich dark chocolatey brown, with shoulder-length hair as thick as it was black. For several years she'd been married to Jackson, our unofficial stepbrother. She suspected him of having an affair with Ruby, a single woman who lived with her child in the shed connected to the back of our house. In the haze of the TV's flickering light I glimpsed Denise walking trancelike through the living room and out onto the back porch, where we later discovered she had placed a five-gallon container of gasoline. She dowsed the low roof over Ruby's room and set fire to it.

Absolute pandemonium! People running in every direction. Tar paper crackling, sizzling, exploding. Propane tanks being ripped away from the burning building. Children whimpering. Adults shrieking. One of my brothers on the burning roof with the garden hose, its ineffectual trickle doing nothing to stop the relentless spread of flames. Me in my parents' bedroom, smelling the burning tar, able to see the glowing flames, trying single-handedly to maneuver a double-bed mattress out the door.

Nothing connected. Why was this happening?

Later, crouched barefoot outside, one side shivering in the night air, the other singed by the heat, I stared into the blaze that was our kitchen, but I was snatched out of this revery by my mother's sharp command, "Get your behind in that car!" Head wrapped, nightdress flying open, eyes crazed, she rushed all of us children into the Ford. I understood that her intention was to get us down the hill to Harris's house, but her wildness made it feel as though she was going to take us much, much farther.

She drove like hell through the woods, moaning, then shouting, as we clutched one another in the backseat. At a desolate turn in the road, the Ford stalled. Estella sat there, one hand gripping the wheel, the other lying heavily on the horn, then she flung open the door, tripped on her nightdress as she got out, and clambered to her feet in the middle of the dirt road to scream, "Mama. Mama!"

No one to hear but the sky, stars, night animals, and us.

THE SINGLE-STORY, cinder block building that my father had built to house "the crew" became our home for the fall, winter, and spring that followed as he slowly reconstructed what was left of our house on Miller Road. We lived in the rebuilt house for a year or more until Gus and Estella decided to "change their luck" and open a restaurant on Main Street in Wayland. Nine of us moved into the five-room apartment above what was to become the Kennedy Inn. (Estella, galled by those "bigotty so-and-sos" who never gave a black man a fair break, had decided to name her restaurant in honor of the man she recognized as a liberator second only to Abraham Lincoln.)

She was going to serve good southern food—fish, ribs, fried chicken, collard greens—although there were not that many people who lived in

Wayland who would even consider setting foot in a joint run by the likes of us, let alone eating such food. Zero customers during the week, but on Friday and Saturday nights, colored people from miles away transformed the place into a juke joint with their drinking, dancing, and carrying on.

Running down the street one midsummer afternoon after playing ball in the park, Steve, Gus, and I saw a well-dressed though obviously drunk white man sitting in a late-model tan Chevy parked across the street. He called to us. "Hey, you guys, c'mon over here."

We looked at one another. He took a drag off his cigarette and gestured even more emphatically, with a big smile, as if to say, "Don't be afraid." Something wasn't right, but we were curious. We crossed the street. With a crooked smile he hissed conspiratorially, "There's some really good-looking girls in there. I'd sure like to meet one of them. I'll give you a quarter if you'll go get one." With his cigarette smoke we inhaled the nauseating realization that he was talking about our sisters.

On the playing field or basketball court young locals, a year or so older than I, would smirk knowingly and say, "We hear a lot's happening down at your place on Friday nights."

Then there was that afternoon when my mother came home, let herself into the apartment, and was grabbed from behind by some drunken farmer who, needing a piece of action, was convinced that this was the place to find it. We applauded wildly, if sadly, as Rhodessa told us of waking in the middle of the night and finding some drunk low-life black guy lying on the floor by her bed massaging her foot. Her kicking and screaming had come so fast and furious that it was only once he was down the stairs headfirst that she realized that she had broken her toe in several places.

It was true that "things" happened at the Crossroads, that juke joint near Bath. We just understood that women, particularly poor women, might have to do "things" to feed themselves or their children. And, yes, sometimes things got out of hand. Look at Edna, a fine, independent, hardworking single woman who happened to choose the wrong man to get drunk with and ended up having to go to the hospital when all the men in the place ran a train on her.

Yes, things happened, but not to us.

But then perhaps we young ones couldn't know what really went on. I'd found a used condom out back once and asked my mother what it was. She raged. "You think you grown, boy? Ain't none of your business what it is."

One day, state troopers swaggered into the restaurant and tossed a morgue shot of a young child onto the counter. She must have been six or seven. Her eyes were swollen shut, and there was some sort of corruption or decay at the corner of her mouth. A trooper said, as if talking to a child, "Estella, this isn't one of yours, is it? Do you know whose it is? We found her over in the river in Cohocton. Somebody had his way with her, then strangled her. When we opened her up, there was some oats in her belly, the kind they issue from the welfare department. We thought you might know who she is."

For weeks and perhaps longer, this picture of the dead girl stayed propped up between the bottles of pickled eggs and pig's feet—just in case someone might come in and recognize her.

◆　　◆　　◆

I DIDN'T GO south again until I was twelve and Sammy Bailey came through Wayland on his way to see his family in Lakeville, Florida.

My brothers and I, out of school so long our hair had grown woolly and wild, were running through the streets one stifling August afternoon. A black man pulled up in a new blue Oldsmobile. In that rural environment, to see anybody—no less a black man—in such a flashy car was shocking. And he had on racy sunglasses, a blue floral print shirt, and a sharp straw hat with a small brim. When he pulled up to us, he called out, "Hey, what's your name?" We were told never to speak to anybody we didn't know. He laughed. "You don't know who I am? I'm like your brother, I'm Sammy Bailey." And indeed, we did know who Sammy Bailey was. My mother considered him like one of her sons—he'd fathered one of my older sister's children. We just hadn't seen him for a long time. Sammy Bailey gave us a ride back home. In my memory, everything about the car seems blue—powder blue—the vinyl interior, radio, cigarette lighter, steering wheel.

We tumbled out of the car, fighting to be the first to tell Estella that the legendary Sammy Bailey had arrived. She squealed in that high girlish way of hers when she saw him. He ran to her, called her Mama, and picked her up off the ground, all two hundred pounds and more of her. After sitting around gossiping for a while, Sammy said he wanted someone to drive south with him. "Well, take Billy. He's a good one. He'll keep you company."

So it was that one moment I was playing on the streets of Wayland, and the next I was heading back to a place I could barely remember with a man I hardly knew. In those days, the two-lane highway, Route 15, stretched all the way south. That first afternoon, Sammy didn't talk much, just played the radio. I sat watching the signs go by until night came and I fell asleep. When I woke up the next morning, we were somewhere in the mountains. There was a fine mist on the road. Home felt very far.

Sammy asked me a bit about myself and, proudly, I told him I was a champion runner in the fifty-yard dash and that I loved poetry. "Could you tell me a poem?" he asked. I made something up about how miles unfolded, how each billboard was a person trying to get your attention. As we drove, I watched the way that the sun seemed to move—first in front of us, then in back of us, to our left, to our right. I thought about Columbus and wondered about the people who believed that the earth was flat.

Eventually, Sammy needed a rest. When we got to Norfolk, Virginia, he asked a black person where the colored section was. I'd never heard of such a place before. "Take this avenue down two blocks, take a right, go over those tracks, and you'll find a motel for colored people." We pulled into the motel in the early afternoon, and a pretty light-skinned girl with straight hair checked us in.

"Get undressed, boy," Sammy told me. "You sleep on this side of the bed and I'll sleep here." He was now lying in the bed wearing just his T-shirt and undershorts, and I was nervous. I lay next to him smelling his Aqua Velva and feeling very small, skinny, not a man. He snored quietly and soon I dozed off.

When he woke, we went to a restaurant. It was my first time in a big-city restaurant, with all big-city black people—black waiters *and* black customers. The women, their hair straightened and swept up to one side, with flowers tucked over their ears or chokers on their necks, wore the latest early-sixties dresses. When they laughed, they threw their heads back, revealing long necks and delicate bones under their brown skins. The men, wearing sport jackets, rested their big jeweled hands possessively on these women. Couples moved through the room as if they had nowhere to go and a lifetime to get there.

After dinner, Sammy ordered me a huge piece of chocolate cake and a parfait glass of multicolored ice cream with a little umbrella stuck in the top. My brothers weren't around and I didn't have to share it with anyone.

When we were someplace in Georgia, I said I had to go to the bathroom. We found a gas station and pulled in, and Sammy spoke to the attendant, who pointed around to the back. Now having to go really bad, I ran in that direction. And there, stinking of shit and buzzing with flies, was a rest room. The door was locked and a sign said "Out of Order." I came back and asked Sammy if I couldn't go in the other room, labeled "Men's," which I had seen.

"No. Didn't Miss Estella tell you about that?"

"No," I said, and he looked agitated.

We got back in the car and drove a bit farther, pulled over onto the side of the road, and he told me to go in the bushes. I was afraid of snakes and of poison ivy. "Go in there?" I asked.

"You ain't gonna piss in my car."

"Boy, you grew up your whole life in the North," Sammy said when I returned. "You gotta learn about this."

Estella had drummed into us that we were as good as any white people, that it was a free country, and that if ever anything was denied us and we suspected it was because of our race, we should make a big to-do about it. But now I was being told not to make a fuss. This was the South.

The air stank of pulpwood and there were acres and acres of pine forests like those that my father had run through. I saw tiny shacks lining the highways and in these shacks lived people, their half-naked children sitting on the shanty steps.

Finally, we pulled into a town that was set off the main highway. This was Bunnell, the place I had named so many times when people asked me where I came from. We cruised around and found my brother Roosevelt's bungalow in a new development of cinder block houses. And there he was—a tall man with a knowing air, a friend to all men and a lover to all women. He had turned his front porch into a barbershop, where locals sat around talking while they waited to get their hair buzzed and clipped.

Roosevelt was delighted to see me. He kidded me for talking funny and admired my new shiny blue shirt with the pearl buttons and navy blue gabardine pants with a matching vinyl belt that Sammy had bought for me on the road. The same pants and shirt that I would wear day after day for the rest of the summer and for the whole of the next school year.

Later, Sammy drove me across town to the old neighborhood, which they called "the Quarters." This was where my father had built his home and where my grandmother stayed when we went north. We pulled up in front of a nondescript, cinder block house and I saw a large, heavy-boned woman bent over, digging in her garden. She was wearing a long skirt and there was something in the way she moved that reminded me of my mother.

"Big Mama, do you know who this is?" Roosevelt asked her. She squinted, reached over, and grabbed me by the back of the head. "It's one of my grandbabies from up North," she answered, pulling my head between her huge breasts, which smelled of tobacco, flowers, and fried fat. She planted a snuff-scented kiss on the top of my head before examining my ears as if I were a prize calf.

Big Mama. The last time I had seen her was in 1957, when she had taken the Greyhound north to visit us. During the visit my sisters had been embarrassed by her. Waiting for the school bus on an early-spring morning, they were trying to live the fifties image in their bobby socks and poodle skirts. Out came Big Mama, hair tied, turned-over slip-slide shoes, a jaw full of snuff, huffing and flustered. She was carrying their winter coats, demanding, "Stop that bus, I don't want my grandbabies catchin' no cold. Stop that bus!" Seeing such a woman in upstate New York was something like seeing a

Himalayan tiger pacing the streets of Brooklyn. But in Bunnell on that August day, she was at home.

"He talk so pretty. Talks just like a girl."

I winced and smiled.

"Say somethin' else, boy."

I began to talk.

"You comin' to see me every day, ain't you?"

I stammered out, "Yes, ma'am . . ."

"Let me hear you do some arithmetic."

I performed, obviously to her satisfaction.

"Boy, you so smart. Such a smart boy. You like melon?"

I could barely say yes before she went on.

"My grandbaby is gonna have some melon."

When the watermelon truck drove through the neighborhood, Big Mama bought several and all of the neighborhood kids came crowding around. "You all ain't gettin' none of it," Big Mama announced. "It's just for him. You gonna stand there and watch him and he's gonna eat every bit that he wants." She cut one open, carved out the heart, and offered me this sweetest part. It was delicious and I felt privileged. Of course, the other kids hated me. Their taunting continued well after the melon was done. They challenged me, said I was stuck up. And I have to admit that I *was* different. I was shy. I had been living with white people and it showed. But, as the week wore on, I found a way into the community. I was a good runner, and by beating them at foot races, I earned their respect. And I had a crush—perhaps my first—on one of the girls. I remember chasing her and she disappeared, then reappeared behind a hedge, grinning. I pursued her again. She vanished. Sometime later, after I'd gone inside, she materialized across the road from Roosevelt's house, smiling. I dashed outside, but she ran away.

It rained one afternoon. I had never seen such a downpour. We played in the cloudburst, scurrying in every direction, sliding and carving troughs in the wet sand with our bare feet. The raindrops were missiles landing with such force as to explode in tiny craters in the dust of the road and on my forearms. The rivulets of rain running down my arms revealed my skin under a layer of grime. I saw how black I had become in the sun and I loved it. I thought, I could live here.

That week the astronauts made their first orbit of the earth. "This is a historic moment," I said to my brother Roosevelt, placing heavy emphasis on "historic."

"Listen to you, boy. What you talking'bout?"

I didn't know what I was talking about, but I said it once again, just for effect.

"This is a historic moment."

Roosevelt looked at Cora, his wife. His amusement was infectious and soon we were all laughing.

AFTER A WEEK, Sammy Bailey came back to pick me up and we went on to Lakeville to meet his people. We drove past the town proper and out to what looked to be swampy woods. There I saw a shack—a couple of rooms suspended on poles above the ground—and lots of the palest-looking black kids I'd ever seen. Sammy's little niece, a pretty girl with green eyes and sandy hair, his coffee-with-cream-colored nephew, and another boy, with the palest gray eyes, were all out playing in the yard. And Sammy's sister was there too—a very pretty woman with a small waist, green eyes, and "good" hair.

I had never met high yellow people before. I had always assumed that high yellow people were like white people—that they were guaranteed privileges—but here I was confronted with a colony of green-eyed, nearly blond-haired individuals who were poorer than we were. They lived in a shack. Yet they were so beautiful. I felt the easy acceptance with them that until this time I had only felt with my family. I slept in the same bed with the children and when I had to leave, I promised them all—and myself—that I would come back.

As we were driving home, Florida seemed flat and boring, but when Sammy picked up an old friend to help him drive, things became more interesting. I sat between them in the front seat as they talked politics and expressed viewpoints that I'd never heard before. Sure, my father spoke about FDR, said the black man had a chance under FDR, said FDR was a savior for the country, but here were two younger men talking, "Man, yeah, in Russia your family gets taken care of by the government." I knew who they were talking about, knew—this being the era of the Red Menace—that these were the people with missiles directed at us, that these were the people who wanted to bury us. To my twelve-year-old ears, this was blasphemy. I had the uncomfortable realization that perhaps my father didn't know everything.

Returning home, I was changed. I knew about "for coloreds only," elusive girls, and black people with blond hair and green eyes. I'd seen mythical Big Mama herself. I'd slept in a motel bed with a grown man, I'd tasted southern rain on my tongue, and I'd heard things about the world even my father didn't know.

◆　　◆　　◆

THE MOVIE THEATER in Wayland was a pedestrian rectangle of bricks—originally an Elks' club, I believe. *Charade*, with Cary Grant and Audrey Hepburn, was playing. Rhodessa asked me if I would go to the matinee show with her. She seemed upset, but I didn't ask her any questions. To be alone with her was a particular pleasure.

She was a coffee-and-cream-colored fifteen-year-old at the time. She wore a red wig and one of those sixties jersey dresses, the kind that came rolled up in plastic containers from the five-and-dime. It was green. Everything about her was ripe and lovely.

I was proud to be with her; perhaps she needed my protection, I thought. As we sat in the theater she held my hand and cried all through the movie. She was crying as if her heart was broken. I guessed it had something to do with the black college boy she was seeing. I was afraid to ask. These girls, my sisters, were always getting their hearts broken.

A day or two later, when I heard my mother's tirade, I understood that it was more than a broken heart. "You heifer. You shoulda' known."

How could she have known? How could any one of them have known? All they'd been told was "Watch out, a skunk will spray you and you'll end up cryin' and bring my house to an open shame."

It was in private moments with my father that my sisters—for this happened to each of them in their turn—found comfort. He would quote the Bible, recount the story of Jesus and the woman at the well who didn't have a husband and had been cast out of her home.

"Stretch out your tent and multiply, and I will be your husband." These words in his mouth soothed and pointed the way.

And Estella, though accusatory and hysterical at the start, would become a reliable guide, advising my sisters on how they should sit, stand, and sleep. Having birthed and raised twelve healthy children, she was supremely well versed in the nuances of pregnancy.

Adoption was never an option. "Cast my blood out in the world. You must be crazy." The babies came and were always cause for celebration. Leading a ceremo-

Rhodessa and Saundra on the porch at Miller Road

nial procession inside and out, Estella was the first to acquaint the newcomer with everything she owned, which was now theirs.

61

◆   ◆   ◆

THE RESTAURANT FAILED. No one had the expertise to manage books, supplies, and advertising. It wouldn't have helped anyway. Friday and Saturday nights couldn't sustain it.

We returned to Miller Road.

I was fourteen or so when my father was stricken with tuberculosis and had to be hospitalized in a sanitarium in Mount Hope, New York. We had all tested positive to the tuberculosis bacteria that year, and Rhodessa's three-year-old daughter was hospitalized as well, so my father never felt too far from us.

I take pleasure in knowing that both my parents were born under the sign of Gemini. It's amusing and touching to think of them as twins—twins who, despite tearing at each other relentlessly, share an undeniable bond. Every Sunday of that long year, Estella took us to visit them, stewarding Azel's 1965 Chevy Impala much as she stewarded the family. It was then that I began to understand what she meant when she said she was my father's "helpmate." She was the mother of his children and until such time as he could come back home and continue their twinful struggle, she would do everything in her power to hold this family together. (Granted, our numbers were much diminished by this time—most of the older ones were on their own—but to take their places my mother had inherited two if not three grandchildren, whom she raised while their mothers went to the city to make a living.)

I think my father enjoyed the attention lavished on him by the nurses and doctors. Estella loved seeing him in his clean starched shirt, relaxed in a pair of soft hospital-issue slippers, smiling, joking with the staff. Gus was always glad to see her. She'd dress for him as if she were going to church—put on her favorite wig, best dress, polished shoes. She would bring him whatever he wanted to read or wear for the week that followed. It was around this time that I first heard Gus refer to Estella as "gal," and I think it delighted her. The two of them would sit together those long Sunday afternoons, then she'd gather us all up for the hourlong ride back home, to another week of parenting, creditors, automobile breakdowns, and—for her—loneliness.

Adversity was an intense light, revealing the hard, strong bones of my parents' love beneath the flesh of their relationship. Their rapport would become a paradigm for all loving relationships.

MY FATHER'S BOUT with tuberculosis left him unable to work. He received a compensation from a factory job he had taken when farmwork had failed. My mother and Rhodessa worked for a while at a local toy factory.

Small-time contractors, remnants of the now defunct migrant labor force, survived by hiring single women, old men needing money, and a handful of youngsters like us willing to pick potatoes. The work was seasonal and convenient as summer jobs, providing a vital part of the family's income. Spence and his wife, Helen, were such contractors. We would climb into their truck shortly after sunrise, shiver the thirty miles or so to South Avon, and trade sore knees, cut hands, and sunburnt bodies for twelve cents a bag. I was proud and quietly satisfied to know that I, like my brothers before me, had become strong enough to be one of the young men who loaded the truck. Yet we all realized that we were replaying a scenario. It was not our future. I did the work halfheartedly, knowing that "real life" was waiting.

Mornings always came too quickly. I'd drag myself out of bed, glum with the prospect of another day in the endless dusty fields—unless, of course, Rhodessa agreed to come. Then there would be conversation, laughter, singing, but Rho was eighteen—"grown"—so our parents didn't make her go.

One morning I hopefully asked Rho if she was going to come with me. My mother overheard me and said nothing—nothing until I returned home later that day, by which time she had found a way to make an issue of it. When we were young and did something she didn't like, she'd whip us, but as we grew older, she'd shame us. "Just 'cause you smellin' between your legs don't mean you grown and can talk to me like that," she used to say when we spoke our minds. But my sense of humiliation was especially keen at the time, and I mustered the grandest impertinence I could and spat it at her in reply. Then, with all my dignity intact, I turned my back to her and strode off the porch.

A cardinal sin.

Estella grabbed a nearby broom and started after me. "Who you think you walkin' away from?" she bellowed. I was bigger, stronger than either of us realized. I snatched the broom with one hand, which started a tug-of-war. With a grunt, I tore it away from her. My next impulse was to strike her with it.

Our eyes locked. I choked, threw the broom down at her feet, and ran. Such tears one does not share with one's mother.

ENTRANCES

AT THAT TIME, dance was an impulse. It was Marvin Gaye taking the word *baby*, tossing the *a* up into the air, stretching it out long and slow, and snapping it back into place with a little cry and a smile.

Something happened when Azel and I saw *West Side Story* at the small movie theater on Main Street in Wayland. Walking home after the show, we threw ourselves at the air, more like going for a lay-up than executing Jerome Robbins's choreography. At that time, dance was about this body and what it wanted to taste, what it wanted to say. Who knew that a body could talk?

MRS. SHAPEE WAS Wayland Central's drama teacher. She let me call her by her first name, Mary Lee, outside of class. She wore miniskirts and outsized jewelry, was an atheist, and didn't care who knew it. In a classroom discussion about the merits of television, she said, "I don't need someone to show me how to clean my toilet." She was hip.

In the fourth grade and for eight years afterwards, she served as a compass and guide. In high school, I would liinger in her office during the last free period of the day and we'd talk about Shakespeare, Gwendolyn Brooks, the civil rights movement. Despite her liberal ways, when I told her that my brother Azel was marrying a white woman, she looked at me a bit strangely and said, "Is she a pretty girl, because usually those girls are real dogs."

I once asked her what she thought of homosexuals. She said that she knew some "fags," a friend of hers had taken her to a gay bar, and she thought gays were pathetic. I wasn't about to argue. Not at this time. I had once intimated to her that I had a deep secret. With good humor, she rolled her eyes towards heaven and said, "Oh sure you do. At fifteen, everything seems deep." We laughed.

But in contrast to so many other teachers, her interest in me seemed free of liberal paternalism. I remember the Monday morning following Martin Luther King's monumental oratory on the steps of the Lincoln Memorial. I was proud. Respectfully, unsentimentally, Mary Lee said that there were those who felt that his speech would take its place next to the Gettysburg Address. I was impressed by such immediate insight in recognizing greatness, and by the fact that she thought enough of me to express her opinions as if I were an equal.

The Wayland Central School Drama Club. Bill is in the upper-left corner and Mrs. Shapee is in the lower-left corner.

As a freshman in high school, I watched classmates I knew stand in the footlights in cowboy clothes and pancake makeup, pretending to fall in love: "Oklahoma, where the wind comes sweeping down the plain, Where the wavin' wheat, it sure smells sweet . . ." The somber beige auditorium became a glowing temple. I wanted to belong there.

During my sophomore year, the Drama Club was going to present *The Music Man*, and I, starved for any activity that might allow me to pretend, was honored when I was invited to join the club. A real-life couple—talented and elegant, with star quality—had the leads, and Mrs. Shapee had me read for the part of Marcellus. And read again. She then asked me if I would work hard to learn the part, if I would be willing to sing and dance. A tremor rose up through the sturdy cement floor of the drama room, registered in my knees, and had its effect on my "I'll do my best."

Wayland had its problems, and one of them was that no one there would have known how to deal with a black fifteen-year-old playing the randy lover of a white ingenue. In one of our afternoon chats, Mary Lee explained this to me as if it were absolutely reasonable. As a solution, she offered that I dance a solo in place of the romantic duet called for by the script. I was without the confidence to reason her into revolt and I wanted the part no matter what, so I agreed.

"Sha-poopee" was the big production number where Marcellus sings out like a caller at a square dance about the virtues of a woman who won't kiss after the first, second, and third dates. I hadn't seen the movie version of *The Music Man*, so I sang the song from the Marcellus I imagined—a humorous, self-effacing man, a sexy blacksmith. Having no partner, I was unsure as to what I would do with the dance. I was told that a dance major from a nearby college would come and choreograph my part. During the rehearsals in the meantime, I pulled out all the old tricks, from our living-room contests, moves I had seen James Brown do, things I made up.

The choreographer never showed up and before we knew it, it was opening night. I was under the lights, center stage, and it was "Sha-poopee" time. I dove into the dance, trying things I had never tried in rehearsal, nor in the living room. I did my version of Estella and Gus's "Throw-It-Out-the-Window," a bit of buck-'n'-wing, the Jets' gliding step from *West Side Story*. And more. The audience stood up as my solo came to a close. For a brief instant I didn't know what they were applauding. I was out of breath and out of myself. I was everything and nothing. I caught myself with a slight dip of the head and shoulders as acknowledgment and glanced to the wings, where Mary Lee, hiding her laughter, urged me to get on with my next line.

FOR YEARS after I graduated from high school, I would go back to see Mary Lee Shapee. She was always a bit reserved, never overly enthusiastic about my visits. I think my sixties rhetoric of free love and free speech rang hollow in her ears, much as the whole alternative culture did. I can't believe that she didn't know I was gay, but she never deigned to discuss it. Instead, she would look at me as if to say, "At your age, how can you be so sure about anything?" Once when Azel and I were stranded somewhere in Utah, I called her and she wired me twenty dollars. I promised to pay it back. "Get real, Jones," she said, and asked me to just let her know that I'd gotten back to school.

I made it back to school. I met Arnie. Years passed.

As our daydream began to take on the contours of a serious career—even with my first write-up in the *New York Times*—I still craved her approval. I wanted her to know. I called the number I had not called for a few years and got her son—who in my mind was still a platinum blond seven-year-old but by then was probably seventeen and on his way out with his girlfriend. He put his dad on the phone. They had sold the house by the lake, he told me, and Mary Lee had died of cancer a year or so before.

◆　　◆　　◆

I WAS AVERAGE academically. I tried not to write a single term paper in all of high school. I was an actor and an athlete. No one could beat me running.

Head thrown back, arms pumping, I fly towards and never reach the trees in the far distance. I love adrenaline. Azel notices and encourages me towards elementary school track competitions. I am temperamentally suited for sprints—ecstatic bursts over the immense green fields that lie in back of the school, short races that ask for everything at the start and are over in no time. I grow familiar with the infinitesimal shift in both psyche and biology that is the secret to pulling out ahead, the rasp of cinders beneath my feet, the particular sound of competition. Between my ninth and eighteenth years, I find winning addictive.

I run out the gymnasium door, past the edge of the new wing, past the garage where the school buses are parked, to those trees that, when younger, I only dreamt of reaching. Beyond the trees, down a slope, I reach a troubling place out of sight from the school. I am straining. My muscles are the only conveyance I can rely upon to carry me back to the locker room. I am so tired. What had been enjoyment in strength becomes a grinding fight against the disgrace of hawking phlegm, collapsing in the grass, rolling eyes towards the autumn sun, and saying, "I quit. I can't. I won't." And yet I run.

Senior year has been a good year. The best runners from the region compete in the State Sectionals and I am one of them.

In the hundred-yard dash the other favorite is a hazel-eyed runner. All watch us as we prance in and out of the blocks. We are respectful of each other, good sports through and through. I have already taken two medals, but can barely contain the desire to get it on, to have it over, to find out what we have to find out. Watching my competitor take the crouch, strain into the blocks, shoulders tense, I am distracted, tantalized.

He's fast, but I'm faster. The last ten yards. His feet powder the cinders to the rhythmic rush of breath as we move in perfect counterpoint. Breast to breast, I see him naked, offering me the same generosity that he had expressed in the warm-ups. I want him but I will never let him beat me.

There is a spot behind my solar plexus, connecting my pelvis and legs to the place where tears come from and beauty is perceived. It says "Now" and I pull ahead of him. The finishing tape snaps across my pectorals. This is the only thing I want, the one thing I have to have.

Running for the Wayland Central Track Team

The crowd erupts. Coach Richie is jumping. We lift each other. He kisses me. "Good boy. Thatta boy, Billy." I turn around. My competitor comes towards me, arms thrown open. "Man, you were fantastic. I'll never forget it." I mumble something, look directly into his eyes. I *see nothing but respect. At that moment, his double—honey-haired—slips her arm around his waist, kisses his neck, fixes her blue eyes on me, offering her hand and a congratulation. They are gone. Richie tugs me over to a group of his colleagues. I have taken the day.*

"Now" still comes to me. Sometimes, dancing on a stage or standing at a lectern, I hear it. It pushes me. I get a second wind, reach another level of association. One meaning becomes its opposite. When I was a seventeen-year-old sprinter, the cable connecting the "Now" to my heart and legs was strength and sinew. These days, "Now" is anchored in my body by a complex latticework of memory, ambition, and fear. I am no longer a seventeen-year-old sprinter. There is no finish line, no reassuring snap across my pectorals. But there is a curtain call and applause.

◆   ◆   ◆

I REMEMBER WATCHING one of my sisters trying to pee while standing up like a boy. We had discovered our bodily differences early on but the exploration never ended. I am not sure when we started "mooching"—rubbing against each other—but it was common until we were ten or eleven.

One Saturday afternoon, we had visitors. I noticed that my two younger brothers as well as my other young relatives had disappeared. I found them all in our bedroom upstairs. One of the girls was on her back and the most brazen boy was playing with her "pocket." Since I was the oldest, it was my duty to raise a halfhearted protest. But my body had its own agenda and before long I was on top of her, moving against her softness with my pants around my ankles. There was an initial nervous embarrassment but it turned into a warmth, a tingling that spread from my fingers up my arms, ricocheted through my chest, and filled my head with a worrisome warmth. I blanked out. Sometime later, I remember waking up outside in a daze, staring blankly at a little green leaf growing out of the rotting tar paper covering Shirley's back shed roof.

My first girlfriend had the most graceful, selfish little brown feet. At fourteen, she smelled like something fresh to the world. Her eyes were almond shaped and she knew what film sirens have to be taught—that special way of dropping her chin and gazing up at her admirer. At fifteen, to touch her nipples and witness touch's effect on her breathing was an act both dangerous and divine. There was no distance I wouldn't have traveled, no climatic condition that could stop me, if I knew I'd be allowed to cup those tiny breasts and hear her startled breath in my ear. Unfortunately, an older relative also developed a taste for her. He had a car and money and although she enjoyed my youthful enthusiasm, I was no competition.

There had always been girls with names like Caroline, Colleen, and Linda. I had known them since that first day when the yellow school bus had taken me away crying so hard, fearing I would never see my family again. At first they were soft little things with blond curls and Campbell's Soup kid's cheeks. We shared cookies and milk. They wanted to stand next to me on line in the school cafeteria, and later they touched my hair and squealed that it was like sheep's wool. These little girls grew up into young women.

At home it was a generally recognized fact that if a young man was slick enough or foolish enough, he could mess around with white girls. But it was the sixties and I needed the more public acknowledgment that comes with being seen carrying a girl's books, having her wear my ring, or holding her in a slow dance. And it was the era of *Guess Who's Coming to Dinner*. Azel had already ventured beyond the illicit late-night encounters in the backseats of cars by marrying Mary Ellen.

Prom time came. I had felt close to Paula. She was gentle and mature and I asked her to go with me. She said she had to speak to her parents and she did. They told her that it wasn't a good idea—that it would make things hard for her, me, and my family. This seemed a logical, justifiable response. I didn't challenge it. Marlene, a short, aggressively built young woman, accepted my invitation. She came from a family with liberal leanings. We felt very "with it." We made our entrance at the prom, danced together, laughed with our friends, got drunk, and even made out a bit. It was enough to assure me that I was all right, that I had done what should be done on prom night.

Marti was tall and blond, popular and intelligent. Her parents were Christian Scientists and though they may have worried about her involvement with me, they would not prohibit us from seeing one another. Maybe my being well liked by the teachers, an athlete, and successful in the drama club made our relationship a little easier to tolerate. Caressing against the background of Joan Baez's pure soprano, listening to Marti's alto-pitched voice talking about the nature of right and wrong, about destiny and ultimate beauty offered me some of my most intensely sensual moments and a temporary refuge from the banal brutality of my surroundings and age. She was the beginning of a bridge to what would become my future.

◆　　◆　　◆

VOMIT EVERYWHERE. In my nose, in my hair. Was it two six-packs or was it three? I can't remember. I drank them all down and they all came back up. I was visiting Azel and Mary Ellen in Rochester for the weekend. I was seventeen. I adored them, their conversations, records, books, and their parties, too.

But it was now the morning after. Azel had cleaned me up and put me in bed. I was heading for the toilet, lurching down the hall, one hand against the wall for stability, when I made a wrong turn, into Azel's room. He was still sleeping, one muscled arm sensuously cradling his head, legs akimbo. His penis was fully exposed through a large rip in his pajamas. He was stunning—as a teenager he used to boast that he had classic Spartan dimensions—biceps, waist, calves. And I suppose many would say his penis was the black man's penis of the imagination, sleeping as he slept.

I was aroused and deeply ashamed. I ran.

◆　　◆　　◆

IT WAS THE MID-SIXTIES, and into a house that had listened to the Temptations, the Four Tops, Muddy Waters, and B. B. King, Azel, then in college, brought Bob Dylan, Joan Baez, and the Beatles. Into a house governed by root workers, the Bible, and the realities of race, Azel brought the rhetoric of Marxism, mind expansion, social change, and political protest. And when the age of Aquarius reached its zenith during the "Indian" Summer of Love, we were ready.

When I heard about the gathering at Yasgur's farm, I was wearing my green corduroy pants. I tied a Guatemalan sash around my waist, pulled a vest over my naked chest, put an old felt hat on my head, and got into the car with Azel and Mary Ellen. We headed south.

At school they had tried to warn us about all kinds of dangers we might encounter. I remember one film in particular—one of a girl cooking an omelet. She sees a beautiful blue flower and reaches out to touch it, but the flower is flame and her hands are burned. As we drove to Woodstock, we all agreed that we wouldn't touch LSD—"too risky" and besides, "What about our chromosomes?" After several hours of working our way into the traffic jam that was the festival, we found a parking spot and I, eager to explore, struck off on my own. I soon came upon a U-Haul rental truck full of week-end revelers from Penn State. It didn't take much coaxing before I swallowed a tab. Not long afterwards, the famous Woodstock storm broke loose and we retreated into the U-Haul. There, in the clammy intimate pitch blackness of the windowless moving van, I sat among strangers and wondered where I ended and the outside began.

On the last morning, the festival of love, peace, and music was a chaos of beer cans, ice-cream, cookie, and macaroni containers, soup cans, and cig-arette butts. Scattered around the litter-strewn fields were pockets of people. Some of us gathered at a pond to bathe and enjoy the sun. I, never one to enjoy mud or the possibility of encountering water snakes in their natural habitat, sat on its banks. The pond seemed another hallucination, a place of infinite love at the harmonious center of the universe. Around me were top-less blond girls with pink flowers painted on their breasts, and an old Beatnik wearing an Australian infantryman's hat and nothing else. A pregnant woman hummed softly to herself as she carefully picked her way through the reeds into the water. I wasn't naked, but Azel was. I watched him—my magnificent brother, with his athlete's body—as he waded into the pool. He carried himself formally, almost as though in uniform. Everyone watched him. Something brushed past him and he flinched. I saw my brother at that moment as a beautiful object. As an icon.

I think that even those of us who have no notion of what the auction block was can still feel it, as if the memory of it is handed down to us through our mother's milk. It was there with Azel as he moved through the water. It is there with me when I dance before you on a stage. My eroticism, my sensuality is often coupled with wild anger and belligerence. I know that I can be food for fantasy, but at the same time I am a person with a history—and that history is in part the history of exploitation.

We all carry this history inside and it costs us.

◆　　◆　　◆

THE WRETCHED SOULS was a garage band of young longhairs from the neighboring town of Cohocton. They were interested in performing Wilson Pickett, some James Brown, and Jimi Hendrix, so they were looking for a "colored" lead singer. I joined.

One Friday night after we had finished our final set at the Grange Hall Dance, I asked a girl named Janice if I could walk her home. Janice was small, not pretty but pleasing to look at. Her skin was a smooth nut brown. Her bowlegs gave a swing to her hips as she walked.

"Suit yourself," Janice answered to my request. "Sure you don't want to be back there with those white girls?"

Needless to say, this wasn't what I wanted to hear, but at least it served as a start to candid and, eventually, intimate discussions.

Estella had mellowed by this time. She'd let us have friends—white and black, boys and girls—over, and we'd hang out in the spacious mahogany-paneled living room. Late into the night we'd listen to music and sneak joints when we could. The first time I invited Janice over, she came dressed in a flattering skin-tight halter top and bell-bottom pants. As the evening wore on and we grew more comfortable on the couch, I became bold—quite insistent, in fact—in trying to undress her.

While my sisters had been warned, albeit cryptically, about "skunks spraying on them" and other dangers, the sexuality of the boys in my family had been all but ignored, save the occasions when something was described as "manly" or "unmanly." We were admonished, "Stand up and be a man because someday you'll have to take care of some woman's daughter." It was left to the older brothers to instruct us on the nuances of all things sexual, and their teaching was potentially disastrous. I was told, "When a girl says no the first time, try sweet talk. When she says no the second time, she means try harder, so put your hands on her. When she says no the third time, it's your responsibility to 'take it,' because that's what she really wants."

"Why do you have to do that?" Janice asked.

"Don't you love me?" I questioned as millions have questioned millions at such a moment.

Feeling between her legs, where I found a loose thread. I worked this loose thread until the seam gave way and I was able to get at the panties' fine mesh then the sticky warmth behind them. At first, she seemed to be in a kind of agony. And then I thought she wanted nothing more than to throw herself open to me, that it was only a steely resolve that kept her fighting. I had freed my penis and when I overpowered her, I jabbed myself through the opening I had made. She gave in briefly and then rallied herself, pushed me away, stood up, and prepared to leave. At that moment, Estella was coming down the stairs and, utterly unaware of what had just taken place, said, "I was just comin' down to see if you was gonna take this gal home."

Janice smiled politely and told her she was just leaving. As I walked her home, she asked me why I'd taken it so far.

Still rigid, I cajoled, "You can't tell me you didn't like it."

It wasn't that night, but not long afterwards that Janice told me about a boy down in Georgia who had forced her. She was disappointed to see me acting like him. I am not sure she ever forgave me—perhaps it is the sort of thing one can't really forgive—but love made allowances.

Seldom in the time that has passed since knowing Janice have I been embraced by such thin, strong arms and such a profound sense of acceptance. But like most nineteen-year-old boys, I hardly knew what to do with Janice's affection. Being Woodstock-wise, I wanted to redesign her—wanted her to wear military drabs, drop acid, and listen to Jimi Hendrix's screeching metal guitars, to transform her into a hip black "chick," a suitable companion for the hip black "dude" I perceived myself to be.

In the summer of 1970, after I graduated, Azel, I, and hordes of others hitchhiked cross-country "in search of America."

When I called home during that trip, my mother would tell me, "Boy, that chile's gonna be your wife. I can't throw out dishwater but she's standin' there, lookin' so pitiful, askin' if I'd heard from you and when you comin' home."

I witnessed all of this with a callous, casual acceptance, thinking simply, "It's her trip." Summer ended, we went away—she to a local community college, I to the State University of New York at Binghamton. She talked about transferring so we could be together. It was then that I had to tell her that although I loved her, I didn't feel "normal," that I was more than curious about having sex with a man. She allowed me the dignity of my ambivalence, but it wasn't long before we both had to acknowledge the limits of my love.

◆　　◆　　◆

WHILE I COULD SAY I had left Wayland with no plans to go home again, it would be more accurate to say that I had *no* plans. Binghamton was as good a place to start as anywhere. I arrived there on a Greyhound bus one Sunday night in August wearing my counterculture uniform—the ubiquitous felt hat, bell bottoms, and an army surplus overcoat. I sat in front of the rundown Art Deco bus station waiting for the Special Admissions Program (SAP) counselors to arrive, determined not to be impressed by them nor the importance of this occasion.

After all, I had spent much of the previous year at Rhodessa's house in

Rochester. She and her Irish Catholic lover, Dennis Riley, were the duke and duchess of the Troupe Street hippie community. We'd hang around smoking pot, dropping acid, and listening to the latest Crosby, Stills, and Nash albums with real Hell's Angels who would roar up on their Harleys to pay Rhodessa and Dennis homage. The arrogance of the "Tune in, turn on, drop out" credo had rendered the world stodgy, misguided—hardly worth engaging.

Most of the students receiving financial aid through the SAP program were black and hispanic—from Brooklyn, Harlem, or upstate New York. There was a sprinkling of whites, too. We'd been given the option of integrating ourselves into the general student population or living on two floors of one dormitory—the "Third World" corridors. Hoping to leave behind social ambivalence, I chose to live on one of these corridors.

But fitting in with the brothers and sisters meant, to a certain extent, reassessing the identity I had cultivated since kindergarten. The 1969 takeover of the Student Union at nearby Cornell was a recent memory and militancy was the fashion—the method, perhaps—that a lot of young black people employed in order to deal with the academic challenge and social displacement that being at Binghamton represented.

I remember sitting in my room with one fat, friendly brother, in an unusual moment of camaraderie. I asked him to listen to Joni Mitchell. He conceded she *might* have something, but her voice was lacking that indescribable essence that he was in tune with. As the conversation continued, one thing led to another and he asked bluntly, "Why don't you rap to the sisters? Why you always hanging with white women?"

None of my corridor mates had ever met Janice. She lived 250 miles away, and I never insisted on making her blackness known to them. But at this moment, perhaps in rebellion, I didn't deign to defend my position.

"I don't think the sisters are interested in me," I answered, thinking back to an incident in the cafeteria when I'd offended a stern-faced young black woman by asking her to "please pass the salt shaker." It was a request phrased far too formally—whitely—for her taste. I assumed that I was viewed as an unauthentic, white-dependent Negro. He said that wasn't true, that he knew a "down" sister who fancied me. I was dumbfounded. I later wondered if this woman—who listened to Nina Simone, who wore a gailai, who was on all of the black student committees—could have helped me find a way to integrate my history, my temperament into the black culture of that time. But I never found out.

CIRCLE IN DISTANCE

———◆———

I'm gonna love you till the heaven stops the rain
I'm gonna love you till the stars fall from the sky,
for you and I.
C'mon, c'mon, c'mon, c'mon now,
Touch me, babe,
Can't you see that I am not afraid?

The Doors

When he died, I'd been with him for seventeen years—nearly as long as I'd lived with my family, nearly half my life.

Our partnership began with the giddiness of exploration as we sought our bodies' potentials for pleasure—sometimes five times in a day. The last time we made love was one evening three or four weeks before the end. I was sitting with him in the hospital. I put my hands to his face, his palm rested against my cheek. There is no way to express the satisfaction that I took, and that I think he took, in a relationship that had come to this.

I loved him.

His is the name that is always there, only a slip of the tongue away. Even now, when I say it, I expect him to answer. I am always expecting him—expecting to hear his voice on the other end of the telephone line, expecting to meet him at the airport, or wait for me in a theater lobby. I am always expecting him to share my dressing room, to sit across the table at a tense meeting or at my mother's

With Arnie Zane, Johnson City, New York, 1972 (BARRY BUTTERFIELD)

Thanksgiving celebration. I am always expecting to find him feeding his dogs on the front lawn of our house.

I am always expecting him.

"Experience" was the word we used to describe every new event—and every new experience was an event to be observed almost clinically, categorized, and contextualized into a sort of self-mythology. I resolved to "experience" sex with a man. I told Azel. After all, he had introduced me to James Baldwin, whose writing about black men and women, white men and black women, black men and white men sleeping together had been a revelation we had shared. Or so I thought.

Azel's response was unequivocal. "It's just a phase you're going through." I insisted that it was my destiny. (We spoke in such terms. The language of the counterculture, though easily parodied and often failing to express life's more challenging questions, allowed us to give every observation its appropriate heroic proportions.)

During the first semester at Binghamton, I found a yellow mimeographed sheet posted in the Student Union: GAY?? COME OUT AND MEET YOUR BROTHERS AND SISTERS!! In smaller print, I found the details about an on-campus gay liberation consciousness-raising group hosted by Larry L., a blond man of feminine demeanor who seemed the self-appointed consciousness of queers on campus. It was two years after Stonewall, and people were beginning to emerge from their closets—some timidly, others like Larry, defiantly and flamboyantly.

The coming-out meeting took place in a large room, upstairs in the Student Union. A partition divided the men from the women. People sat around cross-legged listening to Broadway show tunes and talking about who was or was not gay on campus, about some hot new disco in New York, and about how pathetic the gay townies were. Larry had broken the ice by entertaining us with very funny, very camp anecdotes about his infrequent trips to the gymnasium. With time, others in the room reflected on the difficulties of being Italian-American and gay, or being Jewish and gay. I took a deep breath and volunteered that it was particularly hard for me to come out because blacks saw being gay as—and I chose my words very carefully—"the ultimate emasculation of the black man."

For a long moment, my statement just sat in the middle of the circle like a stone, then everyone quickly moved on to other, more consequential topics, the most important one by far being the party that they were planning at Larry's apartment for the following weekend. I went. It was like almost any other party of the time—pitchers of sangria, bowls of Lipton's Onion Soup and sour-cream dip, potato chips, dishes of raw vegetables, and carrot cake. No one spoke to me—not until I was getting ready to leave. Then a hairdresser from town tried to pick me up. It seems he had hoped to get me to go home with him without the others noticing. I refused.

The next night I went out to the campus pub with Mary Ellen. There I saw the same hairdresser again and next to him sat a small man with strong Mediterranean features, close-cropped hair, and a clean-shaven face, which, in 1971, was a rather rare sight. He wore a colorful blue and red hand-knit vintage sweater.

While I had never seen him before, I recognized him. A few years earlier, I had met a singer at a high school choral competition. "Just a premonition of what is to come," I had written grandly in my secret journal at the time. Here, in the pub, was a man whose height, build, and hair were like that singer's.

I'd never cruised anyone in my life, so I decided that being as suggestive as possible was the way to go. I'd get his attention by licking the lip of my plastic cup of Schlitz—that must be how it's done. I must have looked quite ridiculous, and not knowing how to follow up, I left.

True to what would be his form, Arnie discreetly stopped Mary Ellen and asked, "Who was that man you were with? Tell him I'd like to meet him."

STARS SPUN ACROSS the walls and ceiling, projected by the psychedelic lamp I had lit to set the mood. Arnie and I had met later that evening in the Student Commons. I was very direct. "I'd like to sleep with you."

I brought him to my room on the Third World corridor. I put on the Rolling Stones, then Bessie Smith. He tolerated my music, although he would have preferred Barbra Streisand.

We kissed as Bessie Smith shouted, "Captain, tell your men to get on board . . . It's rainin' and it's stormin' on the sea, I feel like somebody has shipwrecked poor me. . . ." I didn't know what the hell I was doing. I was just doing.

I remember how easy and continuous everything felt. I lay down beside him and he wrapped himself around me. I didn't overstay the moment. It was one unto itself, unlike anything I would ever experience again. Arnie knew what I didn't know—that this was to be home for the rest of his life.

I held him in my arms gently, and he arranged himself so that he was pleasured. I found great joy in his appetite for me. Lying on the two mattresses pushed together on the floor, the half-light filling the room, I watched him in his sleep. His coloring was pale, in a southern Italian way. There was a certain richness in his short black hair. His eyelids were of a perfect convex delicacy, his lashes full, long, and curled. His eyes were brown. Later, when I saw pictures of his mother and her sisters as young girls, wide-eyed and scared, fresh off the boat from Vilna, I understood them. His skin was soft and there was the barest suggestion of a beard around his mouth and chin. His neck was long and graceful and I would find that he was rather proud of it. He had a small triangle of curly black hair on his chest. His waist, though not slender, tapered nicely into strong hips. His legs were those of a Jewish peasant, and his feet were trusty, sensitive.

I remember everything about the next morning, but most especially, him leaving. I watched from my window as he walked down the path past the pine trees. He wore his gray overcoat—backwards, I'm not quite sure why. His shoulders—always a bit tense—were hiked up and his arms were crossed and folded in front of him like a woman's. A small, delicate man who was obviously gay, he moved with a determination and precision that is most associated with manliness. Later on, I would call him "my prince" because of an imperiousness and near arrogance he often projected with his carriage.

Did I ask him if I would see him again? I believe I did. And that he said he'd be back.

The world seemed a different place the next time I went out into it.

◆　　◆　　◆

MARTHA GRAHAM'S COMPANY came to Binghamton that year.

I knew who Martha Raye was. I knew who Martha Washington was. But who in the hell was this Martha Graham? I didn't go to the performance. The following day, I saw photographs of the dancers in the school newspaper. While akin to that of *West Side Story*, with its faux Puerto Ricans strutting down the street, snapping their fingers, slicing the air with their left hands while striking the ground with their feet, this dance ran much deeper. Its implications were ancient. As ancient as the rites and pageantry inscribed on Hellenic urns. These dancers, these men and women were not mortal at all, but the creatures of legend and myth. Their heat and exuberance, their pasts and futures were caught in the images reproduced on the newsprint. Even my untrained eyes could recognize this.

Soon, time that I was supposed to spend researching and writing papers I spent poring through books on the arts—painting, architecture, theater, music. And the dance books needed no captions, no explanation. I lived the images that I found in them, commanded them to move in my body, in my imagination. When I saw a dancer's arm reaching towards heaven, I reached too. When I witnessed the impossible pitch of a Gambian shaman dancer, I experienced the giddy defiance of gravity.

I saw a film of Balanchine's *Tchaikovsky Pas de Deux:* Suzanne Farrell ran forward without warning, threw herself upwards, backwards into the air, trusting her male partner to catch her. They stopped. The music stopped. This perfect emphasis suggested the possibility of a body suspended in air for all of time. I was suspended. I wanted this possibility. I wanted to pitch and turn, lunge and strike down the halls of the Fine Arts Building or across the campus.

I soon found myself in brightly lit, low-ceilinged, wooden-floored rooms filled with white women in black leotards, pink tights, and little pink slippers, who stretched at the barre. They tried, for reasons lost to me, to get their legs higher and higher still, counting, *Down on one, then up on two, and down on three.* This was a world of signs, gestures, and events that I knew nothing about.

I wanted to be in the air, wanted to fly, but stretch? triplet? point? I didn't want to understand that this discipline was the way to dancing.

Martha Graham said that it takes ten years to make a dancer. What does it mean, "make a dancer"? I felt like a dancer when I walked down the street, when I ran around the track. Wasn't I a dancer? Mrs. Grandy, whose job it was to teach Cechetti ballet technique on Monday and Wednesday afternoons, and Humphrey-Weidman the remainder of the week, said I was not. My body needed more flexibility and far more training.

My feet were big, flat, and did not have high, supple arches. I was not lithe and swanlike. My buttocks were hard and pronounced. My chest was barrel shaped, and it jutted forward. My shoulders were muscled with great affinity for my ears. My carriage was low, grounded, and round, not pulled up, elongated, and gracefully vertical, as I would have wished. But I wanted to move through space on my toes, to turn effortlessly. I wanted a nineteenth-century sense of *plastique*—to strike a pose ephemeral, transcending the natural world.

I would use my heavily muscled thighs to lift my tense feet over the wooden ballet barre and try to emulate the young women near me who, while seemingly removed and uninvolved, were receiving from their bodies exquisite cooperation and articulation. These were exercises in futility for me. The mental and physical tortures of the dance studio offered no connection to any sense of lyric flight. Instead, they suggested a spiritual and physical threshold through which I could not pass. My muscles were not so willing to redefine their familiar organization to one another or their relationship to gravity. The ballet barre became the site of a battle between what I was and what I willed myself to be. But that battle in itself became a dance—a dance that I chose to hide, as do many other dancers. I'd improvise alone in the empty dance studio, enjoying the curious comfort of watching the way my body, reflected in the mirror, affected space as I changed my position. I would sing quietly to myself as I wafted and soared about, my imagination ignoring all thresholds.

In these moments, I was creator, performer, and audience. I experienced the deep truth of movement. How to share this with others was something I would struggle with for years.

When members of the Utah Repertory Dance Theatre came to Binghamton to perform and give master classes, Mrs. Grandy divided us into two groups—those who were allowed to take classes and those who could only watch. I could only watch.

Tim Wengerd stepped out on the floor. He was a strongly built man with an ample square face and wide-set, almost Asian eyes. He inhaled sharply, then attacked the space before him. With both arms outstretched, his left foot took his weight while his right leg came up sharply as if to kick. Then, with an unexpected change of intent, it bent at the knee and ankle, swiveled viciously in the hip socket as his foot—with the precision of a bullet piercing a target—found the floor and invited his massive body earthward. He had sailed serenely in an arc of such sureness and purity. An imitation of his movement I would never achieve, but its essential nature was mine from that moment on.

◆　　◆　　◆

WHEN I WENT to Binghamton to begin my freshman year, I treasured the image of myself as a nomad. The university was simply a way station. As freshman year drew to an end, I decided that I didn't want to return in the fall, that I wanted to go back to San Francisco. Arnie suggested that we go somewhere I'd never been—Amsterdam, maybe. He'd been there just before I'd met him and had friends living there. All we needed was the money.

By luck and happenstance, Ralph Hockings, a professor at the university, had just gotten a grant to open an experimental video center nearby, and he hired Arnie and me to move the bulky videotape recorders, tapes, and files to their new location. We were allowed to borrow the state-of-the-art portable equipment sometimes and we made videos of each other. I remember two of them in particular.

In *The Devil's Gonna Get You*, I wore a vintage polka-dot dress and straw hat—both of which suggested Bette Davis's rejected wardrobe in *Now Voyager!* I lounged about against the Binghamton skyline to Bessie Smith's admonishment "Devil's gonna get ya, Chile, just as sure as you born!" And *Women in Art* featured Arnie. His hair shoulder length, full and black with a streak dyed platinum blond, he wore a pair of pink 1950s pedal pushers and nothing else. He held a hand-painted plaster relief of the Madonna and executed a dance that was a cross between a religious ceremony and a slow sexy shimmy. Placing a kiss on the Madonna's lips, he let the sculpted image slide suggestively down his body as he undulated to Gil Scott Heron's insistent wailing, "Who'll pay reparations on my soul," in the benign morning sunlight of our third-floor walkup.

By the end of the summer we'd amassed enough cash for plane tickets to Amsterdam and were planning our departure. There was one catch, though—I had no passport. I needed my birth certificate, which was stowed somewhere in the hallowed innards of my mother's steamer trunk.

Arnie and I had hitchhiked up to visit my parents for the first time earlier that summer. I was casual and discreet with Arnie in their presence and Estella treated him as she had treated any of the friends I often brought home. The visit had been pleasant. Thinking that a confidence I shared with them would stay between us, I let my sisters and brothers know about our relationship. After we left, Flossie, overwhelmed by the news, told Mama.

When I called Estella to ask her to please send my birth certificate, she refused. "I want you to come up here now," she ordered. "You and me got some talkin' to do, and anyway you'd best stay in school."

So I knew there was going to be trouble the next time we went to Springwater, the town just a few miles from Wayland, where the family had moved a few years earlier. The morning after we arrived, Estella exploded, and in a terrifying and sad display began whipping Steve with a broom. This was something she would never normally have done in front of a stranger. Once she had collected herself, she commanded me upstairs. As I followed her up the curved, wood-paneled stairway, I felt the kind of weighted portent that I had experienced only once before, when the police had picked up a carload of us college students who, home for Christmas, were all smoking pot.

Estella led me into her bedroom—the inner sanctum. The light, filtering subdued through the drawn curtains, added to the serenity. My mother always insisted upon sleeping on top of three—at times four—mattresses, in what I understood to be a southern style. And on this afternoon the bed was, as always, immaculately made. It was covered with the familiar chenille bedspread that had peacocks worked into its vibrant pattern of blue, puce, and lilac.

My father had followed us and the two of them sat on this high, thick bed, as I positioned myself on the steamer trunk in which my mother kept the family Bible, old photographs, our yearbooks, and, somewhere, my birth certificate.

"You gotta tell me somethin'. What you doin' sleepin' with a *man?*"

Shocked, mustering what defiance I could, I stammered out, "I don't have to answer that."

Gus Jones was typically quiet. His hat rested on his knee and his foot tapped on the floor, as it would whenever he sat thinking. He seemed almost in a trance, trying to process this recent revelation. Or maybe he was thinking about himself—remembering his own rebellions, remembering how much he had loved the open road. Surely, he must have been thinking about the effect of all of this on his wife. After all, he was there to support her.

Slowly, he began to speak. "Sweet, let the boy do what he's gonna do. He's a man."

Estella was always allowed to—and often did—veto any decision my father made that was contrary to her own. But, to my surprise, on this occasion she acquiesced. With a shrug she said in a husky voice, "Go, bring the gentleman up here." I went down and asked Arnie to come upstairs.

How formal he looked, shoulders pulled way back, chin lifted, as he entered the room. Although he was no newcomer to a fight around such issues,

I think he was moved by the gravity of the ritual and what it meant to be invited into my parents' bedroom.

Arnie took a seat beside me on the trunk. "I know this must be shocking to you," he began, speaking in an even, clear tone.

"I never heard of nothin' like this in my family," Estella answered. "Are you a man or a woman?"

Arnie assured her that he was a man.

"If you is a man, then, how do I know you ain't gonna take my son over there across that water and leave him?"

"Mrs. Jones." (Arnie called her that until he died. She would certainly never have allowed "Mama," nor even "Estella.") "Mrs. Jones, I give you my word, I won't abandon him."

"I'm trustin' you to take care of my boy. He thinks he knows everythin', but he's young and he don't know nothin'," she said, looking over at me.

My father sat, nodding his head, in a quiet consent.

"I give you my word," Arnie repeated.

She extended her large brown, feminine hand. He placed his small, pale masculine hand in hers and they shook.

Arnie was a big surprise to the rest of the family. Reactions ranged across a broad spectrum. There was the stunned disbelief of my sister Flossie, who had blown the whistle. There was the gracious, loving curiosity expressed by Rhodessa. There was the characteristic chin-scratching scrutiny followed by a provisional acceptance from Azel. My younger brothers, Steve and Gus, were taciturn and withdrawn around the issue, perhaps overwhelmed with concern as to what would be their own destiny as men, as sexual beings. My brother Iry had the most militant response. When the news traveled to his distant point of observation in Seattle, he wrote an infamous missive saying he was going to come and beat my behind until he got my head straightened out.

Over the years there were many uncomfortable encounters. One Christmas dinner at my mother's house, my oldest brother, Harris, swaggered in as was his custom and, when introduced, referred to Arnie as

"Miss." Arnie bristled and curtly corrected him. And for years, my mother and Arnie would fight every time a Christmas card or thank-you note was sent, because she invariably "forgot" to include his name.

I believe that collectively my family saw Arnie as a sort of dragon who had encircled me with his influence. We would never bring to the family the things that it fed on—offspring, obedience, and dogma. We were a big, uncomfortable question mark stuck squarely in its craw. By the late seventies, Arnie would stop visiting my parents altogether. There was a tacit agreement that my family would give me a little bit of what I wanted from it if it could ignore that part of me that belonged with him.

The truth that my family didn't love us was the dried crust of bread we bit into regularly, so Arnie and I became the most conflicted of snobs. In the spirit of the times, we had said no to all conventional affiliations. And now we said no to family. Yet family, home, loyalty—even tribal identification—formed the matrix of belonging we were raised to believe in. Removed from it, we became everything for each other. Sometimes we'd allow a few individuals like my sisters to come into our existence. We couldn't afford more. Our attitude became "We'll show them. We will thrive and we will conquer. And won't they love us then!"

I MET ARNIE'S PARENTS, Edith and Lon Zane, on the way to the airport, bound for Amsterdam. Passing through Queens, we stopped at their card shop and diner. I sat on a stool at the counter beside our friend Craig Duncan, a long-haired musician. Arnie was in the kitchen with his mother.

"So, which one is it?" Edith whispered with trepidation.

"The black one."

Easy enough, it seemed. But there would be more.

AMSTERDAM

———•◆•———

Twas flight 'cross the Atlantic that made me aware,
we're constantly suspended in the thin, thin air.
—a journal entry, 1971.

I WAS NINETEEN and on my way to Amsterdam, riding in an airplane for the first time. I remarked upon being "suspended in a rarefied air." I had liked the sound of "rarefied air," but "suspended" was the most important feeling. It would come to define the whole Amsterdam experience.

Landing in Amsterdam, I felt I was free. Having left of my own volition, I was truly outside my family for the first time.

We went to stay with Ingrid, a friend of Arnie's. She had agreed to let us sleep there until we found a place of our own. I don't remember much about her tiny apartment except that it was a typical bohemian Amsterdam dwelling—orderly and functional, with kilim rugs and Persian carpet-covered pillows in the living room, chipped plates and saucers, faded dish-cloths, odd bric-a-brac, and the essential teapot in the kitchen.

Past the kitchen was a small stone garden with some scruffy geraniums, chrysanthemums, and rose bushes sharing a corner with empty milk crates. It was there that I whirled my arms like the propellers of the jet that had brought us over that day. I sang a song that was little more than a wordless nasal droning punctuated with yelps and gut-level grunts of release, my

In Amsterdam, 1972 (ARNIE ZANE)

knees pistoning up and down. My naked torso dropped towards the ground, reached up towards the stars, then stretched towards the living room, where Arnie, Ingrid, and a few others of their friends were being reunited. I pranced, lunged, scuttled around that courtyard for an hour or more before I found the comfort of the empty milk crate and allowed the damp Dutch air to settle on my sweaty body and fill my lungs.

"This is it," I remember saying to myself. "You've really done it. You flew away."

FROM THE TIME that Arnie and I decided to share an apartment on Clinton Street in Binghamton the summer following my freshman year, our lovemaking and our fights took on a relentless dependency. It was there in the way we walked together, and in the way we shared each other's clothes. It was there in the way an idea was completed only when one or the other of us had taken it in, and sampled its integrity before returning it to its creator. Amsterdam intensified this mutual dependence, perhaps set our roles in the relationship for the seventeen years that would follow. *BillandArnie* or *ArnieandBill* rolled off the tongue of any person who met us.

One night we went to see Maria Callas's film debut in Pasolini's *Medea*. We boarded the streetcar at the Overtoom and headed over to the Alhambra Theater. Arnie wore a pair of women's platform shoes, a denim jacket, and jeans with pink sequins appliquéd up their sides. Perched on his head was a KLM blanket fashioned into a gargantuan rhinestone-and-peacock-feather-bedecked turban. We held hands, walked through the center of the tram, exited at the movie theater, and stood on line arm in arm. Only when we were seated in the theater did someone comment, "Could you please remove your hat, we can't see the screen."

Amsterdam was a peaceful kingdom. Its openness and tolerance had drawn people from all over the world and impressed us greatly.

Things became tense with Ingrid and we needed to find our own place to live. Arnie was single-minded in the search—obsessed, in fact. Soon we were sleeping spoon fashion in a bed that filled a room so small that

I could touch one wall with my head and the other with the soles of my feet.

As our money began to run out, we looked for work. Arnie tried to return to the job clipping magazine articles for medical journals that he had had when he was in Amsterdam before, but it wasn't available. He didn't seem to care. It meant we had more time to spend together. I was as glad. Unable to speak the language, I was ill equipped for full days on my own in such a city. In fact, I had no true sense as to what I was doing in Am-sterdam at all, other than passing time with Arnie. Eventually, we found night work together, cleaning a bank. It wasn't very hard work—three hours of dusting and mopping, eating the butter cookies we'd find in the clerks' desks, and drinking the thick Dutch milk from the office refrigerator.

"Krentenbollen" are warm, crisp fritters, embedded with sweet currants. First thing each day, Arnie and I stopped at a bakery to buy some for breakfast. Then we'd wend our way down the busy Leidsestraat to the Waterloo Plein flea market. Here anything and everything could be bartered for, haggled over, and won with the right skill. Delft china plates with patterns of lone boatmen beneath willow trees and entire eighteenth-century fireplaces stood alongside 1920s Rietveld living-room sets and fifties Disney memorabilia. One afternoon long before I knew more of this genre, I came upon a stall displaying graphic drawings of Nazis with enormous dicks, gang-raping a young biker. This was my first glimpse of Tom of Finland's work, my first encounter with homosexual pornography. In the teeming marketplace, my arousal and confusion were at once more intense and more embarrassing.

Arnie and I would spend the rest of the day visiting artists, composers, and designer friends. Many of them dressed in vintage clothes and lived in apartments that, with their brass-potted plants and immense hookahs, looked as if they were stage sets for Mozart's *Abduction from the Seraglio*. Some created strange installation art by arranging odd or evocative objects—timepieces and stuffed birds from junk shops and flea markets—with flowers, vegetables, and fruits, changing the arrangements each day. One designer friend specialized in elaborate beadwork. We would gather at his apartment, to drink tea, smoke opium perhaps, and gossip about what had happened the night befor at the D.O.K., the nightclub of the moment, as he hand-stitched thousands of sequins into a pattern of tiny fishes among coral in a sea of blue bugle beads. Then we might make our way across the city to another friend's houseboat, where we'd find him waking late in the afternoon from a night of revelry with one or more lovers. (As David Bowie was defining the meaning of "Glitter Rock" and redefining rock's social and sexual agenda, Amsterdam was demonstrating it.)

In keeping with the tone of the city and the time, the cast of characters in our lives was rich and colorful. There was Ingrid, Nordic blond priestess, tall and gaunt, a mime and street performer who always wore a line of

Maria, Amsterdam, 1971 (ARNIE ZANE)

greasepaint down the center of her face. Nettie, an elegant, attenuated presence who might well have been imagined by Egon Schiele, was herself an artist, etching tortured depictions of plant life, rock formations, and embryos. And Maria, a pretty blond woman with a harelip, clothed in Fortuny

"Flying," Tonia, Amsterdam, 1971 (ARNIE ZANE)

tunics or silk chiffon clouds of the palest dusky rose, graced the parties and afternoon soirées of this subculture. Maria was often accompanied by petite, voluptuous Tonia, with the whitest white skin and the full plum-colored lips of Theda Bara. Like many of these refugees from proper Dutch middle-class families, Maria and Tonia excelled especially in the skill of being beautiful, young, and "suspended."

Living in Amsterdam, I never felt the tension and fear I'd grown accustomed to in America. I encountered racism, but it seemed so innocent compared to that which I found at home. When I went for a job at a modeling agency, I was told flat out that Holland was not the place for Negro models. "Our clients advertise in small provincial cities. These are places where people have never seen a 'zwarte' and we don't know how they would take it." And, one night when the work shift at the bank was completed and all the Moroccan workers were punching out, I was last coming down. The woman in charge said to Arnie, "Well, of course, he's black and they just tend to be slower."

One incident went to the opposite extreme of racial sensitivity. Arnie and I had struck up a friendship with a hardworking Dutch woman who ran one of those meticulous laundries—a place where, when you brought your wash in, they not only took your clothes but as if in exchange gave you a cup of deliciously sweet coffee with Dutch chocolate. We went to a party at her flat one night, and the next day she called us, saying, "Don't ever come to my house again. You're not in America anymore. Nobody here cares that you're a Negro. Why must you be so suspicious?" I wasastounded and told her that I didn't recall talking about such a thing. "It's just the way you acted," she said. I still have no idea what it was I did that offended her so.

ALL THE WHILE that we were living in Amsterdam, Arnie was madly taking photographs and I was his primary model. One time we were in the Vondel Park. Arnie stood beneath me as I perched on a low shed roof wearing a Moroccan jellabah, trying to look as though I were somewhere in the middle of the Sahara. Another time he took two blankets. The first he wrapped around my head. The second, an army blanket, he draped around my waist. He sat me on the stone-covered roof of our Overtoom garret and I projected "the other," the imagined Bedouin. Printed in sepia, the photos looked like glass-plate transfers from the turn of the century.

One of our most ambitious and provocative shoots took place at the home of our friend Peter Schneider. We arranged Peter's Japanese screens, silk fabrics, and lamps into the semblance of a boudoir. The lamps, made of white fur, were strikingly surrealistic. They opened like Venus flytraps in an oddly sexual way from the heat of their light bulbs. Against this backdrop, Peter and I simulated the charged coupling of the exotic black and the delicate white. Arnie acted as director and photographer.

When everything is "suspended," what is allowed?

Max was a photographer friend of Arnie's. I used to visit him in the afternoons and these visits quickly turned into casual sexual encounters. Amsterdam was a place where pleasure and sensation were the goals of existence. An afternoon sharing a bed with someone was almost like sharing a meal or going to a gallery or museum. Or so I thought.

But Arnie was deeply wounded by my relationship with Max. And I, more to assert my independence than because of any sort of profound attraction to Max, refused to break it off. Arnie packed up and moved out with a flourish. "I wish you well and will always love you," he said.

I was stunned, sitting there alone in that room no bigger than a closet. But somehow I expected to be able to get on with my life, to move on. Max invited me to move in with him. I refused. I kept my job at the bank, and Arnie and I did our best to avoid each other.

One night I went to a B. B. King concert. Surrounded by the faces of young Europeans, while listening to music that reminded me of Estella and Gus, who were thousands of miles away, I felt even more displaced. After the concert, I walked home through the Vondel Park and set out to attract as many needy men as I could. It wasn't long before I was surrounded. It was a devilish feeling—being the focus of so much arousal. Just at the moment when one of them thought he would enter me or I would enter him, I said in my rudimentary Dutch, "Excuse me, I have to go," and sauntered away, leaving them to deal with their erections. I felt soiled, lonely, and something else I had never felt before.

Is everything allowed?

A few days later, leaving work, Arnie, as usual, rushed to avoid me but I wouldn't let him get away. As I was crossing a bridge about six feet in front of him, the wind conspired so that neither one of us could saunter. The dampness from the river below fingered its way past my coat collar, I stole a glance over my right shoulder. There Arnie was, walking in his particular fashion, arms folded, shoulders hiked. Enough.

We were two puppets running head-on. There was something angry in the embrace. Something like crying, a relief. We felt ridiculous and happy. We went back home together and set about living down Arnie's sense of betrayal, accommodating ourselves to the revelation that we needed each other more than independence.

No longer suspended in thin, thin air . . .

IN AMSTERDAM, I had gone to a performance by young choreographers from the Nederlands Dans Theater doing works in the style of Hans Van Mannen. Though enjoyable, this performance offered none of the great mystery of Martha Graham—and I complained to Arnie about this. He, always impatient with my dreaming without action, introduced me to a platinum blond Dutchman, Cor, who was a dance teacher.

Slap both knees, thrust the hips right, then left, open arms. Right, left, right. Syncopated rhythm. Head moves in opposition, left, right, left, right . . . 360-degree rotation of the head. Pelvis shudder, skip, skip, turn, and repeat.

I couldn't get it right.

One of my classmates, a statuesque secretary, approached me. "I'm surprised you couldn't do it. I thought all black people could dance. I thought it was a gift from God."

Walking home later on Leidsestraat, I overheard a news bulletin from the ever-present Radio Nord zee about the storming of Attica State Penitentiary. My brother Boot had been there for the last five years on charges of armed robbery. The weeklong standoff with the state troopers had ended in the barbaric letting of inmate and hostage blood. There in the carnival atmosphere of the Leidseplein, I stopped, dumbfounded, my dance class humiliation turning to bile.

A terrible case of bursitis in my shoulder was the confirming evidence that the dampness of the Singel River, the relentless sogginess of the skies had gotten the best of me. When the question of leaving arose, Arnie was ready. We had not found what we'd come to Amsterdam to find and had almost lost each other along the way. It was time to go home.

One thing was missing. Arnie, playing the card he could count on, phoned his parents.

"I want to come . . . back, Mom."

"Where?"

" . . . back."

"Back? Lon, Arnie wants to come home!"

Bewildering as it was to me, the Zanes sent us just enough to supplement what we already had for our passage home. We were gone.

◆   ◆   ◆

COMING HOME WAS to be a profound surprise. This is how I remember it some twenty years later:

The L train to Queens. Sour-faced riders for whom this is just another day on the way to that "damn job." The homeless teen who has been riding the line all night long. A legless beggar. BillandArnie are headed to Maspeth.

The train crosses the East River. Amsterdam's orderly civility is a dream somebody had. "Why is the train so loud?" Metal's misery, a shriek. We're awake now.

"I've always had troubles with them," Arnie says.

"Do you trust them?"

"I guess. . . . They sent us the money."

"Maybe they've changed."

"Maybe."

The card shop/diner hasn't changed. Edith bolts out the front door, flings herself at her son's neck. "Lonnie, he's here."

A pause. "Look at you. What are you wearing?"

"Hi, Ma! You look great. I love your hair color."

"Do you really? I knew you were coming. I asked for a special appointment."

She steps back. "What have you been doing to your hair? Oh my God! Arnold, you've been curling your hair!"

"Ma, wait a minute, it's this way natura . . ."

"Don't tell me, mister. I'm your mother."

"It's true. You always kept it so short, we never . . ."

She pulls him into the shop, laughing, completely delighted. "Lonnie, look at him. The bum. He's finally home."

As if about to cry, "You bum, give your father a kiss. We've missed you."

Lon, all six foot plus of him, hugs Arnie like a bear. Arnie reciprocates but can barely get his arms around the big Italian.

"Mazel-Tov," Lon says as Arnie slips away.

"So what are you going to do with yourself now?"

"Ma, Dad, you remember Bill?"

"Yeah, yeah. We remember," says Edith.

I shift uncomfortably, showing plenty of teeth. "Pleased to see you again."

"Oh yeah, it's about time you guys wised up and . . . ," Lon begins as Edith, grabbing Arnie by the hand, heads for the back of the store.

"Lonnie, give him something to drink. I want to talk to Arnold. What have you been doing? You said you had something to show me."

I, knowing how proud Arnie is of his photos, and eager to share with him this moment he has been anticipating since we left the Overtoom, follow them into the back room. With the pride of a diamond merchant displaying his wares, Arnie opens the leather-bound portfolio—his "European oeuvre."

Edith gingerly leafs through the pages. There they are—Maria, Tonia, me as the Bedouin. Suddenly she's holding her breath, leafing quickly past images as though she is being forced to look at police mug shots or crash-site photo documentation. Here they are—the photographs from that afternoon at Peter's.

"That's you, isn't it?" Edith slams the portfolio shut. "What are you trying to do? These are disgusting. Don't you dare let your father see these," she spits.

The expression that comes over Arnie's face is more shattering than what she has just said. He had truly believed that she'd be persuaded by the beauty of the photographs.

He is wrong.

Lon, out in the diner behind the counter, is drinking a cup of coffee and listening to a ball game.

Unknown to Arnie and me, the Zanes have decided that I will not be staying for dinner, that I will leave and they will set up Arnie's cot in the living room. Everything will go back to the way it was before.

They are wrong.

"Lonnie, Arnold's not staying for dinner."

"What? Why not?"

"He says he doesn't want to stay if the other one can't stay."

"So, he won't stay then."

"Lonnie, we have a lot to talk about with him. I think he should stay."

"Look, Edith, if the kid wants to come here and act like a jerk and then throw a temper tantrum because he can't get his way, then I don't want him to stay."

"Lonnie, I can't believe you're going to let him take advantage of us like this. He has to keep his end of the bargain."

"What bargain are you talking about?" Arnie interrupts.

"You know what I'm talking about," Edith barks back. "He knows exactly what I'm talking about. Is everyone here trying to drive me crazy, or what?"

At this moment, I touch Arnie's elbow. I can see he is beginning to warm up to this scenario.

"Why is everything always about *you*," Arnie says in a voice I've never heard.

"Don't talk to your mother like that, fellah," orders Lon.

"You've always been selfish," Edith interrupts. "You don't just stick in the knife, but you stick it in, turn it, and pull out a piece of meat."

I'm trying to ease Arnie, clutching his portfolio, from the stool he is half-sitting on. He won't move.

"I have my own life. I came here to try to share it with you."

"You don't have any life," Lon replies. "Why do you come to us when your rotten life falls apart?"

"Lonnie, Lonnie," Edith begs. "Don't get upset."

"My life is not rotten. My life *with you* is rotten."

Edith is now part singing, part shrieking, "Lonnie, Lonnie, your heart!"

"You little jerk, you have some nerve coming into my place of business with this guy," Lon continues, ignoring his wife's warning.

"Go on and say it," Arnie shouts. "I know what you're thinking. Both of you are ignorant. Ignorant!"

I, seeing what's coming, have edged Arnie to the door. Not fast enough, though. The cup of coffee hits the ceiling. In a rain of coffee and cream, I see a hefty fist close around a kitchen carving knife. Edith lets out one long, sustained, "No . . . oooh, not the knife." With astounding agility, Lon slams both hands on the counter and vaults lithely across it. Luckily, I have Arnie outside in the street at this point. The sidewalk is too narrow. We are running down the center of the street in the direction of the subway, which is too many blocks away. Over my shoulder I see the huge man striding off the sidewalk. The knife flashes.

He hollers, "I'll show you."

We sprint. Arnie is clutching his precious portfolio.

I encourage him to run ahead. Lon is after Arnie, I reason, not me. I'll try to talk to him, try to stop him. The knife has disappeared. Perhaps he thought better of it and slipped it to his wife. Perhaps she grabbed it away from him. I stop running.

We confront each other in the middle of the street. "Stop, go back, or I'm going to have to hit you," I threaten.

"Get out of my way. I don't want to talk to you. I want to talk to my son."

I swing. My fist lands squarely in his face. He barely flinches. There is blood running out of his nose. He pushes past me, bellowing, sucking in air, spitting out blood. Fist having failed, I try the psychological approach.

"You and Edith are disappointed in your own life. You married each other against your families' approval and now you're taking it out on us. Why don't you leave us alone?"

"Don't you talk to me about my life. You don't know anything about it. I don't know you and I don't want to know you."

Giving up, I sprint ahead to join Arnie. Lon has been picked up by someone in a van and he is overtaking us. This is a scene from a hackneyed police chase in a made-for-television movie. The van swings around, screeches to a halt to cut off our access. Lon is out of the truck in seconds, followed cautiously by the driver, who looks on with disdain and suspicion as I try to protect Arnie from his father.

"Bill, stay away from him," Arnie shouts, stepping between me and Lon. Then, pleading more than defiant, "Dad, leave me alone. Please."

With a brutal, concise maneuver, Lon wrenches Arnie's right hand behind his back and grips a fistful of his hair. A crowd is forming.

"Somebody call the police. This isn't right. This man is twenty-four years old and his parents are trying to keep him against his will," I call out. The crowd of onlookers stares at me, uncomprehending.

"You shut up," Lon screams. "It's none of your business. Go back to Manhattan or wherever you come from. This is my son and I need to talk to him."

There are shouts of "Yeah, yeah, get him out of here" from the crowd.

I think that I'll go get the police myself, but do I dare leave Arnie here?

I pick up a sizable chunk of asphalt and raise it in the air. "Let him go or I'll smash your face," I say to Lon. A woman gasps.

"I'm not afraid of you," he says.

At this moment, Edith steps up. "Give me that," she quietly commands.

Hers is the gentle, conciliatory voice of a mother. I want to trust somebody here.

I give her this chunk of sidewalk. She smashes me with it.

I am bleeding. With a mixture of disbelief and desire to kill, I slap her. There's an audible cry from the spectators. The driver of the van steps forward. "You've done it now, boy. We have ways of dealing with people who hit women in this neighborhood."

The scream of a police car sliding to a halt just outside the perimeter of the crowd's wide circle interrupts him. Withdrawing their billy clubs, two cops push through. They wrest Arnie away from his father and handcuff him. Edith shrieks, "He's our son. That guy over there is the one who hit me."

"They can't do this," I protest.

"We have our rights," Lon says to the cops. "We live here. It's this guy who's the troublemaker."

Arnie, still handcuffed, is shoved into the backseat of the police car between Edith and me. The policemen fit the still-bleeding Lon Zane in the front between them. We head on to the station house.

Handcuffed, Arnie can't sit back. He leans forward, head down, crying. I put my left arm around him. "It's okay. It'll be all right." His mother produces a ballpoint pen as if it were a switchblade. "Take your hands off *me*," she hisses.

At the station house, Arnie is uncuffed. The Zanes are secured in another room. Overwrought, I tell everything. "We are homosexuals. We've been living in Europe together and have just come back. They expect Arnie to stay with them, they want me to leave."

The policeman's eyes are cold and yet strangely nonjudgmental. His mouth a flat line.

"Subway station is a block that way. In five minutes I'm going to release them. I'd suggest that you get on the train as quick as you can and not come back around here again."

The L train to Manhattan. Tired riders on their way home from their "damn job." The smackhead has been nodding on the line all day. A blind beggar tapping through the car rattling a cup. Bill and Arnie are headed to Manhattan.

The train crosses the East River. The Maspeth street fight is a nightmare somebody had.

"I'll never speak to them again."

Metal's misery, a shriek. It is five years before we see Edith and Lon again.

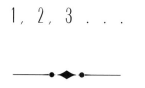

1, 2, 3 . . .

WHILE AMSTERDAM HAD shown me that I didn't know very much about many things, it did teach me that freedom was worthless without the focus of some passion other than pleasure. I knew I wanted to make something, something important. I chose dancing as a way to make it.

It seemed the most certain route towards this end began with a proper dance education, so I enrolled again at SUNY Binghamton. This time, I found myself loving the dance studio, loving to watch people dressed in leotards and tights moving in unison yet unconscious of one another as they examined and critiqued their reflected images.

I again endured Mrs. Grandy's disdain. We were learning Doris Humphrey's *Shaker Study*, a ritual dance with two long lines—one of men and one of women along opposite sides of the room. Enjoying the movement, the lurching forward and back, I lost my place in the men's line and drifted over to the women's side.

"Bill," Mrs. Grandy called out, "you're dancing with the girls. The Shakers would never have tolerated this. Men are men and women are women and they just don't mix."

I had heard that black bodies had an affinity for the Graham technique, so at the end of the semester I went to Mrs. Grandy, hoping that she would take me seriously enough to suggest that I go in that direction. She just said that I'd have to work really hard, implying that I didn't have very much natural talent to work with.

Although I love what Mrs. Grandy loved about dancing, I have come to understand dance in a way that leaves behind the *Shaker Study*, that is not dependent on Cechetti ballet, or even on a well-turned-out leg and a pointed toe. I have made dancing a partner to language. I have danced as a way of traveling backwards, forward, and beside the point of my life. I find myself still dancing at a time when Mrs. Grandy is a barely discernible memory, her voice just a whisper, repeating Doris Humphrey's *Catch and release. Catch and release.*

IT WAS IN the same Binghamton studio that I discovered Percival Borde's African dance class.

Beautiful drummers sat at one end of the room behind Percy, ritual priests to a shaman. A small coterie of black women, with Angela Davis Afros or tight cornrows and perfectly knotted gailais, always demanded the front position as if to say, "This is our culture and we claim it." Behind them were the openly enthusiastic long-haired hippie types, wearing cutoff army fatigues, tie-dyed T-shirts, and Bengali prayer beads, who were there "digging the vibes" of yet another experience. And there were the chunky Long Island girls—daughters of bankers, lawyers, doctors—who, in their fresh, crisp jogging suits, were mingling with different castes of people for the first time in their lives. The expressions on their faces vacillated between consternation and guilty ecstasy.

We were all there to learn the same thing. Shuffle three steps forward, contract the pelvis, release the pelvis, send the sternum forward, and then in the beat somewhere between the contraction of the pelvis and the protruding of the sternum, quickly flutter the elbows up and down, up and down. Each movement had its sympathetic counterpart in the rich topography of the drums.

Percy read our bodies for everything about us. "Hey, big high butt, get it down." Or "Point those big flat feet." Or "You'll never do that. Never. None of you have it. But come, let's try again." So we would try again and just when we'd begun to really enjoy the dancing, just when we thought we had it, thought we were doing it, Percy would laugh at us. "The legs! You've got to move your legs this way. Not *that* way."

While we lay on the floor, Percy would stride about, stalk, cajole, and entertain, then, like cock-of-the-walk, strut past us. He'd twist his handsomely cut Afro into two Satan-like horns and say, "I will only do this a little bit. I'm not as young as I used to be." He'd then nod at the drummers and they would begin to play.

Magnificent arms would open and all time slowed. I saw my history. Dancing as old as the Nile. Dancing that would take me to my grave. When Percy did the *Watusi Study*, the dust of the Serengeti rose about him. His outstretched arms marked the horizon. An impulse that started in his shoulder blades would roll down through his elbows to fuel his virile grasp of the two sticks in his hands. His knees would jack up in counterpoint to his arms, then pull his entire skeleton earthwards at a forty-five-degree angle. These haughty steps came in groups of four, culminated in a precise drawn-up jump, and ended with a thud that ricocheted through his body, causing the torso and head to wag right and then left in response.

Percy said that when the Watusis were on the march, you could hear their feet thumping in synchrony against the earth from a mile away. Then he added, looking at us with something akin to a sneer, "It will take you ten years to learn how to even hold the sticks. But we shall try."

In his Caribbean *Dhambala Study*, Percy's arms—shoulders to elbows, elbows to wrists—would ripple. His golden flat feet would caress the floor to a different rhythm, and start undulations that rose through his loins, his belly, the barrel of his chest. The eyes in his hewad and the imagined eyes of the cobras that were his arms would dart, fix, and burn into us as we watched.

"When you move with this step long enough, the spirit of Dhambala, the Snake God, shoots up from your pelvis through your back and you are possessed. And only when you are possessed are you able to heal."

I understood this dancing. My body recognized its rhythms. And yet when I tried to move to them, I'd miscalculate, stumble. When I danced as one of the warriors in Percy's *Goliath*, a work rich with warlike masculine movements, I had a very high jump. I didn't understand how to coordinate the jump with drawing my knees up, and photographs of me midair showed my long legs dangling down like so much running paint. I would grow frustrated, shy, and long to simply join in with my impression of the movement.

•   While if I wanted to reject Percy's insistence on accuracy in movement and attention to style and detail, I also wanted to be as beautiful as he was. I wanted to hear the story, to live the story that was in those shuddering thighs and predatory arms, that snapping head. I'd practice alone, humming the percussive refrains to myself.

Percy was often disappointed in the students he was obliged to teach. "You lack commitment," he would tell us repeatedly, then chide us with sto-

On the roof of the American Dance Asylum, 137 Washington Street, Binghamton, 1974 (ARNIE ZANE)

ries about real commitment to art—about the night he was told that his father was dying, or had just died, moments before the curtain rose. He'd stare defiantly at the roomful of us, then remark, "You all probably would have broken down and left the theater. But I danced the entire two-hour performance and went to do my duty only when my art had been satisfied."

I had been out of school almost eight years when I heard that Percy had died. He'd walked off stage for intermission and had a heart attack. I thought what a fantastic way to die. It was in keeping with the grand foolishness he had attempted to instill in us. And to which I return sometimes even against my will.

◆   ◆   ◆

PHIL SYKAS was a new friend of Arnie's and mine at Binghamton. The three of us spent a lot of time together reading *The Autobiography of Alice B. Toklas*, exploring the wonders of kitsch, stoneware, and the pinhole camera. Phil was working on his thesis project for the cinema department and we decided to make his presentation a real performance event by adding music and dance and even a little magic. We dedicated the evening to a fictitious character, "Babar Rebus, The Dunwich Horror," (Babar the elephant, Merce Cunningham/Robert Rauschenberg's *Rebus*, and H. P. Lovecraft's *The Dunwich Horror*), and put it up in the shambles of Binghamton's old Elks' hall, where Phil lived.

Arnie and I created a duet—our first—for the occasion. We called it *Begin the Beguine* after a Benny Goodman record we'd found at the Salvation Army store. *Begin the Beguine* began with the lights out. When the needle touched down on the record, the lights came up along opposite sides of the long narrow room, and we appeared shirtless, wearing matching navy pants, swaying—*Right, left, turn, turn, turn. Right, left, turn, turn, step.* The piece grew into a parody of thirties show dancing as the stepping and turning expanded to include pedestrian gestures like brushing our teeth, combing our hair, smelling each other's armpits, mock fighting.

We weren't sure what we were doing beyond thumbing our noses at the "avant-gardisms" of the cinema department, so enamored of the outrages of Andy Warhol and the performance sacrileges of Jack Smith—a mad, gay filmmaker of the 1950s. We decided to show them our own brand of nostalgic outlandishness.

Phil's project was a success, and we gained a rather notorious reputation in the cinema department. Arnie still felt himself to be more of a photographer than a dancer and had danced *Begin the Beguine* as a kind of lark, a way of taking part in the spirit of the evening. But afterwards, he began to create his own solos. His first, *Self-Portrait*, had a sensibility similar to that of *Begin the Beguine*, though less camp. To Caruso's "La donna e mobile" and against a backdrop of sepia-toned magic lantern slides of himself, Arnie— with a shaven head and wearing an antique dressing gown—stood up on a chair. Every time Caruso hit a high note, Arnie would fall violently to the floor, bruising his buttocks and lower back. It was charming, enigmatic, and painful to watch. We saw great value in these qualities.

◆　　◆　　◆

LATE SUMMER IN North Rose, New York, 1972. The milkweed pods about to jettison seed. The air filled with mosquitoes and rock music. Azel and I joined a shaggy assortment of rockers, bikers, and hangers-on that had gathered in a forest clearing in pursuit of an evaporated dream of Woodstock. A fly buzzed around our heads. Sweat trickled down behind Azel's ill-fitting horn-rimmed glasses, held together with adhesive tape. The fly settled on my collarbone.

We were not white. We were not shaggy. But this atmosphere of tribalism spoke directly to our blood. We were revved up at the prospect of our own muscles and outrageous good fortune. Was it the fly or was it the dizzying heat? Azel shot a glance at me. I shot one back. I bolted. Not to be outdone, he followed, pounding the earth with his powerful thighs and feet. We tore through the encampment, causing heads to turn and a small group of people to break into spontaneous applause. There was no finish line. We just ran until ecstasy passed and was replaced with bashful fulfillment.

There's a picture that Arnie took of Azel and me some two years after this mad dash in North Rose. We stand together, bare-chested. I am shielding my eyes from the harshness of the northern California sun. Azel squints suspiciously. This photograph speaks of likeness, of profound intimacy, of union.

My brothers are the tribe that I belong to, a grove of trees of the same structure—these legs, deep chests, and long arms. We all strive so hard for completeness, maleness, and all of us fail a bit. I love my brothers. I do not trust them. We are chronic underachievers. We promise everything to everyone and secretly reprimand ourselves for falling short of our promises. We need someone to draw our hearts out and rouse us from bed in the morning.

I take out the memory of North Rose from time to time, much as I take out that photograph of Azel and me. I wince a bit. I can't afford nostalgia—it makes one flabby in the fierce struggle to live in the moment. It reminds me of what is gone. And I have hurt them. I no longer joyously enter into the mythology of our timeless fraternity. For my part, there is nothing unconditional in our loving. Where can we dash to now? What untrammeled earth is left for us? What relentless and innocent sun? What heavenly denizen in the form of a fly graces the air between our heads? What burst of spontaneous joy can flash between us again?

I stow away this memory of us half naked, glistening, burning the earth in our rush towards the trees, much as my mother stows away those snapshots, school photos, trophies, and birth certificates in her old steamer trunk. Too precious to be displayed, too strong to live with, yet too essential to live without.

◆　　◆　　◆

THE DANCE DEPARTMENT at Binghamton, Percy Borde notwithstanding, could not hold me. I needed a dancer's vocabulary before I could develop my own. I needed to go to a place where I could major in dance, so, at Arnie's insistence and with his encouragement and company, I transferred to the State

University at Brockport. I thought that there I could get serious about the technique of dance—learn to make my legs turn out, to make lines in space, to change directions after I leapt into the air.

We settled into an apartment on Park Street. It had a large wraparound porch that looked out upon overgrown hedges, roses, and a variety of trees—many of them chestnuts. That summer, I was very close to my sister Vileana and she would often bring her brood—Jeanee, Lance Jr., Emeraude, and the twins, Amie and Marie—to spend afternoons with us. Arnie photographed all the little girls in white nightgowns sitting in turn-of-the-century spindle-back oak chairs. They held cracked antique dolls that seemed demented, haunted, next to their serene innocence. And he photographed Mary Ellen, Azel's wife, in our vegetable patch, crouching among the squash in a fifties bathing suit, clutching a photo of Christ. She seemed a modern Saint Veronica.

Every morning I did yoga exercises and then went off to the university for classes in technique and composition. It was in an improvisation class taught by Richard Bull that I discovered that dance wasn't only about pointing my feet or making lines in space. It was about how I could solve problems—how many ways I could cross the room, how I could move without my legs, or tell a story using only my face.

Richard had wanted his students to reach beyond the confines of the university and go directly to the public, so he arranged for us to perform at the Midtown Shopping Plaza in Rochester that summer. I had been wrestling with the mind/body dichotomy, issues of karma, enlightenment, and the journey of the spirit, so I choreographed a piece that I called *Sadhana*. I danced the role of the mind and spirit as one entity while the other dancers were the five senses. I was a showy young performer dancing about the evolution of the spirit, and its cycles of rebirth, as I had danced the part of Marcellus in my high school drama club's production of *The Music Man*.

A burlesque, *Bacon Grease and the Porkchops*, was perhaps more suited to my style. I was Bacon Grease, a very bad vaudeville performer. The Porkchops were my three backup singers.

Hey, good-lookin', what you say? Let Mr. Grease make your day, I shouted at mothers with children whose mouths were smeared with cotton candy, at old ladies with shopping bags who had come to sit by the fountain between stores, at young black kids who loped past us in groups and shook their heads in disbelief.

Afterwards, a man came up, gave me his card, and told me that someday he expected to see my name up in lights. Even as this happened, I recognized it as a cliché from a second-rate movie. I began to laugh, saying "Um-hum" and nodding my head as he went on and on.

My obvious delight at his attention and prediction would soon come into direct conflict with the avant-garde's ambivalence towards showmanship. But that day, it simply felt great. I had a future in dance.

ONE AFTERNOON early on in my time at Brockport, I slipped into the quiet theater and sat down in the back. My skin radiated the warmth of the July sun outside. A young man from the resident dance company stepped out onstage. Wearing tights and a black leotard, he began to stretch out and warm up. I watched his very private ritual.

He sat there on the wood floor, his legs extended straight in front of him. He placed his hands behind his back for support. Keeping both legs straight and feet extended through the arches, through the metatarsals, and out the toes, he slowly slid his legs apart until he was sitting in an expansive V shape. In this position, he carefully lowered his forehead to the floor between his legs and stretched out his back muscles. Then, as if his skull were a heavy weight at the end of the cable of his spine, he swung his forehead to his left knee, and took hold of his foot with both hands, drew his whole torso closer to the knee to feel the elasticity extend from his heel to his buttock, from the tip of his spine to the nape of his neck. Breathing evenly, deeply, he sat upright, then once again dipped to a forward position, and swung to the right leg, repeating the exercise in the same slow motion.

His involvement was total. It was as though he were listening to music, but the music was in every muscle, every sinew, and the pitch or melody changed whenever a joint was flexed or extended. It seemed that he was stretching beyond the reach of mere muscle, was stretching a more subtle body. This young man on the stage had been performing this ritual for a very long time. Without effort, he bridged the distance between his body and the language, the logic of dance technique.

There, watching from the shadows, I thought to myself, "So this is what it takes. This is what a dancer should look like." I didn't look like this. My muscles, though youthful and strong, were shaped for picking potatoes or running track.

This young man's movements had nothing at all to do with those improvisation classes that I took across the quad. His company had been created in the image of Martha Graham and Paul Taylor. It was a company that I knew I would never be able to join. But his quiet rite was a gift to me. I, too, was eager to bridge the distance between myself and the language, the logic—and perhaps, too, the community—that was the world of dance.

One summer day, I brought home a flyer I'd picked up on campus: IF YOU LIKE TO ROCK AND ROLL OR LINDY HOP, DO AIKIDO, OR MAKE LOVE—COME ON DOWN AND JOIN US AT THE CONTACT IMPROVISATION WORKSHOP WITH LOIS WELK. Contact improvisation was a partnering technique developed by noted dancer Steve Paxton.

I had met Lois earlier that week when I walked in on her in a sunny, empty dance studio. She lay on her back in the corner, sweating and listening to the music of Al Green. That strange kind of fear—my mother's fear of a black man alone with a white woman—made me want to run, but Lois was anything but intimidated. With her robustly female body—ample, strong arms and thighs, full high breasts, blue eyes, and a face that was at once hand-some and pretty, everything about Lois spoke of hard work and the integrity of her German-Polish ancestry.

Arnie decided to come with me to Lois's class. It began with warming up, with stretching in yogalike movements, rolling—whatever would get our joints moving. Then we would pair up. "Lean away from your partner," Lois would call out. "Give and take at the same time. Listen to your partner's weight."

Here I came to understand terms like "shared weight" and "counter-pull." Here I found the delicacy of two foreheads together, the contact point sliding across the eye sockets and down to the chin. Two throats then touching at a single point, then clavicles and shoulders, sternums and bellies. Here I saw the wonder in Arnie's eyes as he had his first contact jam with a woman and experienced a host of sensations that ranged from erotic arousal to motherly acceptance. "Better than tripping," he told me after.

In the studio twilight as the sun went down, people would move quietly in twos and threes while others sat along the side and watched. Suddenly, dancing was not only about trying to fly. Dancing was about listening, making sense out of an intensely personal exchange as private as lovemaking.

One afternoon when viscous August had settled over the campus, only Arnie and I showed up for Lois's workshop. If she was disappointed, she didn't show it. We three worked together, loving the sweat, the studio with its window open in the unlikely event that a breeze might pick up. When the sky clouded over, we hardly noticed. I don't know who was gripping, sliding past, or being thrown by whom when the first roll of thunder broke, but we continued our jam, solidifying our future relationship as the sky tore open and poured buckets on the parched late-summer grounds of the State University College at Brockport.

I was ready for contact improvisation, ready for a dance form that didn't ask so much that my muscles change as that I become more sensitive to the qualities of touch, more conscious of the movement of everyday life—of walking as falling from foot to foot, of standing as a virtuosic manipulation of balance. I became conscious, too, of a physical center that was as personal as my own voice. I was ready for this world, with its leaning, its subtly shifting points of contact, its reliance on and defiance of gravity. Give the body a simple instruction: "Step while standing on the right leg. Release your kneecap. Notice what happens. Notice the subsequent shudder and lurch." I noticed, too, the emotion—the only thing that moves faster than thought. Physical awareness was richer than ever before.

With Arnie in Brockport, 1973

FLOATING THE TONGUE

———— •◆• ————

In Brockport, I had become involved with the Krishna Consciousness Movement. Perhaps in its oath of celibacy I sought relief from my socially problematic sexual identity—not that I managed to observe the oath for even two weeks. I wore robes, chanted, and sold "religious" books on the street. Arnie tried to be supportive, but he wouldn't accompany me that far. He'd made a home for us and waited for me to come back to it.

By the end of that summer I found myself struggling. Wondering if I should forsake my desire for a career with all it represented and give myself over to this life of a monk. I tried praying for a sign—something like a car accident, where I'd lose my legs, would have done. My prayers went unanswered and my desire for change, my curiosity about dance, was too compelling to resist.

Lois Welk was going to San Francisco to resuscitate the then defunct American Dance Asylumn, a loose collective of fellow choreography students that she had founded at Brockport some years earlier. She'd spoken of an arts community in San Francisco that sounded fresh, wild, and enticing. We agreed to rendezvous with her to continue our movement conversation.

But more important, my family was there. Azel had made the move some time before, and Estella and Gus had just joined him along with Flossie, who now called herself Flo, her two kids, and Gus Jr. Rhodessa was there too. (When their place in Rochester burned, she and Dennis had loaded up a van and headed to Costa Rica to live on the beach for a while. But when Rhodessa had a vivid dream telling her to "go back to Sodom and Gomorrah," the two of them moved on to San Francisco.)

They had settled into a big red house on Portrero Hill, a typical Bay Area Victorian perched on the side of those impossible slopes. You could, if you imagined, see carriages parked out front and elegant ladies with large hats rushing in and out of the house's large doors with their beveled and stained glass windows. But, as this was San Francisco in 1973, Rhodessa and Dennis called the house "Tomato" and re-created the communal spirit of Rochester's Troupe Street.

Being the place where Rhodessa lived—the same Rhodessa with whom I had shared a bologna sandwich and an orange soda as we watched dust eddies along the shallow trough of a row of unpicked potatoes—Tomato held out a promise of absolute acceptance. Long ago, she and I had decided to live exciting, extravagant, essential lives. We had made our vows through the precious poetry of Sara Teasdale. We'd sealed them with the tears that had fallen on my hand and hers while she, fifteen years old at the time, cried in that darkened movie theater, feeling the painful little secret that was Saundra Lee growing inside her.

And so it was that Arnie and I showed up at Rhodessa's front door. We looked down a long hallway into the sunny kitchen where Dennis's black lab, Darkie, would bask in the glow that was Rhodessa's personality and the pungent smells of healthful food cooking on the stove. Everywhere was the paraphernalia of the time—macramé hanging plant holders and a lace tablecloth sent by someone's mother, a hookah, and many pictures—several of Saundra Lee, now twelve years old, and one of Rhodessa and Dennis. Dennis, pointing to the distance, seems to be explaining something to her with patience and tenderness, while Rhodessa, with the simplicity and sweetness of a child and the furrowed brow of a woman and mother, listens to him.

When I remember Tomato, I hear people talking. I hear Dennis's resonant voice rising in argument, "Jesus Christ, Rho, you gotta understand a thing before you criticize it."

"Well, I just feel that . . . ," Rhodessa would begin. Their tones would rise and fall—as she adopted first the fussing voice of Estella and then the dismissive wit of Gus Jones. Dennis, loving her all the while, kept chairs

Gus and Estella Jones, San Francisco, 1974 (ARNIE ZANE)

from flying and glass from breaking. Soon there'd be laughter and silliness and one of them would say, "Let's go down to the ocean."

The Haight scene had pretty much passed and the neighborhood was changing from seedy to smart.

"Mmmm, chile, today I saw a man walkin' down the street with a mustache and beard, wearin' a gold evenin' gown and carryin' a baby," Estella would say, as she sat on the front stoop of her apartment.

Arnie took many photographs while we were in San Francisco. In one of them, my mother is wearing a huge straw hat. The hat casts a rattan shadow over her immense black face. If you look closely at her glasses you can see Arnie reflected in them, standing out in the Sunday morning sunlight of Haight Street, taking the picture. Estella looks pleased to be having her picture taken. On her right sits my father. He is smaller than she, and has an intense look on his face. He is wearing a bow tie and a fedora.

Azel, who'd always had this vision of the Joneses, that collectively we had a great story to tell and a great talent to tell it with, came up with a plan to create The Jones Company and produce a musical theater work about the Civil War; I (having danced barely three years myself) agreed to be the ballet master and choreographer.

Looking back, I find it remarkable that Arnie and I lived for an entire year in San Francisco and never once went to a gay bar or a bathhouse. Instead we went regularly to the Krishna Temple. I was no longer so single-minded about this as I'd been in Brockport. I had accepted that I was not prepared for the monastic life. But Arnie and I both found ballast in Krishna Consciousness. It underlay many aspects of our life. We kept an altar in our bedroom. I gave Estella yoga lessons in her apartment and proselytized within the ranks of my family, inviting them to "love feasts" at the temple on Sunday afternoons. When my mother and father came to our house for dinner, they were given *prasadam*—blessed, holy food—and they sat on the floor of our austere apartment, eating yogurt, chappatis, and other vegetarian delicacies.

In time, our interest in the Krishna movement passed away, but never completely. In moments of great stress, I still find myself chanting my mantra envisioning a blue-skinned avatar.

◆　　◆　　◆

ONE EVENING, we were all sitting around Rhodessa's table, eating winter casserole and discussing existentialism, socialism, Marxism. Out of the blue, Rhodessa's daughter, Saundra, said, "I was walking down the street today and I wondered what would happen if a person fell out of a window onto their head." We just smiled, knowing how twelve-year-olds say the oddest things. We continued our rumination. The phone rang. It was Mary Ellen, calling to tell us that Vileana's eight-year-old daughter, Emeraude L'Amour Delavante, had just fallen from the third-story window and landed on her head. The child had been rushed to the hospital. Rhodessa and Dennis left to meet the rest of the family there and I was left alone with Saundra.

Saundra wanted me to explain how things like this could happen. She wanted me to tell her if she'd made this happen because she had imagined it earlier. How could I explain? The phone rang again. The child was dead.

Emeraude's ashes were placed in a modest urn. All of us, on a memorably clear northern California morning, went walking out among the sand dunes to the Pacific Ocean. This gathering of relatives, friends, and friends of friends included Rhodessa, me, and Arnie chanting *Hare Krishna, Hare Krishna, Krishna Krishna, Hare Hare*; Azel; and two black-robed Zen monks whom he had invited. And there, face hidden by a black veil, was my mother, her grief so profound she would not deign to cry.

We stood at the edge of the Pacific Ocean. Vileana held the urn with the ashes of her daughter in it. I saw a primeval barracuda-like fish washed up on the shore, its side gashed, its mouth gasping.

We had to push my sister to the edge of the water. She refused to let go of the child. She held the urn tight in her arms. All the women joined around her, took her into their arms, and there she found courage. She took the lid off and reached into the urn with her hand.

She threw a handful of ashes. They blew back into her face, mixed with saltwater. She took another handful and threw it. It came flying back, mixed with saltwater—ocean and tears.

The monks spoke of eternity. Estella looked on with a stony expression.

We were all invited to reach into the urn and throw its contents into the ocean. That which the Pacific refused returned to our mouths and eyes.

And the urn was empty, the sky was a little bit darker, the two Zen monks were still praying as Arnie, Rhodessa, and I, all with shaven heads, danced and chanted.

Eventually we started to wander back up the beach towards the cars. I held back. As the group had all but disappeared over the crest of a dune, more hallucination than real, a blond runner emerged out of the late-morning haze, striding along the shore with both grace and effort. With one smooth motion he plucked up the large fish, which was now still, and tossed it into the waves before continuing down the beach.

◆　◆　◆

WHILE SAN FRANCISCO's informality, its unconventionality could absorb almost anything, its alienated middle-class children distrusted the pretensions of art. It was not in the spirit of people who had walked away from their parents' struggle for security to accept the desire for success in anyone else at that time. But we wanted to dance and we wanted to be successful.

"Lois and I have talked about it and we've decided that nothing's happening here for us," Arnie told me as he, Lois, and I stood on a street corner. "We should go back to where people are serious."

I said nothing. I watched a bus hiss by, sparks flying out from the crude connector and the ink-black cable. A dog skittered out of the way. A wino spat in the gutter. "What do you think, Bill?"

That small clawing animal who lived within the confines of my ribcage said, "Don't answer that question. Don't do anything."

"We can't put down any roots here," Lois continued. "We should go back to New York. Find ourselves space not too far from the city. We could really start to do something important."

The door of a nearby store swung open and inside I could see hash pipes, Day-Glo posters of Jimi Hendrix and Janis Joplin. Patchouli incense mingled with cigarette smoke and gasoline fumes from the street.

"All right. I'll think about it," I offered.

"C'mon," Arnie and Lois persisted. "We've go to do something. *Now* is the time."

Leaving San Francisco would mean leaving my family—one that was quite different from the one I'd left in Springwater when I went away to college. It had finally found peace in San Francisco. Georgia was a lifetime away. The snow and freezing cold of February on Miller Road might as well have been a dream. Here in San Francisco no one remembered that so much had failed back there. We had all moved from that cold north land to the Bay City, where anyone could be anything, where no one expected much of anyone. Here we were together.

As a bus roared and pulled away from the curb, I agreed to leave all of this.

WE SETTLED ON the idea of returning to Binghamton. It was between New York City, where we hoped our careers would take us, and the counter-cultural influences of Brockport, where we'd first formed our working relationship.

Some days later, Arnie and I paid $100 each to make the three-and-a-half-day trip back East, on one of those Gray Rabbit magic buses—a close relative of the very same bus that had picked me up every day on Miller Road, its grinding gears so familiar to both kindergarteners and the varsity basketball team. Here it was—now spray-painted a dubious shade of silver gray. The last eight rows of seats had been knocked out and replaced with bunk beds, space for backpacks, and other essential paraphernalia of cross-country travelers.

The driver was a stringent, cynical old veteran who looked at all his passengers as so much dung. He played Merle Haggard and old Elvis Presley tunes on his tape deck to tune us out. Among the other riders were a Native American recently out of prison for antiwar and tribal rights activities, a long-haired capitalist heading back to New Jersey to open a boutique where he intended to sell clocks and tables made from polyurethaned slices of red-wood stumps, and a young blond woman with her "old man," going back East to deal with "some shit her parents were trying to pull." And there were Arnie and me, shaved heads, quietly fingering our japa beads, trying to build up to the 108 daily repetitions of our mantra.

Barely a day on the road, the Gray Rabbit broke down in Reno, Nevada, and for forty-eight hours we sat in a garage with the others, waiting for it to be fixed, before deciding to catch the Greyhound.

"Self-portrait," Arnie on the roof of the American Dance Asylum, 137 Washington Street, Binghamton, 1975

ACROSS THE STREET

—————•◆•—————

Eliminate or minimize:
1. phrasing
2. development and climax
3. variation: rhythm, shape, dynamics
4. character
5. performance
6. variety and the spatial field
7. the virtuosic feat and the fully extended body

Substitute:
1. energy equality and "found" movement
2. equality of parts, repetition
3. repetition of discrete events
4. neutral performance
5. task or task-like activity
6. singular action, event, or tone
7. human scale
Yvonne Rainer, THE MIND IS A MUSCLE

IN BINGHAMTON, Arnie, Lois, and I, joined by dancer Jill Becker and poet Ira Bruckner, moved into the old Elks' club on Washington Street to reestablish the American Dance Asylum. This was the same space where Arnie and I had performed *Begin the Beguine*. The building was a wreck, the floors completely rotten, the roof barely able to hold out the rain. At night, lying in our bed, Arnie and I could see the stars through holes in the ceiling. But there were gorgeous stained glass windows and big open spaces in which to dance.

Being poor, we bought a fifty-pound bag of cornmeal, and ate nothing but cornmeal pancakes smeared with peanut butter for a month. Lois and Arnie gathered from a nearby apple tree, to add some fruit to our diet. We were happy, though, in this life we had chosen.

We rejected the modern classic techniques and stylistic training employed by Martha Graham, José Limón, and Alvin Ailey. Dance Asylum was about experimentation. We were impressed by choreographer/theorist Yvonne Rainer's manifesto, her rejection of technical display, charismatic performers, and illusion.

Lois drew upon accumulation, counterpoint, and task procedures as she created her work. She organized teams of performers doing very simple things around complex thematic megastructures.

Jill Becker in her *American Wildlife* went in search of the poetic by exploring a highly personal and eccentric movement style and an odd theatrical format. In it, we were animals. Lois, a fleshy woman with a lovely body, wore nothing but combat boots and moved like a seal. I was a bird, naked too except for a pair of shoes. I don't remember the movements of the piece except for one sequence in which we used the wall to lean, leverage against, and literally bounce off. Our audience—perhaps five people—huddled frightened at the other end of our loft.

The pieces that I made at this time were primarily narrative—stories with movement, movement with stories. In interpreting the Yvonne Rainer credo, I said no to heroic themes, no to psychology, and, for a while, no to mythology—no to all the attributes of the classical moderns. *Entrances* was a counting structure. The lights would go off at intervals, and when they came up again, the tempo of the dancers' movements had changed. Or the lights would go off as the dancers stood around the edge of the room, then come up on the dancers halfway to the center of the room. Then off and on again to find the dancers gathered at the center of the space. Interspersed among the lit segments were curious dramatic vignettes. In one Lois assumed the role of a woman being tortured and stabbed. Her bloodcurdling screams pierced the room as the lights were extinguished. The idea behind the piece was to manipulate events as if in a film editing room.

Arnie's take on the manifesto—and he was never one for manifestos—was to look hard at the body. In his photography, he concentrated on portraits of naked torsos cropped below the eyes and just above the groin. In the dance studio, grudgingly at first, he began choreographing the holds, the

Sue Carol Schmidt and Pearl Pease in At the Crux Of . . . *by Arnie* (ARNIE ZANE)

lifts, the passes of contact improvisation into tightly composed stage pictures. He created a piece called *At the Crux Of*, for which he produced a slide that said, "I wanted to make a dance about the body, beyond the medical, the clinical. . . ." One of the many segments of this work involved a tender contact duet between a small curly-haired young woman and an emaciated older one, both of whom were topless.

Arnie had met the older woman, Pearl Pease, one day when we had gone to the local thrift shop to buy old rugs and furniture for sets for *The*

Track Dance, a site-specific work of mine. We were driving across the bridge in Binghamton when we happened upon the astonishing sight of this ancient woman (who we later learned was only fifty or so) wearing a lace *fontange* around her head and a girl's Marie Antoinette–style pink party dress. Pink angel wings were strapped to her back. Her hair was almost white. Arnie stopped and asked her if she wanted to be in a show and she said that, well, she had to think about it. She ultimately accepted, and in *The Track Dance* sat in a parking lot installation fiendishly smoking cigarettes and knitting for hours.

Shortly after the performance of *At the Crux Of*, Pearl went to the state hospital. When Christmastime came, Arnie went to the hospital and told the officials that he was Professor Arnold Zane from the university and that he needed to have Mrs. Pease, who was under his care, released for the holidays. Pearl spent that Christmas with us and from then on, she called Arnie "Professor Zane." Over the years that followed, she appeared in many Dance Asylum performances.

◆　　◆　　◆

ONE SUMMER NIGHT in Binghamton, I rode my bicycle on the north side of town. The sun might have exploded that day and the asphalt was taking its revenge. The trees radiated heat, and the underside of their leaves sweat onto the shabby sidewalks. I rode past the railroad yard. I was happy. It was as if I was about to go somewhere, to leave the next day on vacation, but there was no vacation.

I rode past the matrix of abandoned, rusty trains. Over my head the sky was clear, the yard seemed haunted, uninviting, but I felt that there was a kind of light emanating from me, that I could brighten the darkness.

Ancient cinders crunched beneath the tires as I turned the bike into the train yard. I got off and walked. Wearing only sneakers and a pair of shorts, I could feel my body, the peculiar radiance in my chest, the warmth and heaviness of my groin. Peaceful and agitated, I was pumped like an athlete after the race. Abandoning the bike, I sat myself down on one of those creosote timbers that support the tracks and looked up at the stars. Not like the stars in the mountains that are perfect, crystalline, and remote, but my stars, the same stars that had graced the skies over a sleeping house on Miller Road.

The ancient Phoenicians used to say a man's nipples were his soul's eyes. When I lay on my back, my hands were free to interrogate my body, the flat of my stomach, my pectorals, my soul's eyes. The sky is my lover. My thighs spreading apart advanced our conversation. The stars watched us. They watched my hands move down to open my cutoffs and free my dick.

Here we are again and where do we go now, my friend? Tonight we are not warring. I am not chiding your fickleness. I am not comparing you to anyone. You are not feeling neglected nor overworked. You and I are one. My buddy. I stroke you.

I am holding a conversation, speaking to everyone that I have ever loved. I think of my mother. My father. He gave me permission to love Arnie when he pointed to an old man, then looked me in the eye and said, "He could be a gay and gays can love each other for a long time." I think about my high school sweetheart's tiny breasts. And, of course, I think about my prince, his anxiety quieted when I enter him, his arms wrapped around me, safe. I think about big, beautiful men bathing together, stroking each other, pinching tits, clutching buttocks. I think about power. Men tied, tying, released, crying. And I begin to come. The night's heat is me, spreading in all directions. My semen is aimed at the sky. My semen is aimed, ridiculously, at everything.

What is this?

Wanting to be wanted. To be loved. To be safe. To belong.

Sometimes when I step onstage, I carry in front of me an invisible phallus. And this phallus is to me what the spear was to the Watusis. It is my virility, my right to be, and the assurance that I will always be. I am in search of the dance in which the phallus is forgiven for being a thing that must penetrate, deflower. This dance will be selfish and self-interested, and yet, fulfilled by filling.

Sometimes I dance the dance that one does when one cannot get it up, when one scrapes about, looking for that fantasy, that kernel to set the blood pumping in the flaccid tissue. That dance is a life that is wasted. It is doubt, a set of arms that will never know what it's like to hold and to be held. That flaccid dance is weeping, complaining, alternately helpless and furious like a bleeding bull gathering its strength to charge. I hate that dance as I dance it.

Whenever I stand onstage—whenever a work of mine is up in front of an audience—I'm offering this thing that crashes or slips into the world.

Lying on the creosote rail, cinders pressing into my buttocks and lower back, trying to make the universe pregnant, I was signing a pact. I was agreeing to go on a long journey equipped with nothing more than my body and this hunger.

◆　　◆　　◆

WATCHING LOIS structure her pieces, manipulate events in time and space, juxtapose bodies and music, I began to understand dance as a perceptual exercise, as opposed to a story. I began to think of its participants as materials that could be molded as a sculptor would mold clay or stone. Time was also a material.

I'd look out on the traffic on Binghamton's Washington Street and feel the space changing beneath and between the cars, feel an object—a man, a child, a cat, a piece of paper—move from one side of the street to another. I came to look at city blocks and see every form—the buildings, the sleeping indigents, the police officer, an abandoned shopping cart—as distinct, separate, yet in ever-changing relationship to other.

A man named Walter lived in the flophouse across from us. He would sit at his window for long hours. One day, I watched him pull on his coat, imagined him making his way down the decrepit skeleton of a stairway. He stepped painfully out the front door, into the brightness of the street. Now, where there had been nothing a moment before, there was drama as Walter's fragility crossed the filthy expanse of concrete that was Washington Street on a Sunday morning.

The American Dance Asylum dance studio, 28 Frederick Street, Binghamton, 1975 (ARNIE ZANE)

Walter moved like a squirrel, quickly shuffling, stopping periodically to furtively look around, then continuing his odd, purposeful trek. He reached the center of the street and looked to his right, to his left. Tony Bump materialized.

Tony, a transvestite with bright carrot-orange makeup and hair, wore chunk-heeled platforms and a marigold-colored miniskirt. To watch Tony was to watch a personality unfold in space and, more particularly, in time. Unlike Walter, Tony never rushed. With neck jutted forward at a birdlike angle, arms poised at a distance from the sides of the body like a crazed man-nequin's, Tony glided so slowly, it seemed that scenery moved around him. Tony moved so slowly, in fact, that Walter had crossed the rest of the street, picked up a cigarette butt, checked some trash cans, and was heading back upstairs in the time it took Tony to negotiate the distance between Willis's Pawnshop and Maria's Italian Deli.

It was as if the two of them lived in different physical universes. One existed in small eddies of staccatoed events; the other's sense of time was grandly geologic. I didn't concern myself with why, but where, how, and when. Tony and Walter's dance was complete.

The stage is a bit like that desolate stretch of pavement, and the drama of Tony and Walter traversing it set a standard for all entrances and exits in the language of choreography.

◆　　◆　　◆

Everybody works at my house,
But my old man . . .
　　　　Jesse Fuller

In 1976, I was awarded my first grant, a Creative Artists Public Service (CAPS) award for a work in three parts entitled *Everybody Works/All Beasts Count.*

The piece began with a trio for myself and two small girls from the neighborhood. They wore sparkling, ill-fitting tights and leotards, rode on my back, did walkovers across my chest, and balanced on their heads in a quasi-circus act.

The piece ended with sixteen dancers—all wearing black business suits, some in Pacific Northwest and Native American-inspired headdresses that I had fashioned from papier-mâché—pretending to be in the unemployment line. In increasingly complex geometric patterns, they moved forward to answer perfunctory questions, then get their books stamped.

Between the two sections, I performed a solo.

I got the blues when my baby left me by the San Francisco Bay,
She's takin' an ocean liner and she's gone so far away,
I didn't mean to treat her so bad,
She's the best gal I ever have had,

In the solo of Everybody Works!, *Clark Center Dance Festival at the City University of New York Mall, New York City, 1975* (NATHANIEL TILESTON)

She said good-bye gonna make me cry,
I'm gonna lay down and die. . . .

Then Jesse Fuller would shout *"San Francisco Bay!"* and I'd stride out across the stage. Barefoot, wearing a suit, white shirt, and tie. I was a demented preacher or an off-duty waiter. I directed Jesse's refrain from my feet, thighs, and buttocks to my pumping arms and mugging face. In the fiercely archaic jazz of my imagination, I was dancing to say San Francisco was where I put a life aside in order to invent a new one.

The music changed. Eerie, beautiful vocalizing filled the room. Balkan? Native American? No. It was Arnie and our friend Lynda Berry improvising into a microphone from the hospital bed where she was healing her broken back. Holding up my fingers, sign language style, I counted out my social security number as I danced. When this segment finished, I began to tell a story while repeating the numerical hand gestures. And in this story, I never gave voice to the word *white* when my lips formed the shape of it: *When I was a little boy about twelve years old, I received a little* white *card in the mail. Two, two, five, two, six, three, eight, four, eight.* I repeated this sentence louder, slower, and more slurred. It could have been the sound of a tape recorder failing or a large, retarded child wailing.

Jesse Fuller returned with his foot-tapping harmonica music. I danced.

Another story interrupted by my social security number.

When I was a little boy of about twelve years old—two, two, five—I went back to the place where I was born—two, six—Bunnell, Florida. I was sitting on the steps with my two old aunties—Aunt Mattie and Aunt Purity Roger—three, eight—Mattie said to me, "Billy, you ain't gonna do what your brother Iry did. He went up North and married a white *girl. 'Cause if you marry a* white *girl you can't come down here and visit us no more." And I said, "Auntie, I love you. I love you."*

As I told this story, I stripped to the shorts I wore beneath my suit and ended by spinning in a circle, shouting, *I love you. I love you. I love you.*

After the piece had completed its run in Binghamton, Lois, Arnie, and I were taking a class from Suzanne Klein in New York City and saw a flyer for an audition for the Clark Center Dance Festival at CUNY Mall. On the spur of the moment, I decided to audition this solo.

At the audition, I had to wait for more than an hour, in which time I became increasingly nervous. At last my turn came. In the piece, there was one sequence, a series of contrasting gestures and facial expressions. One of them, a boxing gesture directed at the audience—in this case, the audition judges—was to soften into a smile and shrug of acquiescence, but striving against my nervousness, I became defiant. My clenched fist evolved into an unplanned obscene raised finger and a mouthed curse. I shrugged and smiled. Having had no technical rehearsal, at the point where the lights were supposed to go off I yelled to a young black woman standing at the back of the room, "Hey, soul sister, turn off the lights." The judges sat in shadow. They called the next auditioner. The audition was over.

I never thought they'd want me. At the time, I felt as though I lived in a world where "true art" was made. Manhattan was Babylon, its art world mercantile and corrupt. I would try to forget these judges and this festival.

Back home, several days later, I received a message to call Louise Roberts, the festival director. Abandoning all my artistic convictions, I eagerly rushed to a Woolworth's pay phone, where a coldly matter-of-fact Ms. Roberts informed me that the panel was interested in using my piece but demanded assurance that I would not make "certain gestures," use "certain language," and so forth. "Are you trying to censor my work?" I sniffed.

"Look, young man, you have a chip on your shoulder. New York City is going to knock it off. Do you want to do this or not?"

Of course I did.

The *New York Times* called the piece "humanist," and said I was a "performer worth watching." The *SoHo News* said that I had "an engaging stage presence," although the writer doubted that anyone else could do this choreography, which seemed more about the performer than about dance.

I was invited back to do the same piece the next year at the New York Shakespeare Festival in Central Park, on a program with Murray Lewis and the Joffrey Ballet. It was very heady stuff, finding myself in Central Park, naked except for those shorts, spinning under a sky darkened by a brewing storm.

Aunties, I love you. I love you. I love you.

Arnie had flown Rhodessa in from California for the occasion and she came onstage bearing flowers. As I took my curtain call, the sky opened in a deluge. It seemed to me a benediction.

◆   ◆   ◆

*NO to spectacle no to virtuosity no to transformations
and magic and make-believe no to the glamour and tran-
scendency of the star image no to the heroic no to the anti-
heroic no to trash imagery no to involvement of performer or
spectator no to style no to camp no to seduction of spectator
by the wiles of the performer no to eccentricity no to moving
or being moved.*

Yvonne Rainer, PARTS OF SOME SEXTETS

We still held to our credo, though the actual experience of the professional stage was beginning to present us with a challenge. When I was
onstage, I wrestled with the audience's expectations, wrestled with the fact
that I was a composite of preconceptions, biases, and fantasies—a mere projection. I believed that by talking honestly about my life and my feelings, I
was saying no to illusion and expectation. I understood performing to be
using the body, the mind, and memory to connect with an assembly of people. If I was charismatic, I accepted it as a necessary evil.

After the success of *Everybody Works* in Central Park, I was invited
to perform at Dance Theater Workshop, and the Kitchen, and for a return
engagement at the Clark Center Dance Festival at the CUNY Mall in New
York. How did I understand this? I didn't. I insisted that I appear at the Clark
Center Dance Festival as part of a Dance Asylum engagement, featuring
the works of Arnie, Lois, and myself. I was proud of Lois's formalist command of large groups and Arnie's unwavering visual pragmatism. My per-
sona as a performance "natural" was enhanced and supported by our
collective.

It was the duets I did with Arnie that drew the most critical enthusiasm.
We were exactly what the times called for: structuralists—but with a difference. One of these early duets, *Monkey Run Road*, had premiered at the
American Dance Asylum and was later performed at the Kitchen and the
Warren Street Performance Loft. It was a stark and formal work, a layered
accumulation of gestures. We had modeled the duet after Richard Bull's
piece *Making and Doing*, wherein dancers performed casual acts—wiping
water up off the floor, doing pliés, changing a shirt—and repeated those ges-

138

tures until they lost their origins and became pure movement. Arnie and I also drew upon the films of Michael Snow, Tony Conrad, and Stan Brakhage, films that analyzed the act of seeing through the accumulation of frames, repetition, and the manipulation of speed and inversion. We shared their purpose—the subversion of narrative expectation.

Monkey Run Road was named after a juke joint, Monkey Run, set way back in the woods over the mountain near Miller Road. In the late fifties my parents would go there on some Friday nights. They never described Monkey Run, so my child's imagination pictured a vast tract of land overrun by wild monkeys.

The dance was composed of series of gestures and positions, performed backwards, forwards, then backwards again. Like many of our pieces at the time, *Monkey Run Road* had an improvisational look to it. It was, however, very carefully set. It began with us dressed in black, pushing a large unpainted pine box out onto the performance space. We talked quietly to each other, seeming to disagree about where to place the box. When we found the right spot, I sat down on the edge of the box and Arnie stood between my legs. We remained in this pose for a substantial time before breaking it, taking the box offstage, then returning with it. We performed the whole set of movements two or three times, incorporating small, seemingly spontaneous changes into the structure of each repetition. Arnie would sit between my legs. I would dance a solo. Arnie would dance a solo. And a series of grappling partnering sequences would follow. Each could be taken apart like modular pieces.

The finale found me peering into the box, into which Arnie had disappeared, my face illuminated by the flickering candles that he, out of the audience's sight, was lighting. Here, in the warmth of our relationship, in the glow of candlelight, I quietly began to reflect on the Bay of Pigs crisis and my memory of Gus, Steve, and myself as we lay across our bed waiting for Armageddon in the late summer afternoon light of Miller Road. In the candlelight I could imagine Armageddon's bombers in pastel hues. And so I whispered to Arnie, as much in encouragement as in warning, *Pink bombers, pink bombers, pink bombers.* The ominous had become playful, and then playfully ominous in the male-to-male camaraderie that existed in our constructivist world.

By chilling coincidence, the night that we premiered *Monkey Run Road* at the Warren Street Performance Loft, a March night in 1979, the Three Mile Island accident occurred. Annihilation, even nuclear annihilation, was as close and as far away as the Bay of Pigs.

◆　　◆　　◆

DESPITE ITS COMMUNAL aspect, Dance Asylum was a federation of artists, not a family. We had settled into the Elks' lodge as a creative experiment in lifestyle. Some of us shared an emotional affinity for one another, and some of us did not. A kind of heaviness would overtake me at times. I'd put on Mahalia Jackson, improvise in the studio, and find myself crying. It took me a while to realize that what I missed was the defining backdrop of my family.

I began to make solo works drawing upon my mother's and father's penchant for narration, mining my memories of the family and its history—as if this activity were a substitute for living with them.

My mother's praying was the first theater I ever saw—and the truest. *Floating the Tongue* was not a story so much as an exercise that drew upon these prayers as its rudimentary paradigm. Its title was derived from a Buddhist meditative practice in which the practitioner sits or lies perfectly still and focuses on the simple activity of floating the tongue freely in the mouth. There is a tension between the simple physical task and the ceaseless working of the mind.

In the first part of the dance, I repeated an improvised gesture until it was set—mastered. Then I began to describe my movements as I performed them. Through repetition, the gesture and its spoken description slowly changed. I relished these changes—exaggerated them, in fact, until the movement and its description were related by only the freest association. While performing this evolutionary piece, I found that I entered a trancelike state not unlike that which I had watched Estella enter every Christmas morning of my childhood. Movement granted me access to new levels of emotion and meaning. Sometime later Arlene Croce wrote dismissively, "He works himself into a tizzy." I was hurt by this. And offended. This "tizzy" is something I have claimed as an inheritance. Perhaps in her experience it did not seem genuine, or perhaps it seemed too genuine—embarrassing, even— but for me it is an integral part of the strategy that allows me to make art.

Blauvelt Mountain, *1980, International Center for the Arts, London* (DEE CONWAY)

SHARED DISTANCE

———— • ◆ • ————

"It appears that we don't like each other anymore. Maybe we need to move apart for a while. We might even work together again," I said, interrupting a heated argument between Arnie and Lois. Lois, half standing, half sitting, inevitable morning mug of coffee in hand, was wearing her "controlled" face—a proven defense against Arnie's onslaught. The late-summer morning light tinted Arnie's pallor as I entered the kitchen to hear him shout something about the duration of Lois's boyfriend's shower. This fight was not about a shower, about who did or did not do the dishes. It was not even about us liking one another or not. Just as it had the day on Haight Street when we decided to leave San Francisco, the time had come for a change. Only this time the three of us would be parting.

And there was no air in Binghamton anymore. When I went to the local gay bar without Arnie, finding a partner to dance with felt like finding a partner for the senior prom back at Wayland Central High. I was the only black there and white folk may have been queer but they chose not to be *that* queer. When we performed Lois's environmental extravaganzas in the abandoned parking lot behind the Dance Asylum's new home at 28 Frederick Street, we had to struggle to be heard over the din of neighborhood children and their parents shouting obscenities, banging trash cans, and throwing bottles. The strain was reflected in our collaborative relationship.

Leaving the American Dance Asylum was not unlike leaving a spouse or parent for reasons that were confused, painful, and too pertinent to resist. In New York, we would not have to explain what we were doing and why we did it—or so we thought. *Foggets* or *faggits* had been scrawled on the sidewalks in front of the Dance Asylum. In New York, we would not be the subjects of verbal and graffiti threats—or, so we thought.

NEW YORK would be different. We'd already danced to some success there. We hoped for more opportunities to do the same. But despite its attractions, Arnie and I agreed that we didn't want to move right into the heart of the city proper. We would work there but find someplace safely beyond its reach to call home.

Our friend the singer Jeanne Lee had been searching for a place to settle herself and her brood at the time and she shared with us her list of possibilities. We moved into an apartment over a restaurant in Blauvelt, a town just north of the city and not far from where Arnie had grown up. When the restaurant went bankrupt and our landlords fled in the night, we had to leave. Through a real estate broker who apologized for its being "so wild," we found a house in nearby Valley Cottage, forty-five minutes from Manhattan.

We first laid eyes on the house in the early spring of 1980, the homeliest time of the year for this particular property. The modest cottage's most attractive quality is the abundance of trees and shrubs that camouflage its many defects, and in March these trees were bare. Nonetheless, I knew that this was the home we would share for the rest of our life together. And Arnie, contrary to his habits, deferred to my inclination.

Soon there were hundreds of boxes—boxes filled with Binghamton, Amsterdam, Brockport, San Francisco, the Dance Asylum. And they were all piled in the dank, musty rooms of the little house.

To my great relief, I had committed myself to a three- or four-week residency with the Cedar Art Forum in Waterloo, Iowa. So I was able to leave. (In 1978, I had been accepted into the Affiliate Artists Program, which had been founded with the intention of sending solo artists of various disciplines into small communities around the country.) Arnie stayed behind to do what he was always drawn towards doing. I was so caught up in my own midwestern adventure that I never knew for sure how he did it, but I can imagine. Telephone virtuoso that he was, I'm sure that he cradled the receiver in the crook of his neck and held lively conversations with friends or potential business contacts as he unpacked the endless boxes, and sorted, placed, and arranged their contents. At other times he must have left off his unpacking to feed and walk his beloved Akitas, Rasa and Ali, whom we'd acquired when hostile neighbors had forced a siege mentality upon the Dance Asylum.

Returning home to this soulful little cottage—surrounded by spring's luxuriant foliage, everything orderly inside, freshly cut flowers on the tables, and Arnie, offering a home-cooked meal and the pleasures of himself as master/mistress of our dominion—was an exceptional delight.

But the decision to settle an hour away from our dance life had serious ramifications. It was no longer possible to wake up first thing in the morning, run downstairs to a gymnasium-sized studio to flex, bend, and work out choreography that might have come in a dream the night before. And there certainly were no technique classes in Valley Cottage. In spite of the obstacles, we created our next duet, *Blauvelt Mountain*, there.

In this two-part, seventy-minute-long piece, we continued to draw upon the notion of accumulation as we extended it beyond the body to include the set. We wanted a wall. Bill Katz, an artist and friend, suggested that we build one out of cinder blocks, so we spent an afternoon carrying 150 of them up the stairs of Dance Theater Workshop. The wall these blocks formed was compelling, almost sinister. When, under Bill's watchful eye, William Yehle lit it, the subtle play of light against the textured gray concrete was breathtaking.

The opening sequence of *Blauvelt Mountain* was a meticulously choreographed duet called "A Fiction." Arnie and I knelt upstage left in a single shaft of light, dressed in black thinly striped ski pants and sleeveless shirts that recalled early Frank Stella paintings. I faced upstage towards the wall. Arnie faced me at a right angle. The composer, Helen Thorington, sat behind a mini-fortress of electronic equipment downstage left. Alternately chatting, gurgling, and singing, she recounted *The Emperor and the Nightingale* in a complex and shifting whir of musical tones.

In an almost incantatory series of movements, Arnie and I made a slow traverse along the four-foot-high barrier. I lay on my back, my head to the audience, legs extended in a wide V, as Arnie crouched at my left. He extended one arm and passed it methodically over my prone body. I rolled to change my position and ended balanced precariously on Arnie's back. The movement was seamless, almost matter-of-fact. This introduction ended as we began the first of a series of passes around the periphery of the stage, during which time we conducted one of those whispered conversations that were quickly becoming our hallmark. This traverse conversation was abruptly interrupted by a spurt of dancing on converging diagonals. My own movement—gulping space—focused on leaps and huge arcs for the upper body and legs. Arnie's movement—bound and angular—was an odd blend of martial arts and childlike whimsy. (No one could somersault with greater concision and speed than Arnie.) And then there was the crafted grappling between us that resulted in outlandish lifts—me wrapped around Arnie's waist, Arnie bent over like a mother baboon clutching her baby—as Helen's sotto voce intonations came to a close. When it was silent, we released each other, collected ourselves, and prepared for the next sequence.

There were two pine benches downstage left that served as landmarks on our itinerary as we traveled the stage. As we sat on them—Arnie on his bench and me on mine—we moved through a series of jerky postures that sometimes suggested the broken puppet Petroushka, sometimes Charlie Chaplin's *The Great Dictator*, and sometimes animals removing thorns from their paws. We then rushed away from the benches, doubled back to place a knee on them, and with the opposite foot pushed the floor away, to spin in perfect unison before returning to our traverse along the periphery.

As the piece progressed, Helen's storytelling became more convoluted, more obscured by her electronic sound environment. Our repetition became more elaborate. What had been a sequence of movements performed in close proximity to each other was now separated in space. Everything got faster. The traverse became a run. Against Helen's background vocalization, Arnie and I began a more audible, improvised word association. I would say, *Statue*, Arnie would say, *Liberty. White. Black. President. Communist. Cock.*

Cunt. Sweat. Dogshit. Cat. Mother. Father. No. Then, without ceasing the word game, we'd dash back into the frenzy of our diagonals.

At the end of the piece, only barely interrupting the diagonal dancing, Arnie picked up one of the benches and threw it the entire length of the stage, where I caught it and hung it from a hook protruding from the proscenium downstage left. We performed a brief fragment of the Petroushka and *The Great Dictator* movements. I turned just in time to catch the second bench, which Arnie had thrown. I hung it alongside the first. The word association continued. *FBI. KGB. Jew. Spic. My Country, 'Tis of Thee.* In midsentence, I barreled across the stage, threw myself into the air, and at the height of my jump Arnie caught me. Blackout.

We opened the second section, "An Interview," with Arnie's and my a capella singing of a medieval Swiss-German harvest round that we had learned from a painter friend in Zurich. Both of us wore simple white Greek tunics tucked into light cotton sailor pants. We had decided that there was going to be no partnering, no contact between us, so after the singing we began the contrasting activities that informed this section. With the concentration of a martial arts expert, Arnie, wearing white shoes and huge welder's gloves, disassembled the wall, block by block, and reconstructed it at a ninety-degree angle, dividing the stage in half. I, barefoot, improvised my way from stage to audience to exit and back again. Arnie's gritty shuffle with its staccatoed repetition, the scrape of concrete and the inevitable spatter of falling debris, my erratic thuds in and off the performing area were bound together by the leitmotif of our breathing. In trying to counterbalance Arnie's austere aloofness, I relied as much on my personality as on my flinging and crashing improvisation. Three times the ambient sound environment was interrupted by a tape-recorded conversation between Arnie and myself—a mundane conversation, something about going to a foreign city near water and trying to describe whom we might meet there. At first, it appeared to be a logical discussion, but with successive repetition the relationship between questions and answers became more and more skewed until there was no relationship at all. There were alarm clocks placed under the chairs in the

Blauvelt Mountain, *1980, International Center for the Arts, London* (DEE CONWAY)

audience. They were all supposed to go off twenty-five minutes into the performance. Of course they all went off at different times, but it didn't matter. The piece ended when the last answer was given, the alarm clocks were blasting, and we both stood still as the lights slowly died.

Blauvelt Mountain was a vital performance, perhaps even a defining one. As with *Monkey Run Road*, we had taken our inspiration and impulse for analysis from non-narrative cinema and visual arts. We chose a range of activities, from pedestrianisms like walking, sitting, standing, to complex grappling. We dismantled this material, rearranged it, and manipulated it in an effort to provide an exercise in perception for our audience. And in the free-flowing word association, we in turn were challenged and learned to enjoy a special sense of accomplishment each evening as we solved this particular performance puzzle. We were very proud of the boldness and effectiveness of the cinder block wall. We felt a direct connection between the "constructivism" of our choreographic sensibility and the obvious construction and deconstruction of the wall.

The work received some significant critical attention, and Robyn Brentano, an artist friend, praised it as "a truly beautiful homoerotic work."

Arnie and I were a bit surprised by this and didn't know exactly what to make of it. To us it was that and much more. We had understood our homosexuality to be a *part* of our work, just as homosexual eroticism was *part* of our relationship. *Blauvelt Mountain* was a very athletic piece, not at all as camp as *Begin the Beguine* had been. But it wasn't like a piece danced by a man and a woman or, for that matter, like a piece simply danced by two male contact dancers. It was unlike anything else: dance was a place where the strategies of our relationship and of our art making were delineated even as they commingled. We were serious. We had fun. We fought like hell.

The first half of *Blauvelt Mountain* became a staple of our small repertory of duets. The Kitchen Center for Dance, Music, and Video had inaugurated a mini-festival of performances and invited us to tour with them in Europe. I remember waking up on the morning we were going to premiere the piece in Berlin and finding it remarkable that we were going to build a cinder block wall down the center of a stage there. But the German critics made no particular mention of the wall and praised the piece as a "brilliant depiction of the struggles between whites and blacks in America."

◆　　◆　　◆

What does it say?

There was no air in the bedroom the night before reviews came out. Our throats were dry. We did not sleep.

What does it say about us?

In Binghamton, the people who reviewed us in the local paper were often music writers forced by their editors to cover obscure dance performances. Their reviews were cursory, even naive. But now, we were being judged by "informed observers."

They are watching us.

When we danced in the converted gymnasium of Dance Asylum, we were showing a relatively small group of friends who we were, who we thought we were, and maybe what we wanted to be. But now Arnie and I were dancing before much larger groups of people, now we had public personas like suits of clothes that we put on, or were somehow put on us.

What are they saying about us? About Bill and Arnie?

They were taken with our camaraderie. They didn't mention that we were lovers, but said that the work spoke of a deep intimacy. I was "tall and

Valley Cottage Duet, *1982* (LOIS GREENFIELD)

black with an animal quality of movement." Arnie was "short and white, with a nervous, pugnacious demeanor." We were "greater than the sum of our parts" and our work took place in an "urban clearinghouse where two disparate beings work out some elaborate social ritual."

They were writing our dance down, transferring it to microfilm, discussing it on panels, thumbs up, thumbs down. Composer Rhys Chatham once said to me, "Don't even bother reading what they say. Just measure the column inches." I always read what the reviews said. They mattered because we were now promoting ourselves—promoting a career that was driven by commissions, audiences, and critical approval.

They are watching me.

Suddenly, I understood the way Vess's Mary pulled those men to her. I found myself easily seduced by a set of eyes, learned what it is to engage the expectations and needs of spectators. It made me want to please. Or spit.

"You think I'm going to please you, but I'm going to show you something we both have trouble looking at. It's in my legs and hips, my face filled with clouds passing to reveal the sun, and now clouds again, it's in my voice. Perhaps I am pretending, but this is my habitat, this place of illusion. I have no money in the bank. My life is not insured. I'm not worth much. Your acceptance is my only security."

This was a lie. The truth was that my relationship with Arnie was my ultimate security.

What are they thinking about me?

The more I was watched, the more I looked backwards. It was an uneasy glance. On the one hand, I was convinced that I knew something, convinced that I had a story to tell that was as elemental and as eloquent as gathering potatoes into bushel baskets and dumping them into burlap bags in air as hot as an oven, spiked with dust, defoliant, and desperation. But I was still the five-year-old boy hugging the side of a concrete building. I was still the nineteen-year-old flailing his arms and crashing naively about in a Dutch garden.

What did they say? What did they see?

Back in San Francisco, I remember saying to Rhodessa's companion, Dennis Riley, a writer, that I wasn't interested in writing because too much had already been written, that library shelves were overburdened with dusty unread books. And here we were, Arnie and I, trying like hell to join our voices with thousands of other voices clamoring to be heard, to be recognized, to be written about. Why?

The magic in our love was the shared belief that life was something rhapsodic, heroic, that one should run out to meet. We would do whatever we had to do to serve up this something in dance.

Time, money, and fear were our enemies.

Time. For not having enough of it before the critics and audiences grew tired of us and turned away, not having enough before we ran out of the precious, invisible substance that flowed through us and out into the world. For having perhaps started too late.

Money. It had always been in short supply. But now we were no longer on welfare, no longer hanging on to the odd job—Arnie as a water department clerk in San Francisco or as a go-go dancer in Binghamton, me as a male orderly in San Francisco or at the geriatric hospital in Binghamton stuffing adult diapers at the laundry. We had said to our families, "We are different. We will not work as you worked. We will construct dreams and feed ourselves doing so."

Fear. That we were not going to make it. That our work would go unnoticed. That we would fail each other. Arnie was afraid that I would at the first opportunity leave him for someone who could give me more, someone who was taller, stronger, more beautiful. I was afraid that I would not keep up with his drive and discipline, that I would hurt him irreparably. I was afraid that I would be revealed as empty, having no story to tell, nothing new to add. Afraid that I would run out of courage, as I had once on the athletic field in Wayland when, leading the pack across the cinders, I was overtaken with debilitating doubt, paralyzed with fear, and tripped myself so as to have an excuse for not finishing the race. If this was a race, was I up to it? I was afraid of them—of the ways they could condemn me, tie my hands, and discard me, just as ambitious poor people have always been tied and abandoned.

Arnie and I lived with these three enemies. We set a place for them at the table. They slept all around us at night and would sometimes wiggle unctuously between us. But we could handle them. Between us, we had the guts of Estella and Gus and Edith and Lon, and we'd rather have been dead than give in.

Together, Arnie and I formed some mythical beast. We flew. I had the wings, but it was something about the strength in his legs that got us off the ground. This adventure we were having in the art world could fall apart, but we would still be together. We had no reason to be together, no validation from anyone, no children, nothing but his vision, my arms, his legs, my wings, our loving.

What did they say?

We found that the world had changed—not overnight, not unrecognizably so, but it had changed. Yes, there was still a flow, but there seemed to be more and more times when we were swimming against it, holding on to rocks, debris, and each other. There was strength in this swimming and we were never alone. We were now personalities with a location, even a constituency. And there were clear markers as to where we were going. And so we went.

What did they say?

◆   ◆   ◆

My memory is not my enemy.

It's difficult to report honestly about what happened at the baths of the East Village in the late seventies. There were so many of us doing things we were embarrassed by, yet we were also finding the expression of dreams we'd dreamt for our entire lives. How do others remember them? Do they think about them now in the same way that I do—those men who have not died? I know that they were there. We were all there.

I went with Arnie for the first time shortly after we moved to Blauvelt. This was in 1978. The last time was in the early part of 1982. The Saint Mark's Baths were the most luxurious, not that there was anything particularly genteel about the place. The first time I went, we stood on the long line that stretched from the doorway out into the bazaarlike atmosphere of Saint Mark's Place. The buzzer would go off periodically, the door would open, and someone would be allowed to enter. Out through the open door came a heavy smell—a smell different from the one that filled the locker rooms I had known as a runner, the odor of expectation, the odor of sex as tangible as the acrid whiff of amyl nitrite—poppers.

The management took the occupancy ordinance very seriously, and we were allowed to enter only one or two at a time. Once inside, we joined another line, which snaked up the stairs. Slowly, we approached two mustached young men with military haircuts and tight T-shirts who stood behind tellerlike windows and collected seven dollars for a locker key, twelve dollars for a single bedroom, or fifteen dollars for a "deluxe" double room. Arnie counted out our money—enough for two locker keys.

We were told to go downstairs, that someone would take care of us there. As we walked down the hallway, we passed men sitting at a little snack bar, wrapped in white towels, smoking cigarettes and eating sandwiches. All around us pulsed the tempo of late-seventies disco music. *I never knew love like this before. Love, love, love.* The men—mostly white—were of every age and description. No, perhaps not *every* age. There were very few older men. They knew better than to come here. This was a showplace for the young and delectable.

Downstairs, we were met by an ingratiating young man with a shag haircut, also dressed in T-shirt and jeans, a towel hanging out of his back pocket, another in his hand. "How are you guys tonight? Here're your lockers. The showers are this way," he said, pointing down the hallway to our right. "I hope you enjoy your time." And for handing us the towels and giving us directions, we slipped him a tip.

Undressing in front of your locker, you'd notice that someone else was slowly undressing beside you. He'd look at you. At first you'd be uncomfortable, afraid to look back. But everywhere people were covertly (or not) staring at one another. The challenge, the theater of it, was to slide out of your pants and into your towel quickly, before anyone could see anything.

Attaching our locker keys to our wrists, we moved on to "the Showers," a big, state-of-the-art temple. Some people spent whole nights in them, others would just scrub up, use the douching room, then move on. We showered.

Arnie led me upstairs and guided me through the labyrinth of dark halls that divided the four floors of the Saint Mark's Baths. Lit by single light bulbs spaced every ten feet or so, these halls were painted a discreet, masculine shade of brown, with an equally discreet brown carpet on the floor. Hundreds of little cubicles lined the halls. If their doors were ajar, you could look in and see a man lying on his bed partially covered or uncovered, presenting himself. If you saw a man you wanted, you stepped just inside his door. He would either ignore you, tell you, "No, no," or he'd shift his body in a certain way, look at you invitingly, perhaps even say, "Come in, close the door."

The question at the baths, particularly the first few times I went, was how much could I have? Wandering those halls felt something like roaming the aisles of a supermarket while hungry or enduring that moment before the presents are opened on Christmas morning. I'd never much liked the bar scene—never much liked the illusion of simply wanting to drink and talk when really only looking for sex. The baths were so much more direct.

I try but cannot remember my first encounter. Maybe I found him inside one of those little rooms. Maybe I met him in the hall and he followed me or I followed him to some darker corner, where we stood together. There, nothing being said, our furtive glances might have given way to suggestive looks, and suggestive looks might have turned to frank stares. One of us might have placed his hand on the other's chest, reached beneath the other's towel. We'd kiss.

"Do you have a room?" "No." "No? Oh, this is bad."

We could go to "the Orgy Room" if we didn't mind voyeurs, furniture covered with clammy Naugahyde, and men coupling everywhere. Or we could go to "the Barracks," one of several spaces designed to represent a number of male iconographic locations—the back of a truck, a jail cell, a locker room, a military bunkhouse. There were all kinds of men at the baths—military men, married family men—and one could never know what their fancies were until they told you. Having found a place, we would negotiate who was going to do what to whom, and sex would begin. If you were lucky, you really enjoyed it. If you didn't, you had a choice—either to excuse yourself from the exchange or continue until at least one of you had satisfied himself. Afterwards, you might go take a shower before finding someone else. Then it would start all over again. And again. The ritual was hypnotic.

Unlike our dance at the time, which was energetic, almost assaultive with all of its jumping, diving, twisting, turning, movement down these long corridors seemed to unfold in slow motion. Interactions crumbled and dissolved or took fire and consumed themselves in dark corners, in the tiled glare of the showers, or in the perpetual twilight of the steam room.

Often, you'd come across a cluster of men—a "desirable" surrounded by several others who vied for his selection. Someone would make a move, be accepted or rejected. If he was accepted, the momentum would shift. The men gathered close around the pair turned their desire elsewhere or, if so allowed, joined in the sexual exchange.

There were times when I saw someone and pursued him, but most of the time I positioned myself as a "desirable." I would advertise my body quietly, discreetly. If someone wanted me, I would choose. I often found myself being followed by people I had no interest in—presumptuous men, pushy men, or racist men. But some undesired suitors seemed decent if needy. When they put their hands on me, their entreating touch merited a gentle refusal and an apologetic smile. I'd often stay and talk with these men, to try to change the tenor of our exchange. Sometimes friendships would evolve.

Every once in a while, you would run into friends and you'd experience a sensation not unlike two positive charges repelling each other. "Oh, how are you doing?" you might ask nervously before darting off in opposite directions.

This was a world apart and we liked it that way.

Arnie and I would spend five or six hours pacing to the disco beat and the sounds of sex, being rejected and accepted, rejecting and accepting. When we ran into each other, we'd have a drink and ask, "Do you want to go back up again?" It was time to leave this delicious purgatory only when we were utterly exhausted, hungry, craving the intimacy our private time afforded.

We'd head back to our little cottage and have sex together before falling into deep sleep. It was perfect.

AN INEVITABLE RISK of the baths was falling in love with someone. I fell in love with Ralph. He was a tall, yellow-skinned black man, lankily built, forty years old. A sort of free spirit, Ralph strode the halls of the Saint Mark's Baths with an occult volume tucked under his arm and a look of bemused disdain on his face. He wore beautiful hand-worked silver jewelry that became my habit to wear whenever we were together. When he called me "my pretty nigger," I was gratified and confused.

Ralph's attitude offered many challenges. He felt it would be an insult to his mother to bring home a white lover. He likewise believed that it was impossible for blacks to be racists, since racism was an institution and disempowered people have few, if any, institutions. In the realm of art, he offered criticism. I once demonstrated a solo I was working on that made use of a quick series of arm gestures. He was not impressed. He said, "I can take you to a place where young brothers can show you that, and more than you can imagine." My field of reference points was in flux and Ralph's experience broadened my appreciation of black popular culture. At the time, break dancing and "vogueing" were still exotic, unexplored in the New York dance scene. Ralph provided me direct access to this rich resource.

This infatuation lasted six months and proved torturous for Arnie. The relationship ended when Arnie called Ralph out to the street from his job. I stood a block away and watched five-foot-four Arnie staring up at six-foot-two Ralph and say, "If you don't stay away from my house, I'll blow your motherfucking brains out." I had no choice, I knew where I belonged. The courage, desperation, and pain represented in this threat (Arnie never had a gun) illuminated the depth of his love and what I stood to lose if we fell apart.

It was around this time that we stopped going to the baths.

This is my desire. My desire is not my enemy.

This is my dick. My dick is not my enemy.

When I think of the baths, I don't see my dick leading me down the halls and in and out of cubicles. My dick is not my enemy. Its gentle probe is a part of myself that entered another person for a chance to pull that person closer, a chance to make a promise, "I have something to give you and it would be my joy to give you what I have." No, it was not my dick, but more a pulse behind the breastbone, between my lungs, a pulse that beat in a staccato counterpoint to my breath, which led me. My eyes became simple detectors, scouting, scanning, seeking the curve of a calf, a strong thigh, pubic hairs starting at the navel and cascading past terry cloth barriers. Once found, these things set this blood piston into motion. My legs would follow. My hands, arms, and shoulders would obey.

We were all a little bashful at the baths, but I liked being there. I liked us being there. Contact improvisation in 1974 had encouraged an unselfconscious, direct physical intimacy in which all differences—weight, size, psychological temperament, even gender and race—were negated in favor of cohesion—tissue to tissue, bone to bone, muscle to muscle. I saw our exuberant acceptance of each other naked, aroused, profoundly eroticized as some higher expression of our humanity, of our participation in human history as it is told through sex.

I had romantic notions about the baths. I had to believe we were free.

My desire is not my enemy. Is my desire my own? Does my desire have a history? Does it have a future?

These questions were with us when we rehearsed in the dance studio. They were there with us in the ways we handled each other onstage. They trailed us—perhaps led us—down Saint Mark's Place. These questions were implicit in the ways that we looked at each other and sometimes refused to look. These questions were what every new arousal, every sweet torso, high-curved backside, or spurting penis seemed to ask.

Who would have known that it was just a passing era? Those Friday nights, those Saturday nights, those Wednesday evenings in the time outside of time that was the baths. Only the most beautiful bodies dared show themselves. We had the impression that we were perhaps godlike, desirable, and eternally young. The promised revolution was happening, it would go on forever.

This is my memory.

My memory is not my enemy.

My memory is my enemy.

◆　　◆　　◆

MY FATHER DIED in San Francisco in 1981—twenty years and thousands of miles away from Miller Road, his last great venture that he lost to New York State for five hundred dollars in back taxes.

A year to the day after his death, I dreamt that he and I were back at Miller Road. We were alone. It was a Saturday afternoon and the place seemed particularly useless, lonely, haunted, without the sound of children, without the sound of the radio playing James Brown, without anyone crying, laughing, or making love.

In 1977, my father had had a stroke and lost the use of his right arm. When I visited him, I would massage his cold hand while we talked. In this dream, he was this old man. We hadn't turned on the electric light and the house was gently succumbing to twilight. I held his icy hand, looked him in the eye, then placed his hand in my armpit and asked him how it felt.

"It feels *very, very* good," he said, rewarding me with a smile that I had seen only once or twice.

I awoke from this dream feeling as if I had been given a gift, given permission to get on with my life.

◆　　◆　　◆

Freedom of Information, *1985, with dancers (from left) Julie West, Bill T. Jones, Amy Pivar, Poonie Dodson, Arnie Zane, and Janet Lilly* (LOIS GREENFIELD)

SOCIAL INTERCOURSE

THE FORMALIST AESTHETIC of the 1970s, with its premise of minimal means, maximum distancing from the subject, was the latest incarnation of the works and thoughts of many earlier generations. We read Marcel Duchamp, examined the art of the Russian Constructivists, and watched dance by choreographers as diverse as Merce Cunningham and Lucinda Childs.

In her *Characters on a Diagonal*, Lucinda performed a skipping movement—forward and back, forward and back, forward and back. Arnie had loved the stunning purity of the piece and it influenced his creation of *Continuous Replay*, a work that consisted of forty-five gestures repeated over and over again. *One, two; one, two, three; one, two, three, four, five, six*. Altogether, these repeated forty-five gestures accumulated into close to 4,400 separate movements. Like *Characters on a Diagonal*, *Continuous Replay* is free of personality, free of social context, free of the biases towards content. It is purely about form.

But if minimalism was an influence, so were the impending eighties. Some said they had already started by the late seventies. Skirts were tight and short. Fine-meshed stockings clouded legs that were shaved once again. Discreet spike pumps seemed to sprout from the feet of women who not so long ago had worn chunk heels and Earth Shoes. Any young man-about-town was sure to have a suit or sports jacket in his closet bearing the label of a European or Japanese designer. Food suddenly became a pastime, a barometer of one's sophistication, worldliness. Restaurants sprang up everywhere. Mr. Chow, Florent, the Odeon, Jezebel's, Chanterelle, and others became the proving grounds for a generation bent on the "good life." It was the era of appetites. Clothes, sex, fame, money, and power. Truth was, we sat down to expensive meals flustered, exhausted by having had to decide what to wear, how to get there, how to make an entrance, what table to be placed at, what wine to order, which credit card to use. And the bill was coming. Its specter inexorable, inevitable.

Performance art, reliant upon text and media representation, became the new bright hope of the art world. Painting, only recently declared dead, played Lazarus as artists returned to figuration and the ham-fisted manipulation of paint, image, and metaphor.

Lois Welk used to tell a story about Daniel Nagrin and how he, while rehearsing with his improvisational dance company, the Work Group, had said, "Look, we don't need new ideas. We just need to know what to do with the old ideas we already have." And in fact, this premise served as a sort of sanction for the 1980s art world. People scanned history to plunder, imitate—and the plundering and imitation became both content and commentary. One notable example of this trend came in the form of Sherrie Levine's meticulous reproduction of a Malevich, to which she signed her name. Artists were saying that all art belonged to them, that art had the right to devour itself, that by devouring, it sought new questions and new paradigms.

In the enclave of the dance world, things moved more slowly. Arnie and I didn't have a formal dance company yet—just a pickup group of friends and acquaintances who would come together once or twice a year to perform. In 1979, I invited Julie West to be part of a duet that I wanted to make. I theatricalized and costumed the sandlot gymnastics, rough-house partnering, and homespun sensitivity of contact improvisation and called the piece *Balancing the World*. (A later version of the piece, *Shared Distance*, has since become a staple of our repertory.)

The theatricalization and costuming were in keeping with what Arnie and I were thinking at the time. We had always been in pursuit of an ecstatic athleticism in our dance, but now we were becoming more interested, albeit reluctantly, in technical virtuosity. We wanted to understand elegance. We wanted to dance brilliantly. As a visual artist and photographer, Arnie had always been aware of the way things looked, but now we both became more concerned about production, lighting, sets, costume. Our dancers began to wear makeup and hairstyles became a consideration. Gone were the days of bare feet, and we discovered what could be done on the tops and sides of our feet when we wore shoes.

In 1981, I participated as an "Emerging Choreographer" at the American Dance Festival (ADF). The piece we presented was billed as *Social Intercourse: Pilgrim's Progress*, by Bill T. Jones with Dancers. Arnie acted as administrator and artistic consultant. It was at his suggestion that I had shaped this piece into a fusion of the traditional and the new wave (jargon invented to describe a post-punk era in fashion and music). He invited my sisters Flossie, Rhodessa, and Johari (as Vileana now called herself) to provide a chanting Greek chorus. I wrote the lyrics about one day in the mental life of a New Yorker. Joe Hannon arranged them. Randy Gunn, a tall, perennially pale rocker who traveled with his portable television and electric bass, was the sole musician.

The dance itself was not narrative. What you saw were four people— Julie West, Caren Calder, Harry Shephard, and I—dressed in black, lurching, strutting, rushing from upstage to down, obsessively performing fragments of athletic partnering and dance movements peppered with semaphoric arm gestures against the chanted sound score:

Time to get up! Time to get up! Get goin'! Get goin'! Wash down, zip up! Wash down, zip up!

Go!

Wash down, zip up! Go!

Go! Go! Go! Go! Go.

The man gets into his car.

It's cold. It's cold. My car, yeah! My car, now! My car, my car. Got to go to work, got to go to work.

Go! Go! Go! Go! Go! . . .

The man travels through the morning rush-hour traffic and reaches his workplace, which we discover is a courthouse.

I am the judge. I am the judge. These are your rights. I am the judge. How do you plead? These are your rights.

You are the judge. These are my rights. How do I plead?
What is the law? What are my rights?
Go! Go! Go! Go! Go!
Time to go home 'til tomorrow. Time to go home 'til tomorrow.
Go! Go! Go! Go! Go!

To this chanting and Randy's bass, we danced very upright, aggressive short phrases of movement that were punctuated by hip wiggles and head tosses. There was a karatelike aspect to these gestures but it was uncertain whether the performers were under attack or attacking. Amidst the ebb and flow of defensive aggression was insistent eroticism expressed through embraces, clinches, counterclinches, and the nihilistic smashing of one face against the other in gender-blind variations of kissing.

EVEN AS WE staged works that involved a number of dancers, I continued my solos. For me, that mysterious intimacy between audience and performer held the answer to all questions about product, ownership, and originality. If I could reach an audience, create a moment like no other, my dance could be less than original and still perform the highest function of art, provided that I maintained my authenticity.

Often, I opted for improvisation to accomplish this. I chose to use language in performance as well as movement, and I improvised both. I wanted to challenge the implicit ritualism of performance, acknowledge its boundaries and subvert them. But how?

It was from conceptual artist Vito Acconci, who lay under the floor of a New York art gallery and masturbated, or stood blindfolded in a museum stairway banging a metal pipe against the concrete whenever approached, that I got the idea that performance could be aggressive, designed to alienate an audience. I found this strategy seductive. I rankled at being called a "black artist." Coming of age in the sixties, I had embraced a host of values that placed a premium on freedom from social definition, and being so described seemed an attempt to diminish individuality, to reduce the possible interpretations of what I was trying to express. It seemed perpetrated by racist people. Add to this my deep feeling of alienation from both black and white culture and the implicit social tension between the white avant-garde and black performers, and this strategy became essential.

On closer examination of my earlier work, from *Bacon Grease and Porkchops* to spinning near-naked in *Everybody Works*, I realized that I had unconsciously employed aspects of this strategy all along. But I had always tried ultimately to please my audiences. Robert Pierce, a critic for the *SoHo News* at the time, had called me "an ingratiating demon." With the Acconci strategy in place, I was able to deconstruct this identity. Deconstruction yielded solos that were confessional, often painful, taking unpleasant emotions and exposing them spontaneously in a fashion that was brutal on both the audience and me.

And so it was at ADF in 1981 that I also did a largely improvised solo built on oppositional statements. *I love women,* I would say. Then, *I hate women. I love white people. I hate white people. I'd like to kiss you. I'd like to tear your fucking heart out. Why didn't you leave us in Africa? I'm so thankful for the opportunity to be here.* I said something very personal about Arnie, who was in the audience. I also made reference to an article in that day's paper that quoted the co-director of the festival as saying that careers would be made or broken that weekend.

The solo shocked many. My anger—and my vehemence in expressing it—shaped the way I was perceived for many years to come. I wasn't invited back to the American Dance Festival for ten years.

IN 1982, we mounted a more dancerly six-person variation of *Social Intercourse: Pilgrim's Progress* for Downstairs at City Center, in New York. We still used the three "colored girl" singers, but added an extended prelude that consisted of twenty extras who passed in front of the one entrance to the theater like pedestrians crossing a busy intersection. The audience could enter only according to the fierce instructions of Herb Dade, a handsome young black man in uniform who shouted, *Stop. Go.* It made for a tense, claustrophobic atmosphere that alienated some audience members immediately while energizing others. A bit like the streets of New York, I suppose.

Reviews were thoughtful, but it was then that Arlene Croce in *The New Yorker* first condemned Arnie and me as stars, saying that "Bill T. Jones has marched the New Narcissism right into the fever swamp." I took this criticism as my marching orders.

In 1983, it provided me with a title for the first serious commission I was ever offered, *Fever Swamp* for the Alvin Ailey American Dance Theater, a male sextet to the idiosyncratic pleasantries of Peter Gordon's pop-inspired score. In 1984–85, after the success of *Fever Swamp*, Alvin offered us another commission. Like many artists, including Sherrie Levine, who had been referring to works from the past to explore the careful distinction between imitation and ownership, Arnie and I turned to George Balanchine's 1934 neoclassical masterpiece *Serenade*.

"How to Walk an Elephant" was the first movement of this new piece that was to become *Animal Trilogy*. This title's whimsy paid homage to the avid theoretician Senta Driver. A fiercely intelligent dancer and choreographer, Senta grappled constantly with the implications of history and what she took to be its imperatives—that the truly great artist is an inventor who pushes his or her field forward or outward.

In "How to Walk an Elephant" we quoted freely from Balanchine's masterwork. Balanchine's protagonist was his white female corps de ballet, in and out of which principal female dancers would play. Our corps, Alvin Ailey's predominantly nonwhite company, consisted of both men and women. We replaced Mr. B's lyric flow with rambunctious angularity and discontinuity in body line and overall composition. We wanted the piece to look rough and constructed. The phrases themselves were danced on heels and knees, with arms and backs held rigid, doll-like. The partnering was more like handling, mechanistic, relying on the small supporting the large and a generous degree of partner switching.

A sacred section of *Serenade*, both for its role in the ballet and in dance history, is sometimes called "Angel of Death Pas de Trois." It is a beautiful exploration of the potential existing in the combination of one man and two women. At one moment, one of the women hovers protectively over the kneeling man as he mysteriously promenades the other woman, rotating her by the ankle of her pointed foot. The rapt extravagance of her arabesque and the tender efficiency of his manipulation lend the scene an air of holy ritual. In our version, Danny Brown, a long-limbed black man whose proportions moved me, performed this arabesque. In impassioned protest, a critic wrote, "'Ballet is woman,' George Balanchine declared. Jones and Zane have replaced the ultimate display of female beauty with a gawky male arabesque. . . . It is very much in fashion these days, now that the master himself is gone, to take from his genius. Is it an homage or a parody? Either way they would not have done it while he was alive."

But George Balanchine was our father, too. We loved what he left us and it was ours to partake of. For us then, as for me now, who dances what is just as important as what is danced and how. "How to Walk an Elephant" was our "primer," our index. We modeled it after Senta's piece *Primer*, in which she had provided a guide to her choreographic vocabulary—one that consisted of purposefully awkward grappling and tortured restatements of ballet's petit allegro, in which dancers danced on point barefoot. This was how we walked the elephant of dance history.

◆   ◆   ◆

By 1983, things that had once been personal were being broadcast into households around the world. Perhaps it all started with so many TV assassinations—Medgar Evers, John F. Kennedy, Robert Kennedy, Martin Luther King, Jr., Malcolm X—or in the dinnertime debacle of Vietnam, the shameful war with a shameful defeat, or in Richard Nixon's Watergate, his near impeachment and his resignation. Or could it have been the image of a fetus in the womb on the cover of *Life* magazine, or *60 Minutes'* weekly exposé-as-catharsis, or Phil Donahue's invention of the "reality show"? No matter the cause, media artist Gretchen Bender gave definition to the phenomenon when she said, "Our insides are now outside."

It was a tenuous stretch from this premise to what would be our next work; it defied logic, but we decided the only response to this loss of personal privacy was the pursuit of hyperphysicality. Arnie and I were impressed by the task our friend the choreographer Molissa Fenley had set for herself in developing a body of work that demanded the commitment and conditioning of an athlete to perform. She influenced the development of a dance that explored the limits of our speed, strength, and endurance.

Freedom of Information was a sextet in three movements. For its sound score, composer David Cunningham referenced the spoken narrative of an air disaster in the Potomac River in the early 1980s. The pilot—or perhaps it was a passenger—spoke about how when the plane should have been lifting off the ground, it lost control and slammed into a bridge. There were people in the water. He didn't know how he had survived.

Freedom of Information, *1985, with dancers Bill T. Jones, Janet Lilly, Julie West, Arnie Zane, Woody McGriff, and Amy Pivar; set by Gretchen Bender* (PETER SAYERS)

For movement, we mined—scavenged, if you will—vocabulary of classical modern dance and the protocol of ballet. But we broke them into odd, angular partnerings, subverted them with the egalitarianism of contact improvisation. A great deal of *Freedom of Information* was about dancers being flung across the stage at one moment, rolling across it the next. Bodies on their heads, then on their feet, reaching for other bodies, flinging and falling.

As the man's voice began recounting the tragedy against the plaintive wail of Peter Gordon's saxophone, Janet Lilly, Arnie, and I dropped to all fours and, while the other dancers stood on our backs performing semaphoric arm gestures, we crawled and barked like dogs.

What did all of this mean—this dancing while a particular man spoke about a specific tragedy and the miracle of his survival? It was absurd and shocking. At that time we might have answered, "It didn't have to mean anything." Freedom of information . . . Free of history. Free of minimalism. Free of all concerns for narrative content. Perhaps not for all time, but appropriately, palpably, even frighteningly free.

Freedom of Information, which premiered at the Théâtre de la Ville, in Paris, in 1985, offered the most striking divergence from the Bill and Arnie duet paradigm. The whole piece was less personal, more conceptual. The movement, while a direct outgrowth of the vocabulary we had developed together, was a departure from work rooted in our personalities. Through the introduction of four other dancers with distinctly different qualities of movement to draw upon, our choreography moved towards the depiction of a community, a society.

With the success of *Freedom of Information*, the United States Information Agency invited us to tour Asia in 1986. Sweat was still the currency exchanged. But dancing was now about finding a place in a broader international context. Dancing was about trying to bridge the gap between my exuberant desire to perform and my responsibilities as a member of what had in 1982 become Bill T. Jones/Arnie Zane and Dancers. Dancing was about trying to understand the distance between passion, belief, and commerce. Between dreams, whimsy, and the checkbook. Between inspiration, enlightenment, and deadlines. Dancing was about creating and maintaining a repertory, about the dancers' uncertainty as to what was expected of them, what their rights were, what their position was in the creative dialogue between Arnie and myself. Dancing was about the trouble Arnie and I had understanding how to be members of an open, lively community even as we

Social Intercourse, *1981* (ARNIE ZANE)

tried to maintain a kind of control. We'd find ourselves saying, "Yes, this is a free country and we believe very much in individual freedom, but this dance company is not a democracy."

The world was huge—still is—but at the time we were building a company, it was a place to fly out and meet. The specter of our enemies was more palpable. Money was what we needed, so we had to tour. But the Asia tour—of Indonesia, Malaysia, and the Philippines—was conducted without Arnie. My prince was ailing. Time was no longer in endless supply but fear was.

ABSENCE

———◆———

What does it feel like to swim, when your seams are held together with thread that dissolves in water?

WE DIDN'T SEE Edith and Lon Zane for at least five years after leaving them at the police station in Queens, but Arnie maintained his ties with his mother by sending her bouquets of pussy willows and roses for her birthday every April. I'm sure Edith missed having her middle child around. The two of them shared a crazy kind of passion that revealed itself in a shared love of jewelry, clothing, and "things." I don't remember who made the first formal overture of reconciliation, but by 1977 we found ourselves shoring up our courage and heading off to the site of his parents' latest relocation—somewhere on Long Island or in New Jersey or Pennsylvania. Often these ventures would end in dispute.

"Look, Arnie. Look at the new ring I have," Edith would begin, tossing her hook into the turbulent waters of their love.

Arnie always took the bait. "Oh, it's really beautiful, may I try it on?"

"Yes, you may, but you better give it back to me."

"What do you mean, I better give it back to you? Have I ever taken anything from you?"

"Oh, you know the way you are."

"What are you getting at?" The debate would, at this point, escalate into an argument or defuse into laughter and a face-saving compromise.

Initially, Edith and Lon had been nervous about what their neighbors would think when they read the articles that implied we were a homosexual couple, but eventually curiosity—and perhaps pride—overrode apprehension. In 1982, they came to City Center to see a performance of *Social Intercourse: Pilgrim's Progress* and they enjoyed the cocktail party much more than the performance. While they were decidedly in favor of traditional values, I am not so sure that Edith didn't get a kind of thrill from seeing a shaven-head man in a glamorous black sequined evening gown sipping champagne and chatting urbanely with a statuesque would-be model, or a mogul to-be-art-star with a rockabilly pompadour and glamorous girlfriend to match.

Secret Pastures, "the first dance work of any consequence to acknowledge the influence of MTV on our perception" (Deborah Jowitt, the *Village Voice*), was our splashiest work to date, with sets by Keith Haring, costumes by Willi Smith, and music by Peter Gordon. When it premiered at the Brooklyn Academy of Music, Edith was beside herself with excitement at seeing Andy Warhol and Madonna sitting two rows behind her.

"Now you guys are beginning to go somewhere. If you just don't blow it, maybe you'll get to Broadway," Lon told us.

Eventually, it became a regular ritual to meet the Zanes for supper downtown or to drive out to their home in Easton, Pennsylvania. Sometimes they would visit us. The first time Edith came to Valley Cottage, she was quite impressed. She thought our home was "strong and elegant—the kind of place where two bachelors would live." Arnie was very moved.

When Arnie began to get sick, he and his mother would argue about why he wasn't feeling well. Lon said he was "sick in the head" and that otherwise there was nothing wrong with him. As Arnie grew weaker, their denial frustrated him. It was only when the lymphoma made itself undeniably apparent that Edith and Lon admitted the possibility that their son was truly ill.

Over his hospital bed, Arnie made me swear in front of Edith that under no circumstances would I return to her his grandmother's *shteisel*— her heavy brass mortar and pestle for grinding the bitter herbs at Passover.

Of course when he died, that was the one thing that she demanded that I give her, and I did. This was the nature of their bond. I was a spectator.

◆　　◆　　◆

IN 1981, there was talk of a mysterious gay cancer. Arnie, convinced that he was infected, was terrified. He went to the Gay Men's Health Crisis, where they examined him and said there was nothing wrong with him physically, and that maybe he'd want to see a therapist. They recommended Freda Rosen, who, he blithely informed me, was a lesbian socialist.

"A what?"

"She's a politico and you'd really like her. You should come see her too, Bill. She agrees with me," Arnie announced after his first session. Where I come from you would recommend that someone go see a psychiatrist only if you wanted to drive the person especially mad.

"Don't get so upset," Arnie said, trying to soothe me. "Try to understand. You could learn to stop hitting people when you feel bad. You could learn to enjoy what you have better."

"Okay. I'll go. Once. But I'm not making any promises."

It was hard to sit there in that room with Freda and Arnie. I had been living with the conviction that my dance was an extension of praying and that Arnie was my partner in this prayer. Freda forced me to understand that what I had thought was a great spiritual adventure was an arrangement, a delicately balanced agreement, and that it had existed ever since that day in Springwater when he and my mother shook hands. What had brought us from my mother's bedroom that afternoon to where we were was not the same thing that was going to carry us into the future.

I was wild with anger. Cursing, wanting to rip at things and people.

Why can't I really be friends with anybody other than him? Why do I always feel like I'm running a game, trying to get over, trying to be somebody else?

And Freda would ask, "Yeah Bill, why?"

Sometimes when I came apart—and Freda knew how to encourage me to come apart, she dared me to—Estella's voice would come howling from my mouth, competing with Big Mama's and the defensive, quietly angry voice of Gus Jones.

Why does Arnie want so much? Why is he so business-minded? He's such a white man. He's such a Jew.

Freda would answer, "He's that way because you need him to be that way. You help him be that way because you are so full of that stuff they told our generation about—that freedom from money, obligation, and planning."

Why do I feel so used all the time?

"Because you *are* used. And why shouldn't you be used, since you refuse to use yourself."

Arnie was saying it. He was saying, "I don't feel good." But then he was always saying that. He and his mother had a kind of competition over who was feeling worse. He'd say it again. "I think something's wrong. I don't feel right."

I'd say, *Let's keep going. Let's keep dancing.*

He'd say, "You dance. I'll sit over there on the side."

Exasperated, I'd say, *We've got to keep dancing.*

"I feel too tired. I'll just lie down over here on the side."

And then there were doctors. Lots of doctors. Sometimes seven doctors in a day and I was raging.

How could anything come before what I want to do, what I want us to do, what we have always done?

And he'd say, "I just need to take it easy. I've got to take care of this."

I was coming apart.

If you don't think so much about it, it will take care of itself. You're doing this because you're trying to keep me from moving.

"I just don't feel like it. I've got to take care of this. Are you going to stay with me?"

Haven't I always been with you?

"That's not what he's asking you," Freda says.

"Are you going to stay with me?"

What else would I do?

And she says, "That's not what he's asking you."

"Are you going to stay with me?"

This is crazy-making. We sleep in the same bed. We make the same art. We have the same friends.

"But are you going to stay with me?"

And Freda says, "You're not answering his question."

Why does he have to ask all the questions? What about my questions?

"Yes, Bill, we know you have questions but what about his?"

"Are you going to stay with me?"

He had always been too plump for his own taste. Suddenly, he was too thin. I'd slip my arms around him and sometimes that was enough. I'd kiss his eyelids and sometimes that was an answer.

"The doctor says I have to have a biopsy. Will you come with me to the doctor?"

Yes.

"The doctor says I have to take chemotherapy. I don't want to puke—you know how I don't like anything out of order. Will you clean it up? How do I look?"

You look like a sick man.

"No. How do I look to *you?*"

You look like my life and you are melting. You are running between my fingers. You are just a voice and a huge pair of eyes. Tell me what to do, baby, I'm coming apart. You've always been the one telling me what to do.

"You'll figure it out. I'm so tired I think I'll go lie down."

Tell me what we're going to do.

"You'll figure it out. We have friends."

I started to make a dance called *The Miracle*. There were dancers—Sean, Larry, and the brand-new Arthur. They moved like big inflated clowns grinning. We were going to dance and we were going to grin. I threw big bones at them. I told them to juggle these bones. *Keep grinning. Keep scampering. No, he's not coming into rehearsal today. No, he's not coming into rehearsal tomorrow. I can't do this.*

"How do I look?"

You look like my life.

"No. How do I look to *you?*"

You look like the first time I saw you and you had your coat on backwards and I was excited and embarrassed that you hugged yourself like a girl, but you hugged me—and held me between your legs—you let me into you. As I lay on top of you, you seemed to know there would come a day when our fucking would be your thin hand, so transparent, so tired of needles and medication—against my face.

I was coming apart as he was melting. There was no dance tour to divert me. There was no party, no bathhouse. There were days and weeks of waiting, of carrying ginger ale from downstairs to upstairs, of administering Tylenol to fight fever. There was group therapy that I walked out on when nobody in the group could tell me when the grieving would stop.

We had managed to put up yet another work, the reworked *Animal Trilogy*, at the Brooklyn Academy of Music. There was "How to Walk an Elephant," many of its Balanchinian references still intact but less balletic, tailored for the quirky virtuosity of our dancers. "Water Buffalo: Lifting a Calf Every Day Until It Becomes an Ox," a study in formal pomp, formed the second part, and "Sacred Cow," a reworking of a piece we had done for the Utah Repertory Dance Company, formed the third. This segment was perhaps our most elegant piece to date, with Conlon Nancarrow's player piano music and Cletus Johnson's beautiful sliding panels of ocher and turquoise, which matched Bill Katz's costumes and Robert Wierzel's light.

Every night in "Sacred Cow," Arnie and I had one final grappling match onstage. As I lifted him onto my back and felt the sharpness of his pelvic bone where once there had been only soft flesh, I would think about Berlin, Hong Kong, London, Manchester, Paris, Los Angeles. The whole world had been ours to grapple in. I would think about a time when our dance was nothing more than a conversation between two men, a white man and a black man, a small man and a tall man, a man who knew exactly what he wanted and a man who was afraid to want anything. Feeling his boniness precariously balanced on my back, I thought I saw those two men watching us, expectant, hungry, from the dark of the wings. I was ashamed that we had come to this. I was proud that we had come to this.

How do I look? I ask.

"You look like my future."

No. How do I look to you?

"You look like my hero, but I'm so tired. My veins have collapsed and now they've put a little hole in my chest. I'm so tired. Are you all right?"

And I'd say, *I'm all right as long as you're all right.*

"But I'm not all right. How is the office?"

They're managing.

"Are the bills being paid?"

You can be sure they are.

"I'm so sorry that this is happening."

You're my hero. You're my prince.

"I may die."

Can I come with you?

"Don't be silly. I want you to record my works. You don't have to keep this dance company, but I want you to keep going. Dance alone if you want to. Travel. Find somebody else, because you know you can't live without a partner."

I don't want to do anything without you here with me.

"You are already doing it."

◆　　◆　　◆

IN 1984 or so, Arnie had started to get terrible rashes. I remember performances in which he bled beneath his costume.

In 1985, he had a tooth infection that would not heal. By then, people were becoming familiar with AIDS and ARC. We were scared—he much more than I. It was his body that was changing.

We went to our doctor's office in the East Village for tests and when the results came back, we met with her. She was very official, efficient, yet gentle, too. "Arnie, as you have suspected, you have HIV—ARC, according to the guidelines. And Bill, you are positive too." She then detailed the precautions we needed to take.

I was not surprised by my test results. But being positive was not the same as having AIDS or even ARC. I was able to deal with it. It was easy in 1985.

"What are my chances? How many people live? What things can I be taking? What can I do?" Arnie asked, his voice raspy.

At first, I didn't understand Arnie's concerns—perhaps I refused to understand them—and he would often become frustrated with me. There was no way he could convey how frightened he was. And not just about dying. He was worried about us. He'd always taken care of me.

By May of 1986, two years before he died, Arnie had his first bout with lymphoma. For a while he commuted to the city for chemotherapy. He was fighting, always fighting. It wasn't long, though, before he grew too weak to drive. He would rest in the backseat of the car as I took him to his appointments. For a long time after his death, I'd reach behind me as I drove, not able to believe that he was not there. And still, when I drive past the Triboro Bridge on the FDR Drive, I remember the moment when Arnie told me he had taken a turn for the worse and needed to go back to the hospital.

At one point, he decided to fight with an alternative medicine, megadoses of vitamin C given intravenously. The institute that promoted this treatment was located outside San Francisco, so Arnie went out there with Nadine Lust, a friend who had paid for the trip. Rhodessa arranged to bring as much of my family as possible to the motel to show support for Arnie. None of my brothers came, but some of my sisters, my nieces, a nephew, and Estella did.

Arnie later said that their appearance was a bit like a mirage. He could hear them singing and shouting their way down the long motel corridors before they reached his room. Once there, they engaged in a ritual of prayer, song, and encouragement. Nadine, a staunch atheist and disbeliever in any kind of ritual, was struck by the rite and later related it to me in anthropological detail. Arnie was deeply thankful. He never saw my mother again, although he would speak with her by phone and ask her to pray for him shortly before he died.

The summer of 1987 was to be our last together and I remember it with pleasure. Arnie was well enough most of the time to enjoy the house, our garden, even to participate in Michael Blackwood's film on the downtown choreographic world, *Retracing Steps*. He attended the company's Central Park performance of his most successful later work, *The Gift/No God Logic*. He and I completed what was to be our last collaboration, in the form of *A History of Collage*.

There was very little work that fall but there was a winter tour scheduled. He last appeared onstage dressed in a white leather jacket, pretending to skip stones across an imaginary body of water in *A History of Collage*, on January 10 in Cleveland. That night he became so sick he was forced to fly back to New York. I had to go on to Berkeley with the company.

In the spring of 1988, when the doctor told us that Arnie had perhaps two weeks more to live, we made plans for an ambulance to bring him home. When he left the hospital, he wore the blue kimono jacket that he loved so much. He gave the thumbs up sign to the nurses as we rolled out of the hospital. They smiled at us and patted me on the back. I had passed their human commitment test. He had passed their human commitment test. Arnie sat upright in a wheelchair in the back of the ambulance. The ambulance was blue. I followed in the car.

We had been away from our house for two months. Spring had come and riotous yellow forsythias punctuated the desolation that was no longer winter. My sisters were there to meet us. I had invited Rhodessa and she, in turn, had invited Flo and Johari.

Together, we got Arnie upstairs and laid him in bed. He was glad to be back in his house and he was chatting about freshening up and getting on with his life. Even in a wheelchair, he changed the light and the air. This was the space he inhabited naturally and it seemed to welcome him home.

But things had changed. Our bed, little more than a raised platform, was shoved aside to make room for a hospital bed. There was a nurse on twenty-four-hour call. Arnie needed supplies for incontinence. My sisters wanted to be helpful. I gave Flo and Johari the car keys so they could go buy adult diapers. Not ten minutes after they'd left, the phone rang. They'd tried taking a shortcut I had described, through a parking lot, but they'd misjudged and were struck by a man and his wife who were driving home from church. No one was hurt but the car was totaled.

With some reluctance, I told Arnie about this. He rolled his eyes. He'd been skeptical about Flo and Johari's presence in the first place. At that particular moment, I wasn't so sure about them myself. I got a neighbor to take me down the hill, where I found them understandably bereft. "It's okay. It's okay," I kept saying.

I'd noticed that a generosity of spirit had grown in Arnie even as his illness grew worse, so it wasn't surprising that when we got back home he called my sisters upstairs and, despite his private misgivings, told them how much he appreciated their being there. So it was that whatever had passed between them over the years no longer mattered. My sisters were there to handle the household, to watch over Arnie, and to watch over me. They could now perform these tasks without reservation. I would find them singing to him—gospel, Streisand's "The Way We Were," Motown. During the night, when the heavy medication caused Arnie to hyperventilate, Flo would come in to calm him with lullabies.

Together, these three women, my sisters, were formidable and the effect they had over the proceedings was remarkable. Some of our friends—many of whom had come to visit Arnie each day when he was in the hospital— were offended by the way my sisters wouldn't allow them upstairs to see him. Some friends thought that the atmosphere was too Christian, what with all those prayers and spirituals. Others thought Arnie would want his last moments to be more solitary, not part revival meeting, part post-rehearsal social gathering, part family reunion. But I knew that Arnie enjoyed the way it was always a bit too much when we Joneses were all together. There was a strength and vitality in our gathering. This was why he had wanted my sisters to be in *Social Intercourse: Pilgrim's Progress* years before and this was why they were at our house those last days. When Arnie's parents arrived, Edith was enchanted by my sisters. I had been concerned she would be competitive and territorial but she suddenly understood the spiritual life of my family and thanked them sincerely for caring for her son. Lon found them attractive.

Arnie's morphine dosage was too high. It was decided to shift from injection to an intravenous drip. He went into extreme withdrawal as his body adjusted to the change. He began to hyperventilate again and, in horrible pain, he bleated almost like a sheep. Nowhere could you escape this pathetic sound—not in the house, not outside in the yard.

I spent most of my time in the bedroom with him. Sometimes a dancer or two, or Maya, the six-year-old neighbor whom we both loved, would come in to say hello to him. Watching Arnie, I felt as though I was standing on the shore of a lake in which he was swimming. He would disappear for long periods of time, then, at completely unpredictable moments, he would come up for air. As the day wore on, he seemed to move farther and farther from shore and to surface less frequently. Then he'd bob back up, often when we least expected it. Our friend Bill Katz showed up, and Arnie greeted him clear as a bell—"Hi Bill, how are you?" A moment before he hadn't recognized his mother.

That last afternoon, people from all parts of Arnie's life were gathered around his bed. He had me with him, and his parents, and my family. He had our love and the love of the friends he'd played, danced, schemed, and fought with. He had the love of children, too. At one moment, a sort of spontaneous chant began. We pressed in close to him to whisper, "Let go, Arnie. Let go," as if giving him permission to leave us. Drowsily, he opened his eyes and said, "Give me a break." Our devastated embarrassment was undercut by helpless laughter.

In the last three or four hours, he stopped calling for his mother and me. It was simply "Dad. Dad, help me. Dad, take off my shoes. Dad, help me open the door." His father, Lon, the same big Italian man who had chased us through the streets of Maspeth, Queens, with a butcher knife, was right there. He was holding his son's hand. Our friend Ethel began to sing Yiddish children's songs, and at times Arnie seemed to sing along.

But then his pain grew more and more unbearable. In a panic, I complained to the nurse and she quickly gave him a shot. He became too calm and she called her supervisor, who assured her that Arnie's time had come and that all we could do was to be there with him and let him go.

I stood by the window holding Arnie's head. His mother was at his left side and Lon stood behind her. Flo was next to me and the young girl, Maya, was at his feet. Others were standing, crouching, completely surrounding his bed. Arnie's breathing became intermittent, with long pauses between breaths.

"He's gone," Edith cried out.

I felt a breeze blow past my face and started to sing "Amen," the single word that came to mind. The immediate feelings that followed were those that accompany a birth—a relieved wonder, miraculous and terrible.

Edith asked what Jewish man was present to say the Kaddish. Through tears, Larry Goldhuber, one of our dancers and on many occasions the unofficial chauffeur during Arnie's sickness, took up the task. Larry is not a religious Jew, but it seems there are some things we know in spite of ourselves. In this most difficult performance, he intoned, *"Sh'ma Yisrael, Adonai Eloheinu . . ."*

"Bill needs to be alone now," Rhodessa announced, as she ushered everyone except my sisters out of the room. An aftershock of calmness and clarity came over me temporarily as I began to quietly give instructions.

Arnie's body was bruised from recent heart surgery and bloated from the lymphoma, so I instructed my sisters to cover him with the sumptuous Victorian piano cloth some friends had recently given us. Rhodessa carefully lifted Arnie's head and placed his favorite indigo blue scarf beneath it. Then Rhodessa, Johari, and Flo each kissed me and left. It was peaceful and quiet. He seemed peaceful and quiet. As I held his head in both my hands, I apologized for the indignity that had been imposed upon him.

It took two hours for the ambulance to arrive. The drivers, two suspicious, stone-faced men, had been met in the driveway by Johari and the nurse—imposing, ample-bodied black women sentinels, both of whom breathed urgency. The drivers must have sensed a tribal aspect, a tribe organized around an outcast. In the doorways and windows, they could see the people who had loved Arnie—people of every description, from bleach-haired, pumped-bodied, miniskirted and combat-booted Damien to the swarthy, unshaven, Italian-American Robert Longo.

They refused to enter the house. Lon, nonplussed, used his position as father and white man to make a deal. If he brought Arnie down, they would meet him on the porch and take Arnie's body from there. Under no circumstances were they to let his wife see her son's body placed in a bag.

At this point, I recall things in a sort of cinema montage. Everyone seemed to become animated, motivated to perform any number of ridiculous, necessary, and unnecessary endeavors.

I stumbled into the bathroom as my sisters wrapped the bedsheet around Arnie. I was on the floor banging my head into the tiles, wailing. Our friend Gretchen was beating me with her fists, screaming, "He loved you, Goddammit! He loved you more than anything."

I don't know if I came out of the bathroom on my own or if I was pulled out, but when I emerged, I found them—Larry, Seth, Robert, Lon—trying to maneuver Arnie's body down the narrow, steep stairway. It would have been comical if it had not been so outrageously grotesque—the body draped in a white sheet, slipping from hand to hand.

"Here, let me have him," Lon said. "I'll carry my son. I'll carry my boy." A procession formed with Lon at the head, bearing the shrouded body. Edith—who had performed the ritual ripping of her clothes—wouldn't allow anyone but me to touch her. Three times she repeated, "Look, Bill. Look at Lon carrying his son."

The procession wound its way through the chaos of the living room and out through the lower porch, where, contrary to the agreement, the ambulance drivers stood holding a bright red body bag. Lon, with all the grace of a professional quarterback, deftly slipped Arnie's body to them and rushed back to tackle his beloved wife so she would never see. Arnie was placed in the bag.

My knees buckled. Flo, with a strength I had never before witnessed, pulled me to my feet. "No. You must go on. You owe it to him. You have to walk just this little bit. You've got to say good-bye. I never got to say good-bye to my husband and I don't want you to live with what I have had to live with. You must and you will."

And so I did.

Night had fallen. It was as if my small suburban neighborhood was holding its breath. No one stuck a head out a window. No one came outdoors. All was quiet except for our procession.

Forsythias are not human and on that evening, framing the hearse, they were as irreverent in their intimation of spring's promise and luminosity as small children giggling, playing tag round the ankles and knees of mourning people.

A slip of white coming out of the red plastic bag was the last I saw of Arnie. Bedsheets that catch the shit and the piss, blood, dead skin, the slipping body are not human.

I reached out—and at that very moment, the nervous driver spun the tires and peeled out of my driveway. My hand, extended as if in greeting, suddenly had nothing to do. I looked at that hand, held it up as if to say good-bye, but more to see it against the sky. I looked through the fingers and saw the stars—the same hand that had masturbated, the same stars I had tried to impregnate one summer evening beside the railroad tracks on the north side of Binghamton many years before. My hand closed into a fist. Arnie was gone. His ashes would be mailed back to me in a box a few weeks later.

My friends and family had put the bedroom back together and I woke the next morning thinking, for one brief second, that it was just another beautiful early-spring day. As I sat up, though, my body began to weep even before my mind recognized the cause for grieving. The world would never be the same. Everything I would make from that day on would recall how it had changed. Everything I did for myself would be in the name of what we had been.

◆   ◆   ◆

I DON'T TELL anybody this, don't coach the dancers in this, but when I watch them perform his piece *The Gift/No God Logic*, I see a picture of Arnie and me. Two men hold each other by the face, bend at the waist, then press their foreheads together, as a small woman in a black dress mounts one of the men backwards. Her arms are raised gracefully above her head. Her torso is curved, her eyes downcast. She is still, like some mythic creature turned into a tree. Standing not too far away is a fourth dancer. He'd been stepping away from the conjoined trio, but now, in a measured and matter-of-fact manner, he turns and reaches towards the small woman. He stretches and it seems he will break in two if he doesn't release.

It is me sitting there astride that man's back, waiting for Arnie. He is the gallant one reaching with such intensity. Or I am the one reaching out to him and saying, "Come and let's go make our lives. Come. Show me how to get on with it." But he's in another world.

How do I look? I ask.

"You look like my future," Arnie says.

No. How do I look to you?

"You look like everything I will do. Everything I want to be until the end of my life."

I reach for him and this time he has spun away down the driveway and my hand is extended into the shadows before I raise it to look at the stars. I close my hand into a fist.

◆　　◆　　◆

AFTER HE WAS GONE, I made a dance called *Absence* and I dedicated it to Edith and Lon Zane. The first movement of this dance is a study of two figures, a man and a woman. The woman, wearing only cotton panties, takes a sheet— one of the sheets I had stolen from the hospital when Arnie's nurse had told us we would never find sheets of such quality anywhere else. She wraps it turbanlike around her head, as I imagine a woman leaving her bath and thinking about a child who is dying or dead would. She preens, anoints herself in the secret ritual of the toilette, but the ritual is broken when she collapses beneath the weight of her sorrow. The man, naked and burly, seen only from the back, leans to one side, vulnerable, exposed on a bench. He is like a Roman senator—or one of the businessmen I used to tend at the Jewish Community Center health club in Binghamton, men who ate too much, drank too much, as if to stuff down other impulses. The man rises to an upright sitting posture. Hairy fist raised above his head, he is huge. He is Job

Arthur Aviles, Lawrence Goldhuber, Sean Curren, and Gregg Hubbard in Absence, *1988* (TOM BRAZIL)

petitioning God, saying, "It's not fair." Both figures on stage are isolated by an ocean of darkness. In the last tortured moments of this duet, the man turns and looks with great compassion upon the woman's misery. They fade into blackness.

The next scene finds a young couple, facing each other, stage center.

I, dressed in a floor-length taffeta skirt, come on stage. My movements introduce a vocabulary that is heavily pantomimed—with a bow to the audience and a sweeping gesture of my arm, I seem to say, "Good evening."

I acknowledge the couple—she is young and fresh, he is beautiful. Caressing the air around their still figures, I imply that I am here because of them. I turn away, take a seat, and the beautiful music of Berlioz's *La Nuit d'été* fills the space, as does the rest of the cast. It's a ridiculous wedding ceremony, a party. The giant father organizes the picture-taking. The mother stands aside in aloof observation. Guests mingle. The party progresses. I sit there and watch it as if waiting for something. The right moment comes and I move to take the young bride-to-be away from her paramour. The groom goes cold. Immovable. The bride-to-be breaks away from me and rushes to him, touches him, removes her hand in shock. He's no longer there. My figure in white taffeta reclaims the prize, causing him to go through a series of withering movements before exiting.

The curtain next opens on the women, now dressed in black mourning frocks, in a cemetery against a red horizon. They play a desperate, sorrowful game akin to musical chairs. The would-be bride claims the central bench. The men roll the stiff body of the would-be groom across the stage and exit with him, only to return alone, on their knees. They rise to their feet and join the women in a procession of swooping sadness—all except for the young bride, who remains seated until the very last moment. My figure returns, seemingly invisible, just as the bride joins the exiting procession. I dance a solo to the title song, "Absence." I dance a sort of invitation to the place of sorrow. I am sorrow and sorrow's apology for having visited such a scene upon two lovers. As I resolve the solo and prepare to leave, the stage is inundated with those stolen sheets, now wrapped around the loins of the dancers—all save for one, the groom, who is naked. He remains still while the others, with the inevitability of glaciers, drift past. They are moving past the white silk gauze curtain upstage, going somewhere, and they have forever to do it. They are shadows. They are dead and they have never been alive. They seem to say, "Look. We do this for you. Ignore the naked man whom we are leaving here. Look ahead of us. It's the only place you'll find courage not to sink to the floor as he must. We must keep moving. We loved him. He was one of us, but these inhuman sheets separate us from him. Let go of him. Look at that expanse ahead of us. This is no longer a theater. This is all we're promised."

The naked man spirals to earth as two curtains close—the one that has acted as a screen and now passageway to the unknown, and the other the grand drape separating this parable in flesh and light from the world of flesh and blood.

◆　　◆　　◆

The wall of a cinder block tractor barn, warmed by the sun. A road passed in front of the tractor barn. The road came from somewhere and led somewhere.

I was afraid at night. I was afraid of things that lurked beneath the surface of my dreams. I was afraid of things that came from the sky. I was afraid of things that lived in my mother's belly. I was afraid of my father's cries in his sleep. I have to leave all fear. I dance. My dancing is leaping over a terrain that keeps changing. I see cities—cities that are building up, falling down. I am dancing in both, ricocheting with a dance that begins at the base of my spine, invades my stomach, and cracks my shoulder blades. It is a fierce dance, punishing those who dare to watch. Then a softer dance, calling out to all those who have gone before, begging them to come back. And now it is softer still, calling out to all those who will hear, living and dead.

I lose my footing. I'm clawing at a hillside, complaining about my body and its marriage to time. I am dancing like my mother's prayers. I am asking for the impossible, for peace and acceptance.

I am bleeding. Others are bleeding.

My dance strikes up a smoke. It goes in the noses, ears, eyes, assholes of bleeding people. I have been told that it will heal.

With Arthur in Forsythia, *1989* (MAYA WALLACH)

FORSYTHIA

— ◆ —

FORSYTHIA: (n) *any of a genus of ornamental shrubs, esp. any of several cultivated species bearing bright yellow flowers in early spring before the leaves appear.*

THEY HAD ALWAYS been there. Our first meeting in mid-March 1971 had been played out against the backdrop of forsythias. Later, when we shared an apartment in Johnson City, near Binghamton, Arnie would fill the house with armloads of the yellow blossoms. They were the only flowers in bloom when we first set eyes on our home-to-be in Valley Cottage, and the last witness of his enshrouded exit.

Forsythias gave their name to the first duet I chose to make after Arnie's death.

Arthur Aviles had come into the company through an audition. He was short, grounded, with a simplicity of manner, an unstudied elegance, and grace of movement. One afternoon after a performance that was, untypically, near my home, I half-jokingly asked if anyone would like to come home with me, because I was lonely. He accepted. We had spoken some days earlier about my needing somebody to help me with the house and he had promised to take on the job. But after that night we were inseparable.

Forsythia was as much about the building of this new relationship as it was about living with Arnie's ghost. The duet was based upon partnering ideas and concepts that were informed by Arnie's and my duet repertoire, but here my partner was eleven years younger than I, and unlike Arnie, had had years of dance training. This was not a collaboration—Arthur and I had no grounds yet for mutual creative dialogues. He wanted to be choreographed upon, and I, unsettled by this at first, came to savor the opportunity to mold and direct this inspired bundle of muscle, emotion, and intelligence.

The piece began with Arthur dancing a solo to the tape-recorded voice of Arnie describing a dream. In the beginning of this dream, he and I were moving into a new apartment that we would be forced to share with two other persons. I danced a solo to the remainder of the dream, moving in subtle counterpoint to Arnie's report of a shirtless young construction worker who is crushed by scaffolding and whose brutal death causes Arnie to turn away.

Later, to the supremely melancholy strains of Dufay's fifteenth-century song "Adieu," Arthur and I danced in close canon. I, the unsure architect of the proceedings, attempted to keep up with Arthur's muscular buoyancy, much as I did in our relationship off the stage. At the end of *Forsythia*, we recapitulated our opening solo motifs as Arnie recounted a harrowing dream in which he scrambles to escape a juggernaut of burning logs.

Arthur was a way into the future, an answer to loneliness. He was a dancer who could inspire me, a man I could trust, and a friend who would fight me on principles aesthetic, political, moral.

◆   ◆   ◆

In a dream you saw a way to survive
and you were full of joy.
                    Jenny Holzer

No one ever asked me to become an artist. It would have been no tragedy if I had become a truck driver, raised some kids, and just kept quiet. Why do I insist upon running the risk of failure, the risk of making a fool of myself? Why do I insist?

Because art does for me what religion does—it organizes a seemingly chaotic world. Because it is my way of making sense of the world and its changes.

When I look at what is curious, strangely proportioned, and true, I am no longer the descendant of a slave. I am reminded of Michelangelo's unfailing eye and steady hand as he made marble give up man. A man who is in fact a fawn. A fawn who is in fact an idea. An idea that is in fact a dream, a memory, perhaps of lying in the meadow of an Italian hillside warmed by the sun. The force with which this fawn, this idea, this dream were brought into the world inspires my faith.

When I look at what is beautiful, I am cured of hatred. I am proud. I am greater than Martin Luther King when he said, "I have seen the mountaintop." I am the mountaintop.

These righteous curiosities, these beautiful things ask me, "Would you know us if you were blind, if you were in pain?"

And I say yes, I would know them. All would be the same because the whole of life isn't contained in this body that I am desperately holding on to. These things give me hope and I don't feel so cheated.

When I am in pain, I must know that beauty always has been and always will be. This is as close to eternity as I need to be.

◆　　◆　　◆

AROUND THIS TIME, the Saint Luke's Chamber Orchestra, following up on a relationship we had established a year earlier, offered another commission. Relying on the encouragement of company members with whom I shared the proposed music, I set out to choreograph a work to the first movement of Mendelssohn's *Octet in E Flat Major*.

At first, the piece was a visceral response to the exuberant and seething froth of the sixteen-year-old Mendelssohn's ruminations on waves and water. I wanted the dance to suggest playground antics, mad explorations of the stage frame and of the combinations possible in an ensemble of nine dancers. In its strength and optimism, the music proved to be the best collaborator I had ever had. Making the morning commute into Manhattan with Arthur, we were consumed with analyzing the brilliant structure of all four movements. And then, in intense, workmanlike rehearsals, everyone was asked to solve the problems of vocabulary and interpreting musical structure.

A drama unfolding in our midst would solidify the meaning of the work. Handsome Damien Acquavella, eccentric to the extreme in both manner of dress and dance, began to get sick. He fought back with every possible homeopathic and nontraditional healing method—sometimes two and three at the same time. Still, the KS lesions spread and his remarkable musculature melted.

I had a daydream, almost a vision, in which I saw Damien and a myriad of friends, living and dead, in a body of water. Perhaps it was a lake as vast as the ocean, a lake emptied by an immense and unforgiving waterfall. This company of people was struggling against the current. Some had already drowned, others were grasping their comrades to save them, still others were swimming confidently, almost enjoying their effort.

I tied this vision to Mendelssohn's music and to the work we were doing in the studio, and *D-Man in the Waters* emerged. I dedicated the dance to Damien (whom I affectionately called D-Man) to honor his struggle, which was emblematic of so many others. *D-Man in the Waters* is a difficult piece and we had to strengthen ourselves individually and as a company to perform it.

As he grew sicker, AIDS-related dementia set in and Damien began to behave more bizarrely. He became obsessed with the idea of returning to perform with the company—in *D-Man* particularly. I promised Damien there would be a place for him in the dance. As he could no longer walk by the time of the debut, in 1989, I carried him on stage, offering my legs as he executed the arm movements of what would have been his solo. When Damien could no longer perform, I chose not to replace him in the piece. Oddly asymmetrical groupings now mark his absence.

Damien passed in June of 1990.

Arthur distinguished himself in *D-Man* and was awarded a Bessie from the New York Dance and Performance Award Committee for "an electrifying series of performances . . . sheer physical daring."

The work became a touring staple. It helped us secure our footing in face of the loss of Arnie, poor management, near bankruptcy due to back taxes, and the financial retrenchment of dance presenters around the country. Sometimes, it threatened to become the signature work that the company could never move beyond, but even more, *D-Man in the Waters* made way for new questions and directions.

Last Supper at Uncle Tom's Cabin / The Promised Land, *1990* (JEFF DAY)

LAST SUPPER AT UNCLE TOM'S CABIN/
THE PROMISED LAND

———— • ◆ • ————

HISTORY HAS RULES. One rule dictates that a people whose identity has been forged by violence and deprivation will manifest violence and deprivation.

Such rules must be broken.

But there are some rules that I do not want to break. I find them compelling and affirming, conflicting but unassailable. They may not exist in the realm of empirical fact but their validity illuminates humanity at its highest. If racism rests in the palm of history's hand, if it is like a knife, a wedge, a poison, it is also like a lace collar placed around the neck of a china doll.

In an article in the *Village Voice* maybe ten years ago, Thulani Davis said that "we taught the world how to take a solo." Since time immemorial, we have known how to step outside of the dance that everyone knows, to do that special little dance, that special little solo that can be appreciated only when the larger dance continues.

There is something that we, as black people, have understood and brought to the world. We did not build the Parthenon. Did we build the pyramids? Perhaps. But there is something else—something that has been written in the human experience, something that we have put there that is as grand as the Parthenon, as grand as the pyramids. We have educated the human heart.

I reasoned that if my time was limited, that if I was to follow Arnie soon, I would make a work that articulated all the questions that I have lived with, all the questions that have shaped me. I would speak in a voice that was decidedly African-American. Why? I speak several languages, all English, but African-American is my mother tongue. It is a constant, as loyal as my face, and like my face, invisible to me without the aid of a mirror. In this case the mirror is history, both personal and public.

I made a chronology that charted the origins of this voice:

SIXTEENTH CENTURY: The beginning of "the modern era," as white Europeans—missionaries, merchants, soldiers—penetrate the Dark Continent. Some of them say that the blacks they meet there are the cruelest people they have ever encountered. They speak of blood rites, ritual mutilations, and ceaseless warring between tribes, villages, clans.

1619: John Smith becomes governor of the Jamestown colony in what will become Virginia. The indolent habits of its citizens cause Smith to make a law: "He who would not work should not eat." Slave ships unload their precious cargo in this New World colony a year before the *Mayflower* brings more settlers to what will be Massachusetts. With the introduction of slaves, the Jamestown colony grows prosperous.

1712: Negroes riot in the colony of New Amsterdam to protest their exclusion from schools and from landownership, the interdiction forbidding them to "strike a Christian or a Jew" in self-defense, and the banishment of their testimony in court.

1750, October 2: An advertisement appears in the *Boston Gazette*, offering ten pounds for the return of a runaway slave, Crispus Attucks.

1770, March 5: Crispus Attucks, a black Bostonian, becomes the first man to die for American "liberty."

1773: Phillis Wheatley, the personal slave of Mr. and Mrs. John Wheatley, publishes her first volume of poetry. In addressing the issue of blacks and Christian faith, she writes:

'Twas mercy brought me from my Pagan land,
Taught me, benighted soul, to understand
That there's a God, that there's a Savior too.
Once I redemption neither sought nor knew,

Some view our sable race with scournful eye,
Their colour is a diabolic dye—
Remember, Christian, Negroes black as Cain
Can be refined and join the Angelic train.

1816: Two boats sail up the Apalachicola River to Fort Blount, Georgia, and exterminate all but fifteen of the 311 Negro inhabitants, of which only twenty had ever been slaves. As the two boats move away from the scene of carnage and the officers in charge retire, the veteran sailors gather before the mast and bitterly curse slavery and those officers who constrained them to murder innocent women and helpless children merely for their love of freedom.

1825: Lafayette writes in a letter, "I would never have drawn my sword in the cause of America, if I could have conceived that thereby I was founding a land of slavery."

1836: A representative in Congress from one of the free states introduces a bill giving a gratuity to the perpetrator of the Fort Blount massacre. The bill passes both houses.

1851: Harriet Beecher Stowe, daughter of a prominent abolitionist, writes *Uncle Tom's Cabin.*

Circa 1860: Matt Lee, my great-grandmother, is born on a plantation in Georgia.

1863, January 1: The second Emancipation Proclamation is urged upon Lincoln by the abolitionists and others who wish the Negro free. Because some counties are left out, it does not free all slaves.

Circa 1880: Anna Edwards, Estella Jones's mother (later known to us as Big Mama), is born.

Circa 1890: Ike Jones, Gus Jones's father, is strapped to a raft with his father and brother. Together, they fight starvation and dehydration on the high seas to make their way from an embattled island republic to the "Land of the Free."

1915: Gus Jones is born in Georgia.

1919: Estella Lucivee Walden is born into a household where a man and a woman produce five children under the glare of despotic plantation owners and the terrorism of "night-riders." Their tenant-farmer shack will soon lose Tom Walden, the husband and father.

Estella's first memory will be of her nearly illiterate mother sounding out syllables from the King James Bible. Estella will never remember a time when she didn't know about Jesus, the man with a beard and long gray robes. Her mother tells her about Him, as her mother's mother had told her about Him.

Circa 1920: Embittered white feminists ask, "Will Sambo receive the vote before women do?" and mark the end of the long and fruitful confederation between suffragettes, abolitionists, and freed slaves.

Circa 1920: Gus Jones, who will become my father, watches his father, Ike Jones, flush a bird from the brush and with lightning speed grab it in flight.

1923: Marcus Garvey is tried for fraud.

1940: Marcus Garvey dies in exile in London. Negro Zionism is doomed to failure.

1948: "I love you. I'll take care of you, your four children, and your mama," says Gus Jones to Estella Lucivee Walden, who believes him. They marry.

1948: Gus and Estella Jones go into the business of contracting itinerant laborers, migrants, as the rest of the country enjoys the warm confidence that comes with "having saved the world." The two of them cover a flatbed truck with a crude wooden armature, drape it with an army surplus tarpaulin, fill it with desperate, hopeful people, and take to the road.

1952: Estella's tenth child, a boy named Bill Tass, is born on a night when "it rained so hard that the yard fowl were found sodden, mud-caked, and drowned the next morning."

1952: Gus and Estella vote for Eisenhower, the kind of white man you *had* to respect—"After all, he whipped them Germans."

1955: Joe McCarthy eviscerates reputations and lives.

1955: Gus Jones decides to "become a Black Yankee." He stops migrating and settles his family up North to take some small share of the prosperity "that is the birthright of all Americans."

1961: Camelot at the White House.

1961: Fire on Miller Road. In the middle of the night a young woman who chose not to sing the blues but act them burns Estella and Gus's dream down in an attempt to secure her man from another woman.

1962: Long-haired white boys from England appear on the *CBS Evening News*. They say "Yeah" sort of the way we do, sing "Roll Over, Beethoven" sort of the way Chuck Berry did.

1962: My brother Azel graduates from high school. Graduation is an unusual event in our family. Azel goes away, not to the military, not to the jailhouse, but to college. At Christmas holiday he returns, talking of Karl Marx, and *The Protestant Ethic and Spirit of Capitalism,* and playing albums by Bob Dylan, Joan Baez, Simon and Garfunkel, and Nina Simone.

1964: I hear a nasal-voiced white man confirm what my mother has always said: *The times they are a-changin'* . . .

1965: Newark, Los Angeles, and Chicago are in flames. I realize that Big Mama had been right when she said to her young daughter, Estella, "There's a war coming. And there's gonna be blood runnin' down the streets like water."

1966, February: I, just turned fourteen, walk home in a pubescent trance. An automobile careens through a mud puddle, slapping filthy ice slush into my face. In that instant, gasping, I realize that someday I will die. What if there is no God? What if there are no heavenly mansions waiting for me?

1967: An ex–research scientist and dubious Orientalist encourages us to "tune in, turn on, and drop out."

1968, Christmas: Estella Jones directs her performance to Jesus Christ, her Savior, on behalf of her mother, who has recently passed away, on behalf of the president of the United States and all those young boys whose deaths are reported on the evening news at suppertime, and on behalf of her helpmate and grandbaby recently returned from the sanitarium. The holiday is motivated by nothing more than habit; no one believes in Santa Claus anymore. There are new babies in the house. Their mothers are little more than teenagers.

1968: I dream of lying between my coach's thighs and nestling in the warm, manly fur of his chest and arms.

1968: Martin Luther King, Jr., is gunned down and a bitter malaise settles in where once there had been hope.

".last at free are we ,Almighty God thank ;last at free, last at free", spiritual Negro old the of words the in sing to and hands join to able be will—Protestants and Catholics ,Gentiles and Jews ,men white and men black—children God's of all when day that up speed to able be will we ,city and state every from ,hamlet and village every from ring it let we when, ring to freedom allow we when And

1969: The sweet smell of marijuana forms the smoke rings of my mind. As I peak on Purple Haze, I see raindrops the size of the Koh-i-noor diamond glisten on the fins of a '59 Cadillac stuck in the mud at Yasgur's farm in Woodstock. The 500,000 people gathered on a hillside don't yet know that a dream is over.

1970: I refuse to salute the flag at a high school assembly and am elected the unofficial representative of a spontaneous demonstration to protest the rule forbidding girls from wearing pants to school. I win first place for oral interpretation and drama at the state level, and tell a tearfully congratulatory English teacher that I'm headed for Broadway.

1970: Incoming Special Admissions students at the State University of New York at Binghamton are required to read *The Autobiography of Malcolm X.*

1971: I am picked up hitchhiking. "You must be freezing your balls off. Want to come to my place to warm up?" I hold a man's erection in my hands for the first time.

1971: I meet a small man with the gentleness of a woman. Together, we become Bill-and-Arnie.

1971: Arnie and I leave the State University of New York, Binghamton, to go to Amsterdam to study dance, to write poetry—to never live in America again.

1971: On Amsterdam's Leidsestraat, I learn about the Attica uprising and what a governor with an army of policemen can do to a group of black men when they have the right excuse.

1972: We come back to America. I learn to call myself a dancer and then a choreographer.

1973: We give in to San Francisco's promise of freedom and my need to be near my family.

1974: The Vietnam War ends and Nixon, under threat of impeachment, re-signs.

1974: Arnie and I leave San Francisco to join Lois Welk and re-form the American Dance Asylum, a place of refuge where outlandish ideas and nontraditional body types are welcomed and flourish.

I choreograph and direct *The Track Dance*. It is my first large-group spectacle. The characters include a demented old lady dressed like Marie Antoinette, twenty tough kids from the local boys' club all willing to run, fall, and roll, a man in a wheelchair, and a tall, devastatingly aloof black woman who carries a little white doll. The woman and the doll are shrouded. They resemble drought-stricken refugees from the sub-Sahara. When the man is deposed from his wheelchair, it is ripped apart piece by piece.

1977: I make my New York debut in *Everybody Works*. I spin half naked in Central Park, shouting the memory of my two aunts to the rain-threatening summer skies and to the audience present and future, *I love you. I love you.*

1978: Arnie and I are dubbed a "same-sex choreographic duo," and routinely described by the press as "tall and black, short and white."

1980: We have left American Dance Asylum and are living in Blauvelt, New York.

1981: Bill Schwerdler, a friend, spends the better part of a year and a half in and out of the hospital and nobody knows what's wrong with him. He dies. He is one of the first.

1981: While performing an improvisation at Valley Cottage, I say, "My father died yesterday." Later that night I receive a phone call saying that my father has died. At my father's funeral, I meet several of my older brothers again and see how these giants are, in fact, small boys in middle-aged bodies. I wonder if I will ever be middle-aged. I hear my mother pray and sing once again and it is as if I hear it for the first time.

1982: Arnie and I enjoy great success with *Rotary Action*, which is to be our last major duet.

Bill: *One more story, okay. This one's going to be about separation.*

Arnie: *What do you mean by separation?*

Bill: *I mean the fear of separation. Are you ready?*

1982: Bill T. Jones/Arnie Zane and Company is formed as a not-for-profit corporation.

1984: Arnie runs night fevers and gets mysterious rashes.

1986: The company, now with six members, tours Asia, the United States, and Europe. Arnie is beginning to have chronic infections and cannot always travel with us.

1986: A lump appears on Arnie's right arm. It is lymphoma.

1988: Arnie says, as he has many times before, that his favorite painting is the head of Christ in Leonardo's *Last Supper*. He points out how the horizon line intersects Christ's head in such a way to suggest that He is of both heaven and earth.

Sean Curran, a dancer in the company, brings novelties to lift our spirits. One of these is a deck of soft-core male porno playing cards, "Fifty-two Handsome Nudes."

At this time, Arnie and I are brainstorming for new ideas. Spectacular new ideas. Arnie conjures the image of Jessye Norman on an ice floe, suspended above the stage at the Brooklyn Academy of Music. She is Eliza, the melodramatic heroine of *Uncle Tom's Cabin*. I have not yet actually read *Uncle Tom's Cabin*. With a laugh we declare the title of this next piece will be *Last Supper at Uncle Tom's Cabin/Featuring 52 Handsome Nudes*. I will later change the title to *Last Supper at Uncle Tom's Cabin/The Promised Land*.

1988, March 30, six P.M.: Arnie dies.

1989: *Mama, I'm afraid. What if?* This is the first time I speak publicly about my fear. I am performing in Los Angeles as part of the Black Choreographers' Series. I dance while my mother reads from the Bible with halting intensity.

> *Do you love all people? Do you love white people?* I ask her, trying to trap her, to make apparent the conflict between her Christian philosophy and the tangible racism in her life.
>
> "I try to," she says without missing a beat, to rousing applause.
>
> *Is Christianity a slave religion?* I ask.
>
> Unknowingly, over a century later, she echoes Phillis Wheatley when she says, "We were naked and ignorant over there in Africa. If it took slavery to help us find the Master, then slavery was all right too."

1989: I read *Uncle Tom's Cabin*. I find it to be hokum, misinformation. I find it moving, infuriating, beautiful, embarrassing, and important.

1989: Looking a bit like a homeless person, a bit like a beat poet, R. Justice Allen, on parole after serving a fifteen-year sentence in the Attica prison, comes to an audition for the opera I am directing, *Mother of Three Sons*. I tell him to come back—that there will be a part for him in the next production.

1990: I meet Sage Cowles on a panel in Minneapolis. I assume she is a cold and privileged rich white woman. I know nothing about her. As a sort of challenge, I say I've got a part for her in a work I am making. She takes me quite seriously.

My history is a fragmented chronology that divides me from my past, from my mother's faith, from the hopeful naiveté of the sixties counterculture. I decided that Last Supper at Uncle Tom's Cabin/The Promised Land would acknowledge this division and attempt to go past it. This work, with its fragmented black voice, would strive to speak to the broadest, most varied audience.

It would speak about being human. About how we are the places we have been, the people we have slept with. How we are what we have lost and what we dream for.

> .ring freedom let, mountainside every from, Mississippi of molehill and hill every from ring freedom Let
> .Tennessee of Mountain Lookout from ring freedom Let
> .Georgia of Mountain Stone from ring freedom Let
> .that only not But
> .California of slopes curvaceous the from ring freedom Let
> .Colorado of Rockies capped-snow the from ring freedom Let
> .Pennsylvania of Alleghenies heightening the from ring freedom Let
> .York New of mountains mighty the from ring freedom Let
> .Hampshire New of hilltops prodigious the from ring freedom let So

And our dreams keep changing.

To dream is human. In dreaming we are more alike than different.

I began to do simple studies, things like having two dancers read the chapter headings from *Uncle Tom's Cabin* as they traveled around the edge of a table, debating like senators or lawyers.

Speaker one: *A man of humanity.*

Speaker two: *The property is carried off.*

Speaker one: *Evangeline.*

Speaker two: *Topsy.*

Speaker one: *The unprotected.*

Speaker two: *The slave warehouse.*

Speaker one: *Dark places.*

Speaker two: *The martyr.*

I listened to Martin Luther King's "I Have a Dream" speech again and pulled out notes from an old solo of mine from the 1970s called *I Am Not*

Sidney Poitier. It had never been performed, but for it I had transcribed King's speech backwards:

> *.brotherhood of symphony beautiful a into nation our of discords jangling the transform to able be will we faith this With .hope of stone a despair of mountain the of out hew to able be will we faith this With*

We should all care enough about this speech—a more hopeful one we'll never hear—to take its mangled inversion and set it right. In order to live together it has to be set right.

I had brought two "guests" into the company. They were strong black men with contrasting personalities. And while neither was a dancer, they both had a confidence and naturalness in their movements that could easily bridge the gap between themselves and the dancers. I was also confident that with the right preparation they could give any characterization I gave them a direct and essential portrayal. The production would revolve around these two actors.

In his late thirties, dreadlocked, and with an odd swinging gait that I later learned was due to a grizzly accident during a prison football game, R. Justice Allen became a muse of sorts. Through his experience as a former high school athlete, streetwise urban youth, drug addict, and ex-convict, I found a way to reach and address my grieving for an identity that is ravaged by history and misinformation, by economics and a social order that exploits a man wholesale while keeping him on the fringes of opportunity. Justice had survived this identity. His spirit was resilient and lyrical enough to lend itself to theatrical transformation.

Andréa Smith, handsome, strapping, and gentle, with a rich, resounding voice and a compelling stage presence, represented for me the mellow optimism and sensuality that many black men are able to maintain. Andréa was young in many senses of the word, and the openness and curiosity implied by his youth were necessary in re-creating such a worn, misunderstood icon as Uncle Tom.

Last Supper at Uncle Tom's Cabin/The Promised Land was not to be pure dance, but rather a theatrical construct relying on several mediums. Literary and dramatic conventions of the nineteenth and twentieth centuries were expressed through Ann T. Green's dramatic distillation of Stowe's novel, excerpts of Sojourner Truth's *Ain't I a Woman?*, dancer Heidi Latsky's rumination on credibility, and LeRoi Jones's *Dutchman*.

Music written and performed by Julius Hemphill and his sextet designed as incidental music, martial music, music for a nineteenth-century pantomime, classic jazz, and what can only be described as contemporary American music. Supplementing Julius's composition was a rap song that Justice wrote and performed, my mother's powerful rendition of a different Gospel every evening, and my own singing of a folk song.

Huck Snyder's stage decor placed the work within the universe of a nineteenth-century children's theater. It achieved its considerable effect by relying on the primary color palette, purposefully naive use of two-dimensional shapes, and bold, childlike patterning.

I was also interested in the real-life identities of the participants on stage. In addition to Justice and Andréa, I invited Sage and John Cowles, both of whom have contributed greatly to the civic and cultural lives of Minnesota's Twin Cities. John was a former editor of Minneapolis's *Star Tribune* and continues to display a strong interest in issues social and political. Sage, sixty-five, handsome, had been a dancer most of her life. Both auditioned for the work, and when accepted went about their responsibilities with a great sense of passion and commitment, touring with the company for most of two years.

It was no secret that, within the company's microcosm, I viewed the Cowleses as the "haves," much as Justice and Andréa represented the "have-nots." But in the universe of the work and its parallel in my company, the "haves" and the "have-nots" joined together to become something greater. They asserted my belief in true equality and the compatibility of people.

Through a complex matrix of meanings between the real world and the world of theater, through nontraditional casting and nonlinear juxtaposition of iconographic events, I tried to suggest the disorientation that I, and I suspect millions of others, feel around issues like power, sex, race, religion, and even art. The truth of the piece was in its disorientation.

In *Last Supper at Uncle Tom's Cabin/The Promised Land* I could wrestle with a series of social, political, and spiritual issues (content) and the issues of movement vocabulary versus text, the use of narrative, and the impulse to deconstruct narrative (form). I wanted to ask: Was Uncle Tom a disgrace to his race? A romanticization of servitude? Was he as a Christlike figure a precursor of Dr. Martin Luther King or Gandhi? Is this high-minded, propagandistic literary work of any relevance to us today? What happened to the bold notion of liberty that fueled this novel?

Before I could expect an audience to consider these questions, I had to be sure that everyone was familiar with the themes of the novel. So I backed up and decided to tell the story.

PART ONE: THE CABIN

A gingham drape runs around the entire prosce-nium of the theater, and behind that drape is an-other one, a jagged two-dimensional drape with stylized magnolias and hanging moss. Behind that stands the naive representation of a log cabin.

To the raucous, rasping saxophones of the Julius Hemphill Sextet, the curtain opens and we're introduced to R. Justice Allen as the narra-tor and to Sage Cowles as Harriet Beecher Stowe. They stand apart from the proceedings.

The story starts slowly, introducing the fi-delity of Uncle Tom, the purity of Little Eva, the tragic reluctance of the liberal master Mr. St. Clare, and the twisted values of the evil slave trader Simon Legree. All performers save Justice, Sage, and Andréa Smith, who is introduced as

The whipping of Uncle Tom from "The Cabin" with dancers (from the left) Gregg Hubbard, Andréa Smith, Lawrence Goldhu-ber, and R. Justice Allen (MAYA WALLACH)

The revival meeting from "The Cabin" *with dancers (from the left) Heidi Latsky, Andréa Smith, Arthur Aviles, Andrea Woods, Maya Saffrin, and Lawrence Goldhuber* (MAYA WALLACH)

Entr'acte with the "dogs" *with dancers (from the left) Niles Ford, Arthur Aviles, John Cowles, Andrea Woods (kneeling), Lawrence Goldhuber, and Gregg Hubbard* (MAYA WALLACH)

Uncle Tom, are masked. The novel is told in a ludicrously blunted, stylized fashion, with some performers playing several parts. Larry Goldhuber's girth is exploited both in his mimed portrayal of Aunt Chloe, Uncle Tom's gingham-plaided, deeply sympathetic spouse, and in his rendering of the mean-spirited brute, Mr. Haley, who threatens to take Eliza's precious child away and does in fact sell Uncle Tom down the river. Andrea Woods, lithesome, earthy, and elegant, plays the heroically maternal Eliza, who is chased by Arthur Aviles and Leonard Cruz, representing, with gymnastic virtuosity, a vicious pack of dogs. Sean Curran, dressed as a dandy, executes a witty petit allegro to suggest the kind slave owner, Mr. St. Clare. Heidi Latsky, fragile, small, wearing a white frock and angelic mask with built-in locks of gold, wafts about as the saintly child, Little Eva. Justice Allen doubles as the evil Simon Legree, who ravishes the beautiful octoroon, played by Maya Saffrin, and whips "our Tom" to death.

It's at this point in the narrative that we send the entire proceedings into retrograde. In a "coup de théâtre" we are back at the point where Legree is about to whip Tom. I then take the liberty of inserting a "correct" ending—the one we would like to have seen, in which Tom, instead of dying at the hands of his aggressor, stands up with all the other slaves and resists Simon Legree.

The entr'acte drape is lowered.

Julius Hemphill's plaintive march, which has accompanied Legree's orgy of violence, is now transformed into an upbeat burlesque that ushers on the apron, from both sides of the stage, twin lines of male dancers wearing black T-shirts, jock straps, combat boots, and muzzles. These are the eight "dogs." John Cowles and Justice bark, marine drill-sergeant style, a curious code of figures to which "the dogs" perform an unnerving routine of arm gestures that resemble both military drill and football practice. To the heavy staccato thud of their combat boots, in groups of two they dash from the stage and run out through the auditorium.

PART TWO: ELIZA ON THE ICE

In her book *Women, Race and Class*, Angela Davis takes issue with Stowe's Eliza. She says that Eliza is "white motherhood incarnate, but in blackface"; she runs away from the institution of slavery only as a response to her maternal urge to protect her child. Davis continues by saying that this politically neutered image of the black slave woman is debilitating and grotesquely misinformed. My response to such a compellingly flawed character was to re-create her as a multidimensional polemic.

The entr'acte curtain rises upon a world inhabited by four personifications of Eliza. The four silhouetted women crisscross the stage performing signature movements, then exit, leaving Andrea Woods's Eliza. Sage Cowles, as Harriet Beecher Stowe, stands to the side.

Sage begins to recite Sojourner Truth's celebrated address as Andrea dances:

I have ploughed and planted and gathered into barns and no man could head me! And ain't I a woman? I could work as much and eat as much as a man—when I could get it—and bear the lash as well! And ain't I a woman? I have borned thirteen children and seen them most all sold off to slavery, and when I cried out with my mother's grief, none but Jesus heard me! And ain't I a woman?

The little man in black there, he says women can't have as much rights as men because Christ wasn't a woman—Where did Christ come from?

Where did your Christ come from? From God and a woman! Men had nothing to do with him. . . .

If Justice offered insight into a certain male identity, Andrea Woods reveals a particular female perspective. As we began working together (sometimes fighting together), I learned of her hunger to know about her identity as a woman, as a black woman, and the history bound in this identity. For Andrea, I crafted a "historical Eliza"—one whom Alvin Ailey would have recognized. In a series of lyrical, loping movements that originated in the pelvis, coursed up the back, and resulted in the languorous coiling and uncoiling of the arms, Andrea abstracted the movement impulses that I have witnessed or invented through my mother, grandmother, and any number of women I have been privileged to know.

From stage right, the nearly forgotten corps of "dogs" comes sprinting across in pursuit of Eliza, who exits, leaving Harriet Beecher Stowe to welcome small, fragile Heidi Latsky's Eliza, entering in the dogs' wake. Her movements are convoluted, turned in, interrupted with the sharp slicing of the air by her arms and feet. She appears deeply troubled, if not demented. From the pit a clarinet laments.

Initially, Heidi had felt threatened by the production of *Uncle Tom's Cabin*. The specific origin of the work, its voice, my absorption in Justice and Andre seemed to leave no room for her. She knew that I was giving Justice a platform to tell his story and certainly to voice his rage. Could I be as interested in her story—small, Jewish woman from Canada that she was? Yes, I assured her.

Heidi's solo grew out of a problem I'd given her to solve. She was to take movements from anywhere in our repertory and fashion them in such a way as to support her spoken monologue about anger.

My father,
My father told me to turn the other cheek.
My mother,
My mother told me not to expect much.
They both told me be honest, have faith, be good.
I believed them.
I grew up.
I met him.
I knew something was wrong.
He told me I was crazy, that it was my problem.
I believed.
I believed him.
I believed him.
I believed him.
But he had betrayed me,
He had lied to me to protect himself.
How could he love me and do this to me at the same time?
How did I allow this to happen?
I believed.
I believed.
I believed.

Sage Cowles held a microphone to this hurricane of discontent as Heidi stomped about, slammed a small chair, lunged, then slapped the floor, signaling the appearance, once again, of the ludicrous dogs. Heidi exited just ahead of them.

The third Eliza enters with the

Betsy McCracken's Eliza with the "dogs" (MAYA WALLACH)

dogs and commands them to attention. This Eliza came in the form of Betsy McCracken, tall with long, well-shaped legs, sensuously lifted arches, a body molded by years of ballet training. Arnie used to say she was a Mannerist figure, with her small doll-like head and face, narrow shoulders, and boyish chest tapering into long arms, legs, and torso. And this elongated elegance was curiously blended with a tomboy/cowgirlishness that was, perhaps, the legacy of her Texas origins, of the rivalry with older brothers and a love of horses. Betsy was young, smart, talented, but strangely timid, not always sure of how to command her majestic physical proportions.

She is the Eliza who commands men—part Joan of Arc, part dominatrix, and part martial arts master. Her movements were designed to show the length of her extension, the range of motion in her supple hips, and the glorious flexibility of her back. She strikes the floor with the staff she wields and the dogs appear to leap through hoops like circus lions. And yet there is tension implicit in the fact that she can never turn her back on them. These dogs may be silly, but they are also dangerous. Suddenly, she throws down her staff and bolts. Julius's sextet bays as the pack of hounds rushes off in pursuit.

Andrea Woods, the historical Eliza, reappears with the exotically pretty Maya Saffrin, who is Eliza number four. Maya's Eliza is dressed as a coquette from a turn-of-the-century French postcard.

Choosing to exploit Maya's beauty, I exaggerated something voluptuous and desirable about her. Other than the simple hopscotch she performs with Andrea, who is chased away by the dogs, her movement is not her own. She barely, if ever, touches the floor. Instead, she is passed, pulled, and stretched by the coarse dogs, to whom she is simultaneously a football and a rape victim. Here is an Ann-Margret nightclub act combined with *The Perils of Pauline*.

The dogs abandon her. She is then gathered up by the three other Elizas. And the four together perform a resolution of sorts before leaving to the historical Eliza's proud, rolling gait.

The dogs return and, in counterpoint with their opening routine, burlesque a line-dance—"The Electric Slide." Harriet Beecher Stowe seems to grow weak. She crawls off, reciting Sojourner Truth's address in retrograde. The dogs' exit reveals one more Eliza—in this instance, the six-foot-two Gregg Hubbard, who wears a white miniskirt and struggles for balance in high-heeled pumps. Gregg executes an incantation of grasping arms, jabbing fingers, wobbling knees, and extended tongue before coolly gathering himself to exit with the rolling gait of the historical Eliza who preceded him.

The entr'acte curtain falls.

ENTR'ACTE: THE PRAYER

"The Prayer" *with Estella Jones*
(MAYA WALLACH)

After Gregg's silent exit, Julius Hemphill introduces an oddly propulsive musical figure that rises and falls in cyclical repetition, moving in ever wilder flights of improvisation, before gently reining in its fervor and evaporating.

During this interlude, Estella Jones moves on stage on my arm. She is swaying, humming, incanting quietly to herself, dabbing the profusion of sweat that has already broken on her brow or using her handkerchief as a fan. She takes a seat and waits for the band to finish playing.

She rises, steps forward, plants her feet, clad in that evening's carefully chosen pair of pumps, and addresses the audience, "Here I am again." She swings into her version of "I Shall Not Be Removed." Estella is comfortable on stage. She leads the prayer in her beloved church in San Francisco, a place where, she complains, people have become less and less willing "to stand up, open their mouths, and bring 'the Message.'" She sings:

Jesus is my captain.
I shall not be removed.
Jesus is my captain.

I shall not be removed.
Just like a tree that is standing by the water,
Oh, I shall not be removed.

Ending the song, she calls for understanding, for an end to all argument. She asks the audience to have patience as she blesses the performance. She asks her Lord—whom she addresses sometimes in the voice of a small child, sometimes of an angry woman, and still other times, of a joyous devotee—to bless her son in "whatever it is he thinks he's trying to do."

I dance beside her as she prays. Moved by the rhythm and the meaning of her words, my solo is based on a shudder and a shout that originates somewhere in my hips and like two claps of thunder moves down my thighs and up my back.

When she has completed her benediction, I take her arm and whisper my thanks as I lead her off the stage.

Each night her prayer is unpredictable. Depending on her mood, taking her off stage is at times like being led by a large impetuous child, at other times like guiding an old woman, heavy, swaying with sober reflection.

PART THREE: THE SUPPER

Here's somethin' to think about
feel your brain cells throb
your thoughts scream and shout
here's somethin' to think about.
They call me Justice.

Trip to the past, you know before
to my younger years, the days of yore
Black Power, peace and Freedom Now.
I sang We Shall Overcome, but I didn't learn how.
My father couldn't spend time with me

he had to work, pay the rent, and ten mouths to feed.
The vices of life, they altered my brain
got consumed by the streets and then I went insane.

Young, gifted and black was my identity
but I was deaf, dumb and blind.
No I couldn't see.
From Vietnam came dope in body bags
I started hangin', and bangin', and got hooked on skag.

I lost regard for life through my forgotten tears.
Picked up a gun, stick 'em up, cost me fifteen years.
Hard time is whatyacallit, a ward of the state
in a legal slave system full of death, and hate.
Locked in, shut out for taking a life
innocent or guilty, I paid the price.
A veteran of Attica and tear gas fumes
I walked amongst the civil dead in society's tombs
Out of sight, out of mind, a forgotten man
Victimized and taunted by the Ku Klux Klan
Headed and prodded from block to block
I was just another Nigger in a cracker-box

Slave—three fifths of a man
Bias—is the law of the land
Death—you better fight if you can
Because clubs is trumps in the corporal plan
Time—is the master of illusion
Pain—at the core of this confusion
Love—was an emotional intrusion
Survival tools were my only solution.
So I cleared my mind of all this debris
And took a look at my life realistically

The good, the bad and the in-between
I'm not a slave, I'm a man
So I must be seen.

A new day dawned the day I got out
I had no fear, I had no doubt
My house is glass so I throw no stones
And now I rock around the world with Bill T. Jones.

R. Justice Allen

The entr'acte curtain rises.

The entire company has gathered on the stage. They assume the poses of those gathered at Leonardo da Vinci's *Last Supper* table. This section is an orgy of inchoate imagery: there is a frantic sequence of what appears to be a classroom or a religious observance. Justice and Andre play an undisclosed game. Sage and John move like two spirits through the frenetic proceedings. Like metronomes, the dancers rock in unison on Huck Snyder's fetishistic chairs.

Suddenly all is still.

Justice bounces an invisible basketball, and in seamless and breathtaking slow motion, deftly dribbles, then, with the concentration of a Zen archer, takes aim at an imaginary basket somewhere above the blue-white of Sage Cowles's head, where she stands in Christ's place in the *Last Supper* painting. He then takes his place, matter-of-factly, in the position reserved for Judas.

I meant for this section to be a kind of religious Dada—propelled by the hyperactivity of the dancers but grounded in a friezelike religious tableau. Towards the end, Justice moves downstage right and, with Arthur voicing rhythms as a human "beat box," swings into his rap, "Somethin' to Think About."

The section ends to his shouting "They call me Justice, Justice, Justice," at which time all the dancers who had been standing on their chairs jump to the floor as the curtain falls.

"The Supper" *with dancers (from the left) Betsy McCracken, Lawrence Goldhuber, Sean Curren, Leonard Cruz, Andrea Woods, Arthur Aviles, Sage Cowles, Andréa Smith, R. Justice Allen, Maya Saffrin, Heidi Latsky, and Gregg Hubbard* (MAYA WALLACH)

ENTR'ACTE: FAITH

When the curtain rises again, the *Last Supper* table is still in full view but now the space around it is empty. A minister, a rabbi, or a priest, invited from the community, sits at its right end. I, flanked by Arthur Aviles and Sean Curran, am seated at its middle. My back is to the audience.

The person of faith relates the story of Job. To this recitation and notes of "Round Midnight" played by the sextet, I rise to enact in dance the story of the Man of Perfect Faith, who is tested again and again by God in his wager with Satan. Arthur and Sean initially act as sentinels, performing large, stylized gestures that frame me. At one point, having removed my black jacket, Sean Curran produces a large kitchen knife and proceeds to shred the shirt off my back in oblique reference to the tragedies and sicknesses that befall Job. Later, when Job is vindicated by his faith and God gives back all, I am given a new shirt and my jacket is returned.

With Julius and his sextet pushing tonality and volume to the extreme, I

219

dance Job's ecstasy. When done, I sit at a right angle to the religious man or woman and begin to ask questions—simple, almost childlike questions:

What is faith? Is Christianity a slave religion? What is evil? Does God punish us? Does hell exist? Is homosexuality a sin? Is AIDS punishment from God?

This dialogue was modeled after the onstage conversation I had had with my mother at the Black Choreographers' Festival in Los Angeles in 1989. The one where she had said, "If you believe, if you really believe, then your faith will take you anywhere. It's like a light or a torch in the dark. You ain't afraid of nothing."

While the guest person of faith was most often of liberal and well-meaning inclinations, I'd designed this interrogation so that it could take place between myself and a black Fundamentalist, who would be unafraid to answer in a politically "incorrect" or nonliberal manner. I was not afraid of being hurt. I wanted to conjure this ephemeral, unquantifiable, potentially deadly thing called Faith. In some thirty-five locations, two of them in Europe, I asked these questions. Every person I spoke with I found unflappable, beyond the reach of debate and any sort of objective discourse.

Once, during the long tour, my mother turned to me and said, "Son, you keep asking the same questions every night, when you gonna finally get the answer right?"

SECTION FOUR: THE PROMISED LAND

Each presenter had been assigned the task of finding the most demographically diverse group of people they could from their community. These people, like the religious person, would become part of the work. I then visited most communities and auditioned prospective casts. Two rehearsal directors were dispatched around the country to prepare these groups for our arrival, at which time their sequences would be integrated within the work as a whole.

The curtain opens, for the final time, on this organized group of some sixty or so local people. In the half-light they listen intently as Justice and Andre begin a whispered conversation that is in fact the retrograded "I Have a Dream" speech.

The whispered conversation grows into a heated argument and then an all-out brawl:

.true become must this ,nation great a be to is America if and—"ring freedom let ,side mountain every from ;pride pilgrim's the of land ,died fathers my where land ;sing I thee of ;liberty of land sweet ;thee of 'tis country My"

Then a series of arena-inspired sequences occurs in which the Jones/Zane company performers, divided into two groups, attack one another as the spectators all around them shout raucous encouragement. This noisy, violent episode is interrupted once by the lanky prancing of Gregg Hubbard, performing what I called "Warming Up in Dixie." Gregg's movements are inspired by the image of silhouetted "Darkies" dancing around the campfire on the cover of some sheet music from the early part of the century that I had been given. Gregg finishes with a one-two-three-shuffle-grin flourish and then the onstage pandemonium resumes. When it seems that everyone would keel over from exhaustion, the stage picture reverts back to its original orderliness.

Justice (as Clay) and Sage (as Lula) step atop the table, face each other from opposite ends, and begin to enact excerpts from LeRoi Jones's *Dutchman* while Andre Smith stands below, in the crowd, and recites all its stage directions with his earnest simplicity. Justice and Sage do not touch until the last tense moments of the scene, when Sage's Lula, in a lovely white evening dress, shouts, "Uncle Tom-Big-Lip," which provokes Justice's Clay to slap her as thirty dancers strike the floor with their open palms. The scene becomes calm as Clay/Justice positions himself, back turned to the audience, in front of Lula/Sage, saying "I'm sorry Baby, I don't think we're going to make it." Lula/Sage in a stylized gesture, part dance, part pantomime, suggests a small knife that she plunges into his chest, saying, "Sorry is right. Sorry is the rightest thing you've said." She stands like a vengeful fury over Justice/Clay's prone body as it rests in the arms of a large group of dancers.

John, Sage's bespectacled husband, dressed in a black suit and looking at once like one of Grant Wood's American Gothic figures and the chairman of the board that he had in fact been, stands at the middle of the table. He has looked on as his wife, in the role of a young Jezebel, has seduced and then killed the young man, Clay, who is also Justice, the ex-convict. John's impassive presence on the stage serves as a witness to the replay of the time-honored ritual of sex, power, and race.

The work develops in an ever more abstract direction. Long lines of dancers travel across the stage performing thirteen gestures culled from religious iconography as varied as a Tiepolo fresco in Venice, a bit of kitsch pottery from Little Italy, or an ancient painting from a church in remotest New Mexico. These lines coming and going sometimes break into clusters of individuals partnering, handling each other gently. Sometimes the arena madness returns, as it does in the "Revival Meeting" sequence, wherein one person in each of twelve trios behaves as if possessed and is either assisted or restrained by the two others. This frenetic field of activity coalesces into a statuary through which the fully clothed John Cowles and a naked young woman whom we call "the Innocent" enact a touching, oddly unsettling duet that is part seduction, part confession. Sage stands nearby reciting simple instructions: "He will take you by the hand, and take you to another place. If you fall he will reach out for you. . . ."

Over the course of this half-hour segment of *Last Supper at Uncle Tom's Cabin/The Promised Land* participants could choose to remove articles of clothing until they were completely naked. In the final moments of the piece, the ever-present drive of Julius Hemphill's score mellows to a single saxophone line performing a lulling counterpoint to a stage covered with the fat, skinny, rich, poor, old, young, male, female, Asian, Spanish, gay, straight, black, Native American, and European, naked, singing together. Robert Wierzel's evocation of nineteenth-century stage lighting, which had illuminated "The Cabin" section, is now warm, golden, flattering, supportive as the cast ambles forward and back, sounding nonsense syllables in childlike harmony.

The Promised Land, with its hordes of naked flesh coming wave after wave into the footlights, pubic patches, pert breasts, sagging breasts, wrinkled knees, blissful eyes, furtive expressions of shame, is a visual manifestation of my profound sense of belonging. This was my portrait of us. All of us. And this is who I am too. One of us. It was my battle to disavow any identity as a dying outcast and to affirm our commonality. In it, some one thousand people from thirty cities stood naked, took a bow, and said, "We are not afraid."

Uncle Tom's Cabin was three and one-half hours long, and it toured for almost two years. It was denounced by the Vatican. It was deemed sprawling and full of platitudes, applauded for its reliance on community, the process by which it was created, its humanity, and its scope. It was the largest work I ever made and a work that came out of my desire to sum up everything I believed. It was impossible for it to succeed, but it did not fail.

ACHILLES LOVED PATROCLUS

SOMETIMES, in the dance studio, I look down at my bare feet, dried by the wood resin and the dust, bunions jutting out, unclipped toenails, and those second toes even longer than my big ones.

I think about my mother, whose feet I bathed. She used to say that when a man has a second toe longer than the big toe, he will be a ruler of women.

When she told this to me, I was both proud and frightened.

I like breasts.

I don't have a hidden desire to taste them whenever possible—I think my mother gave me just enough of hers. But they move me when I see them.

They are like a simple promise on a young girl, like the realization that things are right with the world. They can be a burden when gravity begins to have its way with the body of a woman who is no longer young. They are stark and humbling on the body of a very old woman. And when they are removed, a woman's chest is strange, terrifying, even mournful. It dares one to answer the questions *What is this body? Who is this woman now?*

Deborah, one of our closest friends, had just had a child. She was a short, strongly built woman, driven by the conflicting forces of motherhood and a rapacious appetite for sensations and experience. One night at a party, Arnie and I sat enthralled as she breast-fed her baby boy.

"Would you like to taste?"

Arnie went first. He laid himself across her lap and closed his eyes. She cradled his head, as he pursed his lips around her nipple. He swallowed, then a wide grin brightened his face.

My turn. I felt too large as I knelt in front of her, encircling her waist, feeling the gentle encouragement of her small warm hands cupping my head, guiding me. I was too bashful to even glance at Arnie, sitting there holding the child. I was shaken and strangely satisfied, the warm blandness lacing across my tongue and down my throat.

"It's not really milk," we agreed. "It's weird . . . so warm. . . . It's not really food. What is it?" asking no one in particular.

Recently, I have been watching Trisha Brown rehearsing a solo that she intends to teach me. I observe her turn her back to me and raise her arms. I see the supple arms of a woman in her mid-fifties. I see arms that have embraced a man and held a nursing child. I recall Marti's arms against wisteria in the month of May 1969. I recall Janice after lovemaking in Canandaigua, her arms like slack metal bands, secure around me as we receive the amnesty of sleep.

Do I want to possess those arms, that back, those hips, legs, and thighs? Or do I want to be those arms, back, legs, and thighs?

When Trisha crooks her wrist, unfurls a leg, I envy her. I want what she knows. I want firsthand experience of her body's silkiness, its private sequestered motivations, its unfolding. Offering only so much, her feet and her neck bargain with me and my attention. They say, "You had your chance that summer when you were eighteen and our young bodies were a banquet. You were nothing but indiscriminate appetite, slopping about the meal that we were. Now you can look and imitate, but make your own supper."

Trisha's trim belly undulates. I imagine sluicing my finger across it, as if gathering the remains of cake batter from a bowl. She poises on one leg, her right arm bent at the elbow, her shoulder hiked slightly; the hair at the nape of her neck, subject to the gentle pressure of light and air, adheres with sweat.

Her breathing comes from a world where women are pleasured serenely, another world where women go about their lives as if they were some long-legged creatures, part tree, part animal, never rushing but migrating languorously from bed to doorway to window to toilet to dance floor to lover to child.

Trisha's breathing might emanate from another world, but the woman has descended from her one-legged perch and is now splayed wildly over the floor. I want this body and all the bodies it speaks of. I want to do this dance . . . to have it. I want to be this dance. Trisha raises her arms, her alert scapula eases down her back.

I like women's bodies and I need them.

In my universe, dominated by the dangling, heavily veined penises of my imagination, the reality of my sisters' breasts, of Berta's, Janice's, Marti's—and now Trisha's—is something that I cannot live without.

◆　　◆　　◆

IN MY EROTIC LIFE with Arnie, we generally avoided the Forty-Second Street area. Sure, we frequented one particular sex shop, but we never went to the theaters, the Gaiety or the Big Top. These were places we wanted to be free of.

After Arnie died, a friend invited me to go to a show with him. I had seen go-go boys dancing to drunken revelers and old men with nothing but their eyes to satisfy their desire, but this low-ceilinged, second-story New York City room offered something different. It was packed with young men like those I might have seen at the Saint Mark's Baths some years before. A new generation sat there so well behaved, watching a parade of bare bottoms, bulging biceps, and the studied ardor of the young performers—all white, except for a few darker-skinned South Americans and at least one Puerto Rican. There was just enough genuine eroticism, just enough camp and community to give one the impression that we were a part of some vital cultural expression, some defining bond. One Saturday night, I returned with Arthur to show him a "marathon."

We watched man number eight offer himself—on his back humping the ceiling, flipping over to all fours, looking over his shoulder, wetting his lips as he yielded an unimpaired view of his most intimate orifice in a ritual central to my sexual experience.

The repetition of specific basic movements holds me. The movements say, "Get hard now." But every anonymous arousal occurs amidst a clamor of despair—amidst memories of shriveled flanks, gaunt, emaciated faces, lesions, open wounds, and death rattles. To enter anyone's body, I have to cover myself with latex.

◆　　◆　　◆

. . . then so hurling down to the house of death, so many sturdy souls *and so their spirits soared.*

The Iliad

I HAD BEEN too lazy to read the *Iliad*, so I was happy when I came across an audio version of the epic, with Derek Jacobi reading. In full flight down the Palisades Parkway or stymied in rush-hour traffic in my little black car, Arthur and I listened to Jacobi's haunting voice as he invoked the names of Trojan warriors, their wives, their children, kings, princes.

Here are Achilles and Patroclus sharing a giant tent, along with their wives and slaves. Offended by Agamemnon, Achilles refuses to fight despite the pleas of his generals. Patroclus also urges his friend, and still the demigod Achilles refuses. Patroclus then asks Achilles' permission to take up his friend's armor. He goes into battle against the Trojans in Achilles' stead. I found this exchange moving and perverse.

Patroclus was first to hurl his glinting spear.
The blade sank clean through.
The shaft, splintering bone,
Shearing away the tendon,
Wrenched the whole arm out.
Bronze ripping into his flank,
Spearing him up the thigh,
Loosed his limb.
A gush of blood between the eyes.

The spear point cracked through the boney socket.
The tough sinews shredded around the weapon's point
As the dark swirled.
And hewed his neckbone.
The head swung loose to the side.
The eyes brimmed blood.
Down he soared
And red death came flooding down his eyes.

After distinguishing himself with extraordinary bravery and skill, Patroclus is slaughtered on the battlefield. A mourning Achilles retrieves his defiled body to give it a proper burial. He wails, proclaiming to heaven and earth that everything he loved is now dead. He wants blood. Revenge. The story is passionate, chaste, light-years away from the go-go dancers at the Big Top.

Two generations ago the code word "Greek" was used by men to speak of anal sex. I felt compelled to create a dance that would draw a very erratic but specific line between that ancient expression of man/man love and my preoccupation with "Greek" on the new battlefield.

I would make *Achilles Loved Patroclus* personal, make it for Arthur Aviles, my companion, a person I find as removed from decadence as anyone I've ever known. I would give Arthur this solo, as certain societies choose their most prized for sacrifice. For me, Arthur is beauty. His face is like a generous pan of beaten copper. His cheekbones speak of the Yucatán. I have cupped his face and remembered the belly of a baby, its smoothness best appreciated with a flick of the tongue, or tucking one's nose in the navel crevice, blowing air against it, producing laughter.

Composer John Oswald edited Derek Jacobi's rendition into sputters of disjointed phrases describing the devastation of the battlefield—the hacking of limbs, gouging of eyes, gushing of blood, spilling of entrails. At one point in this solo, Arthur, who portrays an amalgam of Achilles and Patroclus, stands in an odd squatting lunge, undulating his hips interminably as he looks into the far distance.

Arthur Aviles in Achilles Loved Patroclus, *1993* (JOHAN ELBERS)

Arthur's gyration, like the aloof obscenity of the Gaiety's performers, is hypnotic. It says that this dance—whether you like it or not—is independent of its outcome. This inviting, erotic object before you is as constant in your universe as the sun, the moon, as inevitable as your birth, your death.

Achilles
loved
Patroclus
died.

After struggling with *Achilles Loved Patroclus* for a year, Arthur declared in frustration that he didn't want to dance it anymore. He didn't like the way it made him feel. It was too hard physically and emotionally. He felt like a plaything.

I understood.

I use Arthur in my art to speak of death, trusting that he will always walk back into life. In this work, I had given him a very difficult task, given him these gyrations, this maniacal, obsessive context of sex leading to death, leading to pain, leading back to sex. I had asked him to represent an indestructible erotic force housed within a body perpetually attacking or under attack, accepting a rude penetration or offering one. I risked letting him embody the bloody sweetness of *The Iliad*, with its glorification of soldiers, war, and man's love for man. And with that same body—through the use of explosive, sometimes senseless gestures and physical feats—I had asked him to suggest the struggle and death of numerous others.

It was a great task. It was not his.

◆　　◆　　◆

REBELLION I ALWAYS KNEW. Transgression I have had to learn.

Demian Acquavella, the dancer, had purple splotches over his beautifully sculpted arms and torso. What did he think? Demian, with the amazing ass and thighs. Someone had looked at him, wanted him, and ultimately shared with him that which would kill them both, which could kill us all.

We were at City Center performing *History of Collage*. It was a costume piece and each dancer was asked to choose his outfit. Demian put us all to shame with his bravado, his sense of style. He had chosen to wear a translucent black chiffon tutu with a dancer's belt and combat boots. I was backstage; suddenly I overheard the technicians, agitated, repulsed, amused. "There's a guy out there with his dick out."

It was a mischievous, angry thing to do. I understand this now. Demian was saying, "This is the source of my power, my sexualized self. Look at me. I'm melting from within, but look at me. I dare you to look at me."

By daring us to look, he said he was not afraid.

When I dance, as when I talk, I strive for candor. I trust that candor offers an essential aspect of a real identity—not my nor anyone else's fiction, not a scenario imposed upon me—but a reflection of what truly is. Yet, as is everyone else, I am afraid of what truly is.

I believe the world is changed by transgression. Arnie's and my collaboration, professional and personal, was transgressive. It embodied an intimacy, a disregard for racial and sexual social strictures. Insisting that a minority's sensibility be included in the cultural discourse is transgressive. One reading of homosexuality demands that we recognize the human body as a place where sexual pleasure exists for its own sake. Homosexuality is thus viewed as a transgressive act—one that elicits visceral responses. The nature of the stage is to provoke heightened response. I can force us to confront fear in its guise of repulsion.

I can play with this fear.

There are things that we do with our bodies that are deemed so volatile we are not supposed to say the words that describe them. The language of homosexuality, of course, provides us with many of these words, and in public discussion, as in performance, I draw upon them freely. "Cocksucker," "butt-fucking," and "fist-fucking" are inappropriate. Be it in language or movement, I can suggest them. If I am skillful (and I am not always), these words, these gestures can engage, demystify the fearfully unfamiliar, and broaden the ever-evolving social discourse.

This is a promise of my dance.

◆   ◆   ◆

I WAS HONORED when I was asked to speak at the opening ceremonies for the Gay Games in New York in the summer of 1994. Uncharacteristically—in part out of fear at the prospect of appearing before thirty thousand spectators, in part in response to the request that all comments be projected via Jumbotron for the hearing impaired—I wrote down my remarks with the help of my new companion, Bjorn Amelan, as we made our daily commute into the city.

The temperature that June afternoon was a daunting 95 degrees, but it did not affect the endless stream of athletes marching into the Lawrence Wien Stadium at the northern tip of Manhattan. At one point it seemed the number of competitors would outnumber those of us in the stands. Before long, the relentless heat of the afternoon gave way to a balmy summer evening, graced with a benign moon. I, with Bjorn and Arthur at my sides, had been moved onto the field and placed at the bottom of a ramp leading to a microphone just as Zoe Dunning, a lesbian from the military, asked for a moment of silence to remember "our dead." I stood with my head bowed until one of the athletes yelled for me to sit down. Bjorn, Arthur, and I dropped to the parched field grass. I absentmindedly scribbled in the dust, my adrenaline racing. I had turned my eyes to the moon when my chaperon appeared to whisper, "You're up, Bill, go on. . . ." I moved up the ramp as Bjorn and Arthur advanced below me on the grass.

I began.

There was a time when as an African-American if you were frustrated, irate, and defiant enough and somebody had the nerve to tell you that you had to do any-

thing, you could always strike back with: "I don't have to do nothing but stay black and die." I heard my mother say it. I read Maya Angelou's report of a conversation in which Billie Holliday said it. And I am sure that I, too, at some point in that hell called puberty said it.

So here we all are, living in a time when everything seems possible, and yet loss is probably the reigning sentiment of the day. If I substitute the word "gay" for "black"—as I oftentimes feel as a gay man a bit like a nigger—"I don't have to do anything but stay gay and die. . . ." Somehow it doesn't roll off the tongue as deliciously, as irrefutably as the original statement.

We'll let the bio-detectives divine if we have to stay gay or not. We all know the second part is beyond question.

I don't have to do anything but stay gay and die.

But what do I want to do?

What can I do?

I came here today because I wanted to see us, and be one of us. I wanted to realize that Stonewall really was twenty-five years ago.

What can we do?

Here we are—and what can we do?

We can congregate openly.

We can have the Love that dares speak its name.

We can have an army of lovers.

We can do it to him.

We can do it to her.

We can do it this way and that.

We can do it.

We can have one lover.

We can find the one and lose him, lose her.

We can find the one and love, knowing life is counted these days in months and weeks, not years and decades.

We can hold on.

We can let go.

We have to.

We can be there for them.

We can be there for them when they are fine.

We can be there for them when they are beautiful.

We can be there for her when "slash, poison, and burn" are her only choices as she faces breast cancer.

We can be there for him when he's lost fifty pounds, is covered with lesions, and the Hickman catheter protrudes through his chest.

We can be there.

We have to.

We can help answer the questions What is a man? What is a woman?

We can be mothers.

We can be fathers.

We can be sisters.

We can be brothers.

We can be sons.

We can be daughters.

We can be the best friend you ever had.

We can be the most evil "son of a bitch" you never hope to see again.

We can get a president elected.

We can be president.

We can make mistakes.

We can make amends.

We can compete.

We can run.

We can throw balls.

We can break world records.

We can win.

We can lose.

We can fall down.

We can get up and do it over again, better.

We can go for it as if we have nothing to lose, knowing we have everything to lose.

We can fight.

We can be soldiers.

We can be victims.

We can be victimizers.

We can make music.

We can take cloth, wood, stone and make it walk that walk and talk that talk.

We can dress a king, and undress him too.

We can remember those that others feel are best forgotten.

We can tear up a dance floor and put it all back together again.

We can talk loud in public.

We can be fierce.

We can be small.

We can be mighty.

We can be too much.

We can be just enough, just in time.

We can.

We have to.

I don't remember walking back down the ramp—only the applause and my blissfully futile attempt to share a high five with several thousand people as I left the stadium. I had never felt so focused, so understood, in any public appearance in my life.

Last Night on Earth, *1992* (BEATRIZ SCHILLER)

LAST NIGHT ON EARTH

———— •◆• ————

I WILL NEVER grow old. My hands will never be discolored with the spots of age. I will never have varicose veins. My balls will never become pendulous, hanging down as old men's balls do. My penis will never be shriveled. My legs will never be spindly. My belly, never big and heavy. My shoulders never stooped, rounded, like my mother's shoulders are. I will never need a son to massage my arms, as my father did.

My beautiful father—who used to be called Red, who charmed the ladies, who was the fastest runner on the turpentine plantation—grew old. I will never grow old.

He sat with Rhodessa at the kitchen table one day. He was pouring himself tea but missing the cup by inches, unaware of what was happening. Rhodessa stared at him, aghast. He saw her face, then realized with deep shame what he was doing.

I will never grow old like my father did.

I will always have those long skinny legs that black men have. I will always have an ass that is too high—but firm like a racehorse's. My stomach muscles will always be clearly defined. My shoulders will always be broad like the day when I was thirteen and my friend Russ's mother said, "You are such a good-looking young man. You have such broad shoulders." I will always be a boy who has just discovered he has the shoulders of a man.

I will never struggle to stand, as some men do. I will never stoop. My face will never wrinkle. My eyesight will never dim. My teeth will never yellow. My head will always be that of a young prizefighter circa 1910. A young prizefighter with intelligent eyes, sensitive mouth, lips not too thick, nose not too flared. Yet not a pretty prizefighter. No, not pretty. And this not-pretty prizefighter will never grow old. This not-pretty prize fighter will always stay somewhere near twenty-five years old. He will always be supple, capable of taking off his shirt at a suitable time to make of himself a sculpture. To make of himself a cipher, a symbol. To make of himself the man who loves numerous lovers, the man who promises numerous people numerous things and yet never really has to deliver anything.

I will never need a wife to ask, "Gus, what's the matter with you?" when I say, "I'm sick. I think I'm very sick." I will never have my youngest son demand that I go to the hospital. I will never say good-bye to my wife for the last time and have her spend the rest of her life regretting that she didn't go to the hospital with me. I will never lie in a bed crying like a baby, screaming so loud that my youngest son hears it from three hospital corridors away and is panicked. This son who has never before heard his dad cry. I will never grow old begging for someone to stop the pain as my heart tries to fibrillate out of my ribcage—these old ribs covered with gray hair, this belly swollen from the last operation.

I will never. Because I exist in this moment.

In this moment there is no room for old age.

I am not protected, remember? Old is for people who are protected. The unprotected have to die young.

❖   ❖   ❖

Give me strength.

As the curtain opens on *Last Night on Earth*, I stand still at center stage, my legs crossed, my arms outstretched in the inverted V of a Brancusi bird, of a jet plane. The lights blaze from behind me, blinding the audience to all but my outline.

I am Eros. I am the possibility of Eros standing before you. I am your future lover. I am every orgasm you are ever going to have. I am my father when he plowed it to my mother in the single cinder block room at Miller

Road. He a perfect, silent instrument. She all squeals and cries as they met pleasure together.

I stand there in a short white skirt—a tunic, really, confusing gender and time.

All of a sudden, loud into the theater booms the barrelhouse voice of Koko Taylor:

Hey, ev'rybody, let's have some fun!

I begin to move and when I move, the skirt flies up, revealing a glittering sequined codpiece and my naked ass.

Hey ev'rybody, let's have some fun,
You only live once, an' when you're dead, you're done.
So let the good times roll, . . .
I don't care if you young or old, no, no
Get together 'n' let the good times roll.

I make a sweeping gesture. Left arm stretched horizontally towards the wing, right arm pinned to my thigh, legs planted firmly apart, summoning the image of the Colossus of Rhodes. Jackknifing forward from the waist, hands clasped, drawn towards the floor, I cast a coy glance at the audience, as if I were Marilyn Monroe in her lace bustier, teasing a bit of cleavage.

Koko continues. My gestures are emphatic, quizzical, and crude. At one moment, my mouth stretches open as if to suck. My right index finger enters the cavity and transforms the sexual suggestion into one of regurgitation. In the next moment, my left hand makes the okay sign but the index finger, removed from my mouth, plunges into the orifice formed by the thumb and index of my left hand. I roll from standing to all fours, grip an imaginary partner, and thrust two times aggressively with my pelvis. I roll, repeat the rutting action, stop, stare at the audience, caught in the act, then continue with vehemence.

I am dancing about fucking. Unfettered fucking. Obscene, joyous, wildly defiant, desperate fucking. I am dancing about sex with no consequences. Sex is not on trial here.

Last Night on Earth, *1992* (BEATRIZ SCHILLER)

The song is over. The mood changes as I fall to the floor, allowing the audience to see me breathing heavily, clearly fatigued.

I am not a god, I am a man.

NINA SIMONE's strange nasal voice now fills the theater. She sings Brecht and Weill's "Pirate Jenny." It is the song of an embittered woman who, as she washes the floor of an old southern hotel, dreams of a pirate ship that comes wreaking revenge on those she serves.

My mother's favorite hymn, the one she has sung all her life, is

I shall not,
I shall not be removed.
Just like a tree standing by the water,
I shall not be removed.

When despair rules, there comes a point when we stop singing "I shall not be removed" and fixate instead on the escape that never comes. This drives us mad.

Noon, by the clock, and so still on the dock,
You can hear a fog horn miles away
Asking me: kill them now
or later?

I am the crazy black who wants to kill everyone, my miserable life has congealed into a malignancy. The voice in the song—shocking, hypnotic—is like the mad person sitting next to you on a subway car cursing under his or her breath. My movements are repetitive, convuluted, a restatement of the song's lyrics, bluntly phrased like a code. This tortured struggle to escape pulls the spectator into madness.

This portion of *Last Night on Earth* ends with the old woman's pitiful plea to be taken away. All of the threats, the insinuations of malice, the vengeful fantasy were a pose, a balm for helplessness.

Then a ship, the black freighter,
disappears out to sea . . .
And on it . . .
Is me.

As the song snaps to a close, I am left alone in the spotlight in a posture of defiance and invitation—an Aaron Douglas silhouette, arms akimbo, head cocked, as if listening, as if startled from someone else's dream.

I TURN TO the audience and ask, *What time is it?*

After posing this question, I embark upon a monologue that can go in any direction. I improvise. I may tell anecdotes, make personal observations on racial, sexual, or spiritual questions. Here, I can change the entire tone of the piece.

I have incorporated into my improvisation a fragment of a solo, *21*, which represents a style of working I'd all but abandoned as Arnie and I built the company and set out to prove to ourselves that we were choreographers. The solo *21* relied on twenty-one curtly defined postures taken from art history, magazines, sports and religious iconography. The postures range from "Apollo Belvedere" to "Pittsburgh Steelers" to a "pregnant housewife."

What time is it?

I begin to dance again, and the dance is basic—the triplets and turns that I learned in Mrs. Grandy's Modern Dance Class for Beginners. I execute a short academic dance phrase, slide to the floor, and declare,

Now I'll explain what I am trying to do.

I repeat the gestures that opened the dance. In the manner of a medical school lecturer, I point to my eyes and say,

These are my eyes.
My eyes are not my enemy.
Placing my thumb on my extended tongue,

This is my tongue.
My tongue is not my enemy.

Matter-of-factly, I touch each nipple with my index finger.

This is my desire.
My desire is not my enemy.

Pointing to my penis, then circling it once,

This is my dick.
My dick is not my enemy.

The audience titters. I continue my demonstration. My index finger describes a circle around my face; when it reaches my right temple I cock my thumb as if holding a gun:

This is my memory.
My memory is not my enemy . . .
My memory is my enemy.
What time is it?

Koko Taylor explodes into song again. This time her lyrics are those of "Going Back to Iuka," about a distraught woman train-bound for Mississippi, where the man she loves is dying.

The train I ride, I ride it all night long.
I'm going back to Iuka,
Back where I belong.

I rush up and downstage, vigorously combining and recombining elements of all the preceding movement motifs. Koko shouts, *Oh yeah, oh yeah,* the guitars slam to a finish.

Moving in a half-squat, flat-footed shuffle towards a white rectangle that has lain to the right of the stage throughout the performance, I execute a series of rapid contractions, recalling Percival Borde's West African dance classes. These come across as a shudder. Sometimes I scream. Then, standing in the middle of the white rectangle, I reassume the Brancusi bird posture and peer out into the confused, involved, sometimes irritated darkness.

What time is it?

I am tired. I lower myself. It is not easy to breathe but I sing a traditional folk song, "Nora's Dove," which looks back on a life with a twinge of regret.

The River Jordan is chilly and cold.
It chills the body but warms the soul.
If I had wings like Nora's Dove,
I'd fly away to the one I love.
Sail away, oh honey, sail away.

On this last line, the lights have cuddled in closer. All that can be seen is the rectangle of white on which my body now lies flat, stilled. As my form fades, four lights on the back of the stage flare up, blinding the audience for an instant.

Darkness. It is over.

The moment before the lights are restored for the curtain call is one of profound self-confrontation. I must admit to myself if the performance has succeeded or not. Even when I would like to run off stage to the security of my dressing room, I know the ritual must continue. When the lights reveal the stage, I am truly exposed as the audience's response completes the dialogue.

Once, I rose up from the white rectangle and instead of taking a traditional curtain call, I struck my chest and clenched my fist high in the air. I felt like my mother when she stands and shouts "Hallelujah!" during a prayer. For my mother, this hallelujah is a joyous testimony. For me, hallelujah is big flat feet shuffling to the music of clapping hands and voices that shriek as much as they sing. Hallelujah is a battered child climbing into a grown man's lap to encircle his neck with infinite gentleness and trust, and place its forehead against his chin's stubble. Hallelujah is a cadaver, putrefied flesh hanging in ropy strips, out of whose mouth comes an eloquent description of spring complete with the fragrance of flowers and the songs of birds.

This dance is about transcendence. I pound my chest to call out to you who support me, "Let us be strong together," to you who believe that we will survive, "Yes, we will survive together." And to you who do not support me, I say, "To hell with you."

◆   ◆   ◆

A PERFORMER secretly believes that there is nothing worth doing other than performing. The entire day of a performance is nothing more than preparation for that one, two, two-and-one-half hours standing in a glorious arena, a circle of transformation, a ridiculous one-ring circus, a black void with artificial sunrises, sunsets, tiny vortices of light, screaming shafts of illumination striking the performer from this side, that side. A world wherein he's completely exposed, relying on minute tricks to hide imperfections and mistakes. The performer who takes the stage must believe that he is fascinating, that he or she deserves being the locus of several hundred or thousand points of attention. The job of the performer is to pull that instant community of individuals full of distraction, expectation, and hope into a timeless dimensionless now. At best, he or she is a conduit, a vessel through which numerous substances are channeled. Sometimes choking, sometimes abrasive or acidic, gouging. Sometimes sweet, surprising. And sometimes, nothing.

The performer feels small triumphs every time the last curtain call is taken and the sweat, like so many familiar salty kisses, pours down the temple, the bridge of the nose, skirts the eye sockets, and seeps into the mouth. The nostrils know the smell of other bodies, tired, demoralized, or ecstatic. The hands know the dusty weight of stage velour, the feet, filthy carpets that they shuffle across to and from a humid environment of shower and dressing room. The performer knows waiting. The waiting for well-wishers, friends, sponsors. Waiting with anticipation when one feels good about the evening, dreading a look of disappointment or an avoided glance when the evening did not go well.

I envy those who have no desire to perform, those who are content with breakfast, lunch, dinner, a good night's sleep, a vacation, a good book, a good fight, children, spring, summer, fall, those who are content with being one of many. The performer wants to be one of many, but even more, he wants to command the attention of many. Poor performer. He or she will never be satisfied. Perhaps dissatisfaction drives the performer. Perhaps dissatisfaction can, itself, be satisfaction. And then it's called wisdom. I hope so.

◆　◆　◆

IN ITS BEGINNINGS, dance was something that we, as a community, enjoyed. It was a way we told our stories. It was a way we expressed what we wanted and what we feared. It is still a ritual, a system of signs and gestures, but we have separated those who dance from those who watch the dance. The dancer and the watcher are held together in a moment. The dancer steps, he pushes the earth away and is in the air. One foot comes down, followed by the other. It's over. We agree, dancer and watcher, to hold on to the illusion that someone flew for a moment.

And, in this way, all dance exists in memory.

This is what makes dance such a supremely human art. It leaves no physical evidence. This is also what I love about it. It suits my temperament, my view of the material world as being a place that exists only in the moment, a place of illusion. I feel compelled to play with this illusion. I am proud to join in its creation.

My vividness will be attached to how people remembered me—how I looked, moved, how it felt to be near me. The performances themselves pass. Last night's performance of *Last Night on Earth* is already irrelevant. I will perform it again and when I do, I'll make it all over again. I'll compare the way I dance tonight with the way I danced last night. I must live with that comparison and with the comparisons people around me will make. But at the same time, tonight's performance of *Last Night on Earth* will—to me on the stage tonight, as to you in your seat watching—be the first and last performance of *Last Night on Earth*. There has never been another one. There never will be another one. The force with which I call upon this belief is my specialty.

Arthur Aviles, Josie Coyoc, Rosalynde LeBlanc, Maya Saffrin, Gabri Christa, Odile Reine-Adelaide, Torrin Cummings, Gordon F. White, Lawrence Goldhuber, and Daniel Russell in "Still" *of* Still/Here, *1994* (TOM BRAZIL)

STILL/HERE

———— • ◆ • ————

It's a long old road, but I'm gonna find the end, . . .
On the side of the road, I sat down underneath a tree . . .
Nobody knows the thoughts that came over me.
Bessie Smith

WHEN HE DIED in 1988, Arnie and I had reached a professional low point. We were definitely no longer "in fashion" and there was very little work. The repertory was uneven and unsure. The company was broke. Its executive director had fled, as had an important dancer. To help resolve the company's IRS problems, I had had to call fifty artists to ask for donations of works so that we might hold a benefit sale. Likewise, we were required to sell off nearly all of Keith Haring's decors for *Secret Pastures* to keep from shutting down.

When talking about the best way of handling the press's role in our survival, Arnie had always said, "Go for the covers." So when *The Advocate*, the most "legitimate" publication of the gay mainstream press, wanted to do a cover story about me, I agreed.

I knew of the writer through an artist colleague. He and I had a good talk.

> "How do you cope with grief?"

Locate your passion, find out what you love, and give yourself to it.

> "How do you cope with the loss of those whom you love?" <

Consider what it was in them that you valued and cultivate those qualities in yourself.

Somewhere in this comfortable conversation I must have mentioned that I was HIV positive—most casually, I'm sure, because I don't think we discussed it or its ramification during the interview. This fact appeared, however, in the first column of this prominent profile. I was concerned. I remember discussing the article with several company members, and it was Gregg Hubbard's matter-of-fact pronouncement—"Oh, those editors—they scooped it. They outed you"—that raised my concern to alarm.

I called the writer, who answered with the voice of a man expecting a tongue-lashing. "Don't you check these sorts of things before you print them?" I asked.

"I'm really sorry. I just handed the transcripts over to my editors. It was their decision, and . . . you did say it."

He was right. To ask for a retraction would have been fruitless and hypocritical.

From then on, every review that would once have said "Bill T. Jones, tall and black, Arnie Zane, short and white" read "Bill T. Jones, tall, black, HIV positive." I had to deal with it.

Sitting with Lois Welk, who had by this time become a symbol of continuity and strength, I asked, "Did you ever want to make a work that summed up everything in your life?"

I tried to answer my question through *Last Supper at Uncle Tom's Cabin/The Promised Land* and found that grand summations only result in more questions. The work implied that only the zealous pursuit of an ideal could deliver us to a place that transcends our racial, sexual, and historical differences. I chose the commonality we share through our bodies as the ideal for that work. The body is born, grows, falls into decline, and dies. All of our lives are variations on this most simple progression.

But if I felt I'd achieved a commonality with *Uncle Tom's Cabin*, the *Advocate* article offered me another difference. Most of us, with or without HIV, are burdened with the perception, justified or not, that being HIV positive equals death. (Once again, I found myself an outsider. This I refused to accept.)

I would shape a work that transcended difference. I would again shape it around the ideal of commonality. But this time, our mortality would be the central issue.

I was no longer willing to ask Job's question, "Why?" I needed to find out "How?" How do I deal with fear, anger, and pain? How can I find the strength to love, plan, create? How can I defeat the perception that I am an abnormality, cut off and doomed?

To find answers, I would go to the widest, most varied group of travelers along the same road.

I believe that the communal nature of *Last Supper at Uncle Tom's Cabin/The Promised Land* was revolutionary in the world of dance. I was changed, as a man and as an artist, by asking the help of presenters and so many diverse individuals to make a very personal interrogation, a shared one. And I believe that they in turn were changed—that getting so many novice performers to disrobe in their communities in the name of a principle was a triumph for them. I wanted this communal aspect to be part of *Still/Here* as well, so I conceived what I would come to call Survival Workshops and promoted them to presenters as an opportunity for their communities to make personalized investments in the work.

Integrating this vision with the dance company would prove another challenge. In some ways *Last Supper at Uncle Tom's Cabin/The Promised Land* had ignored my dancers in favor of the piece's social-political agenda. When the work had finished its tour, I was left wondering if the company was really capable of serving my vision. In my earliest contemplation of *Still/Here*, I considered disbanding the company and forming a group of some twenty or so HIV-positive individuals gathered from different parts of the country. But I considered this only most passingly—as if in fantasy. Arthur was my companion and one of the most gifted dancers I ever had the privilege to work with. Larry Goldhuber's growth as friend and artist, as well as his loyalty and warmth, I would never walk away from. Sean Curran, as always, offered his brilliant performing and unquestionable allegiance.

Relatively new dancers, such as Andrea Woods, Odile Reine-Adelaide, and Maya Saffrin, held a tantalizing promise for me as a choreographer. No, I couldn't have disbanded this group. This was the child that Arnie and I had had, and I would try—at least once more—to supply the necessary information, ask hard questions, and trust that something vital would come into the world.

In conversations with the ever-sensitive and provocative sounding board and dear friend, media artist Gretchen Bender, I decided that I could expand the world of the stage through the medium of video. Arnie and I, like many choreographers of our generation, had determined that video and dance tended to cancel each other out—that the power of video could rend the delicate fabric spun by live performance. But in speaking with Gretchen, I became determined to employ video's cool immortality in this work. She and I would use state-of-the-art audiovisual equipment to capture the testimonies, images, and selected actions of a group of people living with an awareness that is of invaluable importance and relevance to all of us.

But this was definitely going to be dance. The success of formal works like *D-Man in the Waters*, *Soon*, and *War Between the States* had renewed my commitment to movement as a primary form of theatrical expression. The movement for *Still/Here* would spring directly from a very specific experience and set of concerns that Gretchen and I documented in the Survival Workshops. The dancers would reveal themselves as they revealed the movement. They would not impersonate the sick and dying, but the many variations of the struggle I learned about through Arnie's illness and death and the illnesses and deaths of numerous others, through my own experience, and through the experiences of workshop participants. I realized that the resources necessary to cope with life-threatening illnesses are the same as those necessary for truly owning one's life.

We conducted fourteen workshops in eleven cities—two of them for children. The participants were of all ages, classes, races, sexual preferences, and states of health. The youngest participant was eleven, the oldest, seventy-four. All were facing or had faced life-challenging situations.

I would begin each workshop by introducing myself, stating my diagnosis, and reiterating what they might already have known as to why I was there and what I wanted of them.

"I am not therapist nor am I a practitioner of any kind. I am here because I feel that you have information that I, as a man, might benefit from and, as an artist, will be inspired by. And, yes, I need my hand held in dealing with this thing as I take my place in the world."

I would then introduce Gretchen and her camera crew and my new companion, Bjorn, who acted as my assistant. The only other people in the room were usually caregivers or a health-care professional in case there was a problem.

All of the participants then shared their names. And we repeated them, chantlike, until it became a litany of sorts. We then did simple warm-up movements that evolved into exercises of trust. Once trust was established, the group solidified, I would demonstrate my solo *21*, which is so reliant upon specific gestures and their spoken captions. I then encouraged the participants to choreograph a rudimentary gesture portrait of themselves. We linked our gestures round-robin style.

I used various tactics to elicit verbal descriptions of the gestures: *What does that mean? Could you perform the gesture and tell us something you've learned? Could you perform the gesture and tell us something you've never told anybody else before?*

Later in the workshop, we handed out paper and markers. *Could you conceive your life as one smooth line? Where does it begin? And where does it end?*

With that, people made sometimes startlingly beautiful drawings, which were used as "road maps" to guide where they stood and moved in the workshop space. I encouraged each of the group members to hold on to one individual as he or she "walked us" through his or her life. We must have seemed like Rodin's *Burghers of Calais* listening intently as a man or a woman described, in whatever terms, his or her early life, some particularly striking episode in adolescence, the happiest moment and the saddest, the time of diagnosis.

Where was it? What was the health-care professional like? What was the room like? How did you feel at the moment of the diagnosis?

Then the participants would bring us to the present. For most of the re-markable people who took part in these workshops, the present was a reward won by struggle, contemplation, and courage.

"This is the best time of my life."

"I was not living before this happened to me."

"I have good days and bad days, but I take them as they come."

"I'm no saint, but I think I'm a much better person now."

The inevitable next step came in my next request: *Take us to your death. What time is it? Where is it? How do you look? Who's there with you? What are they saying? What's going on?*

Some people resisted every stage of "walk me through your life" and particularly this final questioning.

I would say, *Be a fiction writer. It's your death, make it up as you go along. You won't have this chance again. What do you want to happen?*

The results were almost always moving. Some were shocking.

Assotto saw himself raging, screaming, needing to be held down. James first saw himself hurtling from a bridge, then, changing his mind, he said he'd be in someplace calm, his work published, and I would be there with him. Beverly was going to go with her husband to a favorite spot along the Carolina coastline, sit on a special rock, and look out at the ocean. Catherine, age eleven, never reached the last day—she kept going until she was 674 years old and had to be stopped for lack of time. She was never going to die!

The workshops ended with video portraits of each participant reading to the camera from a short list, a "private reel of concerns," of what each one loved and feared.

Leo worried about his cat. Several wondered if they'd ever have enough money or find recognition in their chosen endeavours. Elizabeth asked why she got sick. Why she got better, and would she ever get sick again? Jason, adopted, Vietnamese, eighteen years old, and with a black belt in karate, declared, "In my future I want a family." Alberto asked, "Will I be part of the water?" Floyd, who had said he liked jazz, went on to say, "I'm concerned about the breakdown of the African-American family, peace on earth, and stop the violence!"

We sat in a circle for a closing exchange.

I'd ask more questions: *Are we members of an elite? That is, do we know something that people not facing life-threatening illnesses don't know?* Initial surprise, then the answer, most often yes.

What about anger?

Most anger came from HIV-stricken persons. During a break in the New York children's workshop, I approached Tamika, fourteen years old, who had been released from the hospital that same morning after her latest bout with AIDS-related pneumonia. In my desire to break through what I thought was her alienation from the rest of the group members, all of whom were in remission from cancer, I reiterated our common HIV status. She looked at me, as if for the first time, then answered, "Yes, but children should not have to deal with this." On the other hand, Antonia, a serene mother of eight, said she might have been fooling herself but she did not feel anger. Her gesture, both arms embracing the air, circling an imaginary loved one and rocking, was captioned, "My entire world is the blessing of my children."

What have you learned?

One sixteen-year-old: "Pain is no big deal!"

Musette: "I set more realistic goals for myself."

Assotto: "People die every day while mothers are giving birth to babies."

Juan, covering his face and smiling: "Life goes on forever."

Keisha, an eighteen-year-old former athlete, who had lost her left leg to cancer, drew a picture of herself whole, the object of a looming, tearing eye, and captioned the drawing with "Society looks at me with eyes full of sorrow and misunderstanding." Her object in life was to help other misunderstood teenagers.

I HAD DECIDED that, as its title implies, *Still/Here* would be in two distinct parts, as if two mirrors reflecting the same object. I chose two composers of contrasting temperaments and sensibilities.

Kenneth Frazelle, a deceptively unassuming man, is a gifted composer in the classical style. Through long and searching conversations, Gretchen, Ken, and I extracted from the overwhelming mass of material we'd collected the concepts and moods that would define the work. Ken fashioned songs: "Prologue: Still," "Children's Song (Mad, Sad, and Sick)," "Eyes/Anonymous Test Site 1," "Slash, Poison, or Burn," "Still in Denial," "Eyes/Anonymous Test Site 2," "Seen," and "Epilogue." In these songs, he evoked survivors' revelations, states of mind, moments of intensity, with a power and specificity only poetry can deliver.

From the outset, both he and I agreed to build the song cycle around the talent of the legendary folksinger Odetta. In the Lark String Quartet, supported by percussionist Bill Finizio, Ken found five sensitive and committed collaborators who worked tirelessly to bring his lush score to life.

I chose Vernon Reid for the second section, *Here*, because, even in his world of rock music, he is singular—self-created as a black rock musician, unafraid of political and social discourse, and equipped to enter the realm of experimental theatrical music. Striking in his personal style, Vernon's demeanor is that of a person familiar with the stage.

Whereas Ken had spent much of the fall and winter of 1993–94 viewing the videos of the workshops, Vernon—sensitive even to accidental sounds, such as the rasp and rattle of the participants moving about the workshop space holding the drawings, the "maps" of their lives—was only interested in the audio recordings. Using up-to-the-minute electronic techniques, he created moody, pop, jazz, blues riffs as a raster through which actual fragments of survivors' testimonies were woven. The deafening intrusion of a pneumatic drill all but obliterated a tearful and touching testimony. He amplified the simple percussion of my feet as I demonstrated a rhythmic improvisation with such vehemence that we chose to call this interlude "Dance Macabre."

I began choreographing long before there was a large reservoir of material to draw from. Relying on the first workshop, conducted in Austin, Texas, I developed sequences for various combinations of dancers as I sought a way into the universe of the work. Initially, Gretchen and I had

Gabri Christa, Odile Reine-Adelaide, and Maya Saffrin in "Still," *of* Still/Here, *1994*
(BEATRIZ SCHILLER)

thought television would play the role of voyeur. In an early preview, five large TV monitors stood as aloof sentinels or were pushed about like mobile markers, displaying a never-ending stream of talk-show audience members—not the hosts, not the actual interviewees of these shows, but those watching. But the TV monitors were too small and could not overcome the public ritual space that is a stage.

We then turned to large-screen projection. That brought another set of problems, one being that in order to be effectively large, the screens had to sit squarely in the space needed by the dance. Gretchen and I decided that the video would be intermittent, that the screens would move in and out of the dance space, in and out of the dance, sometimes carried by dancers. Their presence was choreographed and performed with the same delicacy and matter-of-fact commitment as the most moving dance phrase or poignant gesture taken from the Survival Workshop.

Gretchen decided that all material not directly related to the workshop process had to be scrutinized—that only the most essential iconographic imagery could remain in the work. In *Still*, she carefully chose video testimonies, artfully constructed abstractions built on actual workshop episodes, and portraits of each Survival Workshop participant. For *Slash, Poison, or Burn*, she created a ghastly montage consisting of medical photographs of the body from its troubled exterior to its mysterious recesses. For *Here*, she lined the stage with five screens, each exhibiting a pulsing, blood-red animated heart, then the fractured image of a woman that "explodes" into shards that rain down like glass or snow.

My own process involved the intuitive combining of the survivors' gestures to make phrases, plumbing my own body's imagination, or borrowing from existing forms—capoeira and karate among them—to create expressive dance sequences.

AT THE CONCLUSION of each workshop, I had felt a combination of sober introspection and exhilaration, as if I had taken part in a ritual of sorts. The choreography for *Still* tried to meld these sensations. The choreographic language frequently relies upon a lone performer who is watched, touched, tracked, or supported by a group.

In the prelude to *Still*, the company performs a straightforward exhibition of several survivors' gesture sequences, naming each gesture's author and reciting its verbal caption. This is a blatant reference to the Survival Workshops and serves as a glossary of sorts in viewing the work that follows. Gretchen and I forged the initial video image to suggest a "spirit world" and to introduce video technology as nonthreatening and poetic. The result was three blue-lit screens, floating from the upstage darkness down towards the audience, as we listen to the litany of workshop participants' names. The electronic blue of the third screen suddenly blossoms into the moonlike visage of Lucy, a young cancer survivor wearing a cap; she smiles enigmatically, drops her eyes, and appears to float up and out.

The dance that accompanies the "Children's Song" consists of a sort of "dance club" routine, a virtuosic sequence of athletic movements, part hopscotch, part Brazilian capoeira foot-fight, part race, and is performed by two young women. One girl falls behind and ultimately gives up as the other is swept away by the rest of the group.

This is followed by sequences, all movement-based, that suggest the disorientation and anger of first diagnosis, the agony and terror of breast cancer. We get to know Gloria, self-described "Queen of Denial," through the frank, sometimes irreverent recollections of her son, Lawrence Goldhuber. Through the hysterical scrambling and pyrotechnics of spotlighted bodies, we experience spiritual agony as Odetta wails,

> *I assaulted God!*
> *The next morning He was in me.*

And finally *Still*'s Epilogue. The surging and dissolving groups on stage personify Odetta's soaring pronouncement,

> *Will I be part of the water?*
> *I'm on a wave being moved.*

Lawrence Goldhuber with the image of his mother, Gloria, in "Still," *of* Still/Here, *1994* (TOM BRAZIL)

I'm flying.
I'm still here.

The curtain moves down as the tight group of dancers has fanned apart, revealing Danny Russell performing the one series of arm gestures that came completely from my imagination, before the Survival Workshop process had begun.

Everything about *Still*—Liz Prince's softly flowing costumes in shades of ivory, pale blue, and beige, lighting designer Robert Wierzel's use of video blue, the pageantlike parade of events, and the music's restrained emotion—is designed to evoke an internal world, a world apart.

I TOLD A JOURNALIST, "If *Still* is the interior world of one person or a group of individuals struggling with a troubling revelation, then *Here* parallels the sensation of leaving one's doctor's office with life-altering news, compelled to ride the New York City subway."

For *Here*, Liz Prince designed garments that drape less, promise more through provocative seams, seductive fabrics in shades of red, rust, and orange that at once suggest night life, vivacity, and the color of blood. The screens are relegated to a uniform line of five. Unlike those in *Still*, these screens are never handled by dancers but are flown in and out of the performance space. The world of *Here* seems more spacious—a frontier perhaps. Robert Wierzel had a free hand in dramatically changing mood through coloring the cyclorama orange or acid yellow. At one point he transforms the stage with pulsing areas of light that suggest a disco.

Vernon sets the proceedings in motion by amplifying the sound of the rattling of paper, edgily underscoring a warm, almost folksy guitar figure:

Can you run it?
Can you run it?
Can you run your life?

Here, as in the rest of the composition's forty minutes, Vernon will cut and paste, repeat and reconfigure sounds and voices, suggesting a world that cruises inexorably forward and ultimately soars.

Choreographically, this section is no longer dominated by clusters watching solo performers. Here dance can exist scattershot across the stage, using unison lines, circles, diagonals as ground to solo figures dancing as much to the cadence of what we hear as to its meaning.

Tell me,
Tell me,
Tell me how to fight,
Tell me how to fight this disease because I am going to win.

I would sometimes test my choreography by watching it without sound, to see if it was engaging enough for my eye to stand up to the onslaught of what was heard and intermittently seen on the video.

I've been pondering. I thought, bitch, did you think you would escape? And the truth of the matter is, yes.

At this moment the stage is clear. We witness Torrin Cummings, a well-muscled and attractive young black man, coiling and recoiling, sluicing in and out of the floor with references to workshop gestures, social dance, and an intensely personal vocabulary. The voice is the voice of B. Michael, a handsome, well-spoken, HIV-positive black man, quoting Assotto Saint as a means of describing his initial response to his diagnosis. Torrin is not a sick person—on the contrary, at this point in the dance he is vitality personified. One might say his convoluted solo is in a purely chance relationship to B. Michael, but not necessarily.

Here has brought to maturity a strategy I have employed through most of my solo work. In *Everybody Works!*, *Floating the Tongue*, *21*, and *Last Night on Earth*, I set up a field of movement material and juxtaposed it to a text, thereby challenging the viewers to process what they are seeing and hearing simultaneously. My assumption is that the result is greater than the sum of its parts. However, *Here* succeeds in using movement at various levels of abstraction, to channel and amplify specific spoken information.

I'm stepping in and out of reality.
"Let the film play in your head."
There's a place for denial.

Denial is a concept that was discussed very often in the Survival Workshops. I suppose when I decided not to follow the course of a company of HIV survivors and opted instead for a youthful, healthy group of dancers, I ran the risk of denying the truth about debilitating illness. I have now decided that their vitality and physical prowess are an apt and necessary metaphor for the spirit displayed by most survivors I was fortunate enough to encounter. So, Torrin's bounding resilient undulation *is* B. Michael speaking.

"Will you get to heaven? Will you go to hell?"
There's a place.
"Is it a familiar place?"

In going through notes from *Still/Here*'s early days, I found a small stack of scribbled comments in the various handwritings of my dancers, all unsigned. In the late spring of 1994, I played a first draft of Vernon's score and requested that they do nothing but be still and listen, then hand me their written impressions. I never read these. I was more interested in the dancers' having to find language to describe their early responses. Now in reading them, two of the strongest responses were "Will the piece have hope?" and "I don't know what my relationship is to this piece."

"People say your light will still shine. Sometimes when she looks up, Tawnni finds that little light has the image of a giant locomotive heading towards her to steam her over."

Tawnni Simpson was twenty-five years old, a cystic fibrosis survivor from Iowa City. She performed the workshop gestures, improvising additional movements complete with a cartwheel that should have been impossible for her, considering her thin frame, fluid-filled lungs, and general physical condition. She was only too happy to have the floor.

My name is Tawnni Simpson. I'm twenty-five and I think about sex. I like sex but it's hard and it's been a long time, unfortunately. Getting into the sex. I think about if I'll ever have that companion again . . . that will love me for my abilities because sex is something that's hard for me because of my lung illness. But I wonder if I'll ever be able to share that again with anybody because it can be very beautiful and I don't want to just share it with any Dick. I can't say Jane because I'm not that type. So starting off on the good note, I think about my future because . . .

It was important for me to focus on Tawnni's desires, because it seems that they are desires that most people her age and certainly my dancers share. I choreographed a trio to what Vernon calls "Tawnni's Blues." Josie Coyoc, petite and with the will and ambition of a professional quarterback, is flanked by, flirted with, flipped, vied for, and fondled tenderly and sometimes not so tenderly by two handsome young dancers, Gordon White and Torrin Cummings. Here I indulge my fantasy about Tawnni. Not a monogamous, docile Tawnni, but a young, healthy woman whose lungs and limbs hunger for sensations and experience. The dancers meet the acrobatic sexy demands of this good-natured pas de trois and seem to enjoy it. It is true to their experience and somehow to Tawnni's.

I ask questions. I've grown up in a Christian home and my God is taking care of me and we have the biblical scripture to rely on but who says that biblical scripture is not phony.

My mom would shit in her pants if she heard me say this but it's the truth because she thinks that God is the way to go. I question that sometimes. It's okay to question. It might bring me to honest doubt and bring me stronger in my own religion. But I question my religious growth . . . where it goes from now.

I REMEMBER how grateful and empowered I felt in the final scene of *The Promised Land*, as those naked bodies of every description moved down to the footlights singing. Carl Sandburg has a small boy, in his epic poem "The People, Yes," turn to his mother and say, "What if they gave a war and nobody came?" In *The Promised Land,* as in what Gretchen and I call the video-portrait section of *Here,* the viewer is offered huge, luminous faces in black and white, recalling for me a variation on the boy's question, "What if they gave a performance and *everybody* came?" After an evening of disembodied voices and artfully chosen glimpses of real people, Gretchen and I felt committed to show them, give them faces in a special ritual.

But what about the dance? In an earlier version, this video-portraits section was an interlude when dancing all but stopped and the piece became a duet between these myriad smiling individuals and the ever-present commentary of Vernon's score.

"When I was young, I was impatient. I was selfish. I was a bully. When I became sick, pain overcame me. I overcame the pain to stand up straight and face the world."

"The questions that people who face a serious illness have are questions that all thoughtful adults have but just don't think about. . . ."

As we toured the piece through Wisconsin and the Midwest, I grew more confident that the viewer could simultaneously absorb the continued evolution of the dance, the video portraits, and the score's constantly changing voice. In its present form, video portraits are sometimes obliterated by the dance activity. At other moments a lone dancer is upstaged by a powerful portrait of, for instance, Bob, a black man from Iowa City who, raising his head abruptly, shocks us with the sight of a large white bandage covering one of his eyes.

Suddenly, Floyd whistles an old jazz standard:

No fears, no tears
We both had a lifetime of living
We'll be together again. . . .

Lucy's pale blue androgyny reappears, with her lowering her eyes on all five screens, only to disappear again as the whistling melts into the soporific sweetness of the score.

The screens fly out, not to return. My voice is heard.

Take us to your death, right to your death.

Now the stage belongs completely to the dance as it loops back to its beginning. Here again is the simple formality of *Still*, but the red suggests that that pure introspection may now be coated with blood. Or is it radiating from within?

What time of day is it?

At one moment a line forms on stage. One reviewer said that it suggested Bergman's *Seventh Seal*—the scene towards the end of the film where all the protagonists are seen holding hands on a ridge, like children—or perhaps it suggests the vision I had in 1955 when I watched a line of grown folks come back laden with water as the evening sun poised between the black silhouettes of Estella's and Gus's heads.

Where are you?

The stage darkens. Circular areas of light glow up successively to reveal individual dancers slashing, stretching, falling to the floor, embracing in what we call "dancer's portraits" that recapitulate signature movements.

What's the room like?

Suddenly, Vernon Reid appears; his guitar is like Gabriel's trumpet and what was a melancholy capitulation shifts into a higher gear, lifting the dance.

Who's there?

Larry Goldhuber, little more than a shadow, stands next to a box that he slowly revolves to reveal a color video portrait of me, smiling during a workshop, demonstrating arm gestures, listening and speaking. Gretchen has manipulated my movements so they are oddly unreal, of another time.

This image is my "message in a bottle," a missive best read in the future perhaps when I am no longer here. A viewer at that time might experience my image, as I experience Tawnni, who died two weeks after her workshop, or Jason, who had promised to come see the U.S. premiere but did not show up, having passed three months prior. Gloria is no longer here. At the time of this writing easily one third of the eighty-four who participated in the Survival Workshops are no longer living. The question remains with each viewing of their video portraits, each hearing of their recorded voices, Where is "here"? Where are they? Are they forever suspended in that four hours we spent together in a workshop studio, as I am consigned to this TV monitor?

How do you look?

Larry, like a priest assigned some cryptic, esoteric task, moves the monitor with my image through the wild tangle of the ever-restless choreography. He sometimes sits before the monitor and watches. Then he rises, moves on, and ends upstage. All of the dancers gather around to bask in the firelike glow emanating from the box.

Are you alone?

When I'm tired, depressed, or just afraid, I think about my death. I think it's one of HIV's luxuries, this fantasy about stopping. At my age I should be at the peak of my creative powers. How can I say I want to go to sleep now? Maybe it's beating death to the finish line, this desire to stop all fucking, this desire to stop all desiring? I'm humiliated and ashamed. I want to take the reins away from circumstance. I accept death.

Can you picture your death?

When I was a boy at Bellanger's Camp, there were old cultivators and tractors parked behind the barn where we lived. In the late-summer dusk, their carcasses would blend in with the golden, browning weeds and, if you squinted your eye just so, you could imagine them to be prehistoric creatures or what was left of such creatures—a ribcage, a femur, a skull. The only sound was the sound of a jukebox, of crickets, or maybe of little children up later than they should be, chasing fireflies.

Can you picture it and can you own it? Can you be responsible for it?

The night would come on soft as the well-washed flannel sheet that a young woman spreads over her bed for the man she loves. This worn sheet, so soft, settles on the mattress ticking. She smooths it with her long hands. The evening, the crickets, and the renegade laughter of children chasing fireflies are all one.

The dancers are now a circular dynamo. We wonder, "Aren't they exhausted?" "Is it Vernon's guitar engine that propels them? Or what Larry is doing with the TV?" Larry is spinning it as if it were a top. My face is no longer there. Instead we see red gore—mouths, teeth, eyes, limbs, embryos alternating in an electronic rhythm, too fast for us to comprehend, yet familiar too. We saw these images flashed upon the screen during "Slash, Poison, or Burn" in *Still*.

We know what "it" is. "It" is smaller now, upsetting still, but manageable. We can handle "it."

So, it's the last moment now. This is finally it. What's the last thing you see and the last thing you say?

These prehistoric creatures behind the barn are the chariot I want to become. Let me dissolve into the most dignified, useless rust. Let small boys and girls, hands smelling of body parts, tootsie rolls, and bacon fat, clamber over me all day and at night chase fireflies around me. Let me hear these crickets, these children for all eternity. Let the nightfall have no beginning and no end.

The young woman falls, her man on top of her, both the color of dust, they couple, cry, and dream.

When that part is over, what happens after?

"Here" *of* Still / Here, *1994* (JOHAN ELBERS)

AFTERWORD

ACTUALLY . . .

———•◆•———

10:30 A.M.   We have quite a day ahead of us. We eat our elaborate breakfast in joyful anticipation. It's the usual rush. We have to be in the city within the hour. We stop by the post and toss our unopened mail onto the back seat. We will use the driving time to edit the manuscript.

1:00 P.M.   Bjorn and I see Max Roach and Toni Morrison for lunch. Can the three of us pull off an evening of reading, dancing, and percussion at Lincoln Center in July? Over desserts, coffee, and tea, we come closer to the answer. By the time Toni reaches over and takes a crumb of my apple cake, I am confident we can do anything.

3:00 P.M.   Trisha Brown's choreography, so seductive to the eyes, is hell to learn. I asked for this solo and now, in the warm austerity of her studio, I am stimulated, intimidated by each wiggle, pause, and galumph. I feel I've got to grow a supplemental brain lobe to learn it. Her idiosyncratic sense of body shape and flux is carried forth by a highly personal virtuosity, at once silky and ferocious. She and her assistant, Carolyn, laugh and encourage me. They think it's going to be all right and so do I.

7:00 P.M.   Bjorn and I step out of Trish's building onto the marketplace of lower Broadway and are ushered into a sedate black sedan by the curb as two men stand outside, intently dialing Tokyo on a cellular phone. I am to appear for four minutes at 7:12 A.M., New York time, on January 1st as part of a live three-hour satellite broadcast extravaganza entitled "Symphony for the Earth," hosted by Seiji Ozawa. The restrained urgency of the Japanese, the incomprehensibility of cellular phone technology and speaking across fourteen time zones, tie my gut in a knot. However, the openness of the maestro's speech, full of Americanisms and just enough uncertainty to be disarming, reassures me. It will be all right.

7:30 P.M.   I am driving, filled with the familiar desire to escape the city. The back seat of the car is a jumble of my dance clothes, Bjorn's computer, our yet unopened mail, and shopping bags of what will be our late-night supper. Bjorn is again reading out loud from this manuscript. We leave the George Washington Bridge and cruise along the familiarity of the Palisades Parkway. I stop by a closed exit so that Bjorn can relieve himself. We are immediately accosted by a suspicious highway patrolman who, after confiscating my license, is joined by another police officer. Ordering me out of the car, he announces that I am wanted for armed robbery in Chicago. The police bulletin calls for an incriminating tattoo on my right arm, which they are unable to locate. I produce a recent copy of *Time* magazine with my portrait on the cover. They apologize and nervously let us go. Shaken, Bjorn and I climb back into our car. I thank the patrolmen for their thoroughness as I direct us back into the Palisades traffic.

9:15 P.M.   The car crtunches across the driveway. Laden, Bjorn and I shuffle past the star-magnolia I planted in Arnie's memory. We make our way into the small gray house that we intend to expand in the spring. It's very quiet here, and though many of the giant trees surrounding us have gone into decline, there is still a sense that the house is swaddled in forest.

The pasta with sage and olive oil, accompanied by a glass of red wine, is simple and delicious.

The house creaks and settles into the hillside. The leafless tree branches rasp some tender confidence. Now onto the business of sleep and dreaming. Tomorrow will come. It always has. It will be all right.

CHOREOGRAPHIC WORKS BY BILL T. JONES

—•◆•—

1973 PAS DE DEUX FOR TWO
(in collaboration with Arnie
Zane) Music: Benny Goodman
First performed:
137 Washington Street
Binghamton, New York

1974 A DANCE WITH DURGA DEVI
Music: Tibetan Temple chants
and Bessie Smith
First performed:
American Dance Asylum
Binghamton, New York

NEGROES FOR SALE
Audio Collage: Bill T. Jones
Decor: Arnie Zane
First performed:
Collective for Living Cinema
New York City

ENTRANCES
First performed:
American Dance Asylum
Binghamton, New York

TRACK DANCE
First performed:
State University of New York
Binghamton, New York

1975 COULD BE DANCE
First performed:
American Dance Asylum
Binghamton, New York

DANCING AND VIDEO IN
BINGHAMTON
(in collaboration with American
Dance Asylum, Peer Bode, and
Meryl Blackman)
First performed:
Experimental Television Center
Binghamton, New York

ACROSS THE STREET THERE
IS A HIGHWAY
First performed:
The Farm
San Francisco, California

WOMEN IN DROUGHT
First performed:
American Dance Asylum
Binghamton, New York

ACROSS THE STREET
(in collaboration with Arnie
Zane)
Spoken text: Bill T. Jones
Film: Arnie Zane
First performed:
American Dance Asylum
Binghamton, New York

IMPERSONATIONS
First performed:
American Dance Asylum
Binghamton, New York

EVERYBODY WORKS/ALL BEASTS
COUNT
Music: Jesse Fuller sung
a capella by Arnie Zane and
Lynda Berry
First performed:
Ensemble performance at
American Dance Asylum
Binghamton, New York
Solo Performance at Clark
Center
New York City

1977 FOR YOU
First performed:
Daniel Nagrin Dance Theater
New York City

STOMPS
First performed:
Daniel Nagrin Dance Theater
New York City

WALK
First performed:
Daniel Nagrin Dance Theater
New York City

A MAN
First performed:
Daniel Nagrin Dance Theater
New York City

ASYMMETRY: EVERY WHICH WAY
Music: Lou Grassi
Visuals: Bill T. Jones and
Peer Bode
First performed:
Roberson Art Center
Sears Harkness Theater
Binghamton, New York

DA SWEET STREAK TA LOVE LAND
Music: Otis Redding
Costumes: Bill T. Jones
First performed:
Clark Center
New York City

1978 WHOSEDEBABEDOLL? BABY DOLL
(in collaboration with Arnie
Zane)
Spoken text: Bill T. Jones and
Arnie Zane
First performed:
American Dance Asylum
Binghamton, New York

FLOATING THE TONGUE
First performed:
Kent School for Boys
Kent, Connecticut
The Kitchen
New York City
(1979)

NAMING THINGS IS ONLY THE
INTENTION TO MAKE THINGS
Vocal music: Jeanne Lee
Text and costumes: Bill T. Jones
First performed:
The Kitchen
New York City

PROGRESSO
Set: Bill T. Jones
First performed:
The Kitchen
New York City

BY THE WATER
Text and movement in
collaboration with Sheryl Sutton
Set: Charles Kiesling in
collaboration with Sheryl Sutton
and Bill T. Jones
First performed:
American Dance Asylum
Binghamton

1979 MONKEY RUN ROAD
(in collaboration with Arnie
Zane)
Music: Helen Thorington
Text: Bill T. Jones
Set and Costumes: Bill T. Jones
and Arnie Zane
First performed:
American Dance Asylum
Binghamton, New York

ECHO
Music: Helen Thorington
First performed:
The Kitchen
New York City

ADDITION
Lighting: Carol Mullins
First performed:
Washington Square Church
New York City

CIRCLE IN DISTANCE
Text and movement in
collaboration with Sheryl Sutton
Set: Bill T. Jones and Sheryl
Sutton
Lighting: Carol Mullins
First performed:
Washington Square Church
Binghamton, New York

1980 DANCE IN THE TREES
Music: Jeff Cohan and Pete
Simonson
Costumes: Renata Sack and
Bill T. Jones
First performed:
Hartman Land Reserve
Cedar Falls, Iowa

OPEN SPACES: A DANCE IN JUNE
Music: Dan Hummel, Mark
Gaurmond, Thomas Berry
Costumes: Renata Sack and
Bill T. Jones
First performed:
Waterloo, Iowa

UNTITLED DUET
with Sherry Satenstrom
Music: Dan Hummel, Marcia
Miget, and Dartanyan Brown
First performed:
Recreation Center
Waterloo, Iowa

BALANCING THE WORLD
Lighting: William Yehle
First performed:
University of Northern Iowa
Cedar Falls, Iowa
Amerika House, Berlin

SWEEPS
(in collaboration with Arnie
Zane)
Video: Meryl Blackman
Set: Rosina Kuhn (painting)
First performed:
Zurich, Switzerland

BLAUVELT MOUNTAIN
(in collaboration with Arnie
Zane)
Music: Helen Thorington
Set: Bill Katz
Lighting: William Yehle
First performed:
Dance Theater Workshop
New York City

SISYPHUS
Music: Helen Thorington
Spoken text: Bill T. Jones
Set: Bill T. Jones
First performed:
Terrace Theater,
Kennedy Center
Washington, D.C.

SOCIAL INTERCOURSE:
PILGRIM'S PROGRESS
(assistance by Arnie Zane)
Text and lyrics: Bill T. Jones
Music arranged by Joe Hannon
First performed:
Stewart Theater
American Dance Festival
Duke University
Raleigh, North Carolina, and
The Space, New York City

BREAK
Music: George Lewis
First performed:
Nicollete Island Amphitheater
(sponsored by Walker Art
Center
Minneapolis, Minnesota)

VALLEY COTTAGE
(in collaboration with Arnie
Zane)
Music: Helen Thorington
Text: Bill T. Jones and Arnie
Zane
Set: Bill Katz
Slides: Arnie Zane
Lighting: William Yehle
First performed:
Dance Theater Workshop
New York City

IO
First part: Prologue
Performance for Bicycle, Voice,
Slide, and Dress
Spoken text: Bill T. Jones
IO
Second part: Set for second part:
Bill T. Jones
Lighting: William Yehle
First performed:
Dance Theater Workshop
New York City

AH! BREAK IT!
Music: Jalalu Calvert Nelson
with additional recorded chants
by Bill T. Jones
First performed:
Werkcetrum Dans
Rotterdam, the Netherlands

1982   THREE DANCES
Music: Mozart and Peter
Gordons
Spoken text: Bill T. Jones
First performed:
Harvard University
Cambridge, Massachusetts

ROTARY ACTION
(in collaboration with Arnie
Zane)
Music: Peter Gordon
Lighting: William Yehle
First performed:
New Dance, New York City,
and Vienna Festival
Vienna, Austria

DANCE FOR THE CONVERGENCE
OF THREE RIVERS
(in collaboration with Arnie
Zane)
Music: George Lewis
Collaborations Long Distance
(in collaboration with Keith
Haring, who painted in
performance)
First performed:
Three Rivers Arts Festival
Pittsburgh, Pennsylvania

SHARED DISTANCE
A duet with Julie West
First performed:
The Kitchen
New York City

DUET X 2
A duet with Robe Besserer
A duet with Brian Arsenault
Music: Bach air sung by Brian
Arsenault
First performed:
The Kitchen
New York City

1983 INTUITIVE MOMENTUM
(in collaboration with Arnie
Zane)
Music: Max Roach and Connie
Crothers
Set: Robert Longo
Costumes: Ronald Kolodzie
Lighting: Craig Miller
First performed:
Brooklyn Academy of Music
Brooklyn, New York

FEVER SWAMP
Commissioned by the Alvin
Ailey American Dance Theater
Music: Peter Gordon
Set and costumes: Bill Katz
First performed:
Santa Monica Civic Auditorium
Santa Monica, California

NAMING THINGS
A collaboration with Phillip
Mallory Jones and David
Hammons
Performed with Rhonda Moore
and Poonie Dodson
Music: Miles Davis and
traditional funeral dirge
First performed:
Just Above Midtown Gallery
New York City

21
A solo
First Performed:
Recreation Center
Waterloo, Iowa
(re-created for video with Tom
Bowles, 1984)

CORPORATE WHIMSY
Music: Bryon Rulon
First performed:
Tisch School of the Arts
New York University
New York

CASINO
Music: Peter Gordon
Set: Robert Longo
First performed:
Ohio University
Athens, Ohio

1984 DANCES WITH BRAHMS
Music: Johannes Brahms
Costume: Jimmy Myers
First performed:
Paula Cooper Gallery
New York City,
Leuven, Belgium

1985 1, 2, 3
Music: Carl Stone
Lighting: Robert Wierzel
Set and costumes: Bill T. Jones
First performed:
Joyce Theater
New York City

HOLZER DUET . . . TRUISMS
A duet with Lawrence
Goldhuber
Text: Jenny Holzer
Audio collage: Bill T. Jones
Lighting: Robert Wierzel
First performed:
Joyce Theater
New York City

M.A.K.E.
Audiotaped spoken text: Bill
T. Jones and Arnie Zane
Set: Bill T. Jones
Lighting: Robert Wierzel
First performed:
Joyce Theater
New York City

PASTICHE
Music: James Brown, Eric
Dolphy
Text: William Shakespeare,
Edith Sitwell, Bill T. Jones
Visuals: Found lantern slides
from Arnie Zane
Costume (crown): Marcel Fieve
Lighting: Robert Wierzel
First performed:
Joyce Theater
New York City

FREEDOM OF INFORMATION
(in collaboration with Arnie
Zane)
Music: David Cunningham
Spoken text: Bill T. Jones
Set and visuals: Gretchen
Bender
Lighting: William DeMull
First performed:
Theatre de la Ville
Paris, France

SECRET PASTURES
(in collaboration with Arnie
Zane)
Music: Peter Gordon
Sets: Keith Haring
Costumes: Willi Smith
Hair, makeup, and painting of
fabricated man: Marcel Fieve
Lighting: Stan Pressner
First performed:
Brooklyn Academy of Music
Brooklyn, New York

1986 VIRGIL THOMPSON ETUDES
Music: Virgil Thompson
Costume: Louise Nevelson and
William Katz
Lighting: Craig Miller
First performed:
Chanterelle
New York City
Commissioned for Virgil
Thompson's 90th birthday

ANIMAL TRILOGY
(in collaboration with Arnie
Zane)
Music: Conlon Nancarrow
Sets: Cletus Johnson
Costumes: Bill Katz
Lighting: Robert Wierzel
First performed:
Biennale Internationale de la
Danse
Lyon, France
Commissioned in part by the
Brooklyn Academy of Music
Brooklyn, New York

1987 WHERE THE QUEEN STANDS
GUARD
(in collaboration with Arnie
Zane)
Music: "Verdiana" by Vittorio
Rieti, performed by the St.
Luke's Chamber Ensemble
Set and costumes: Frank
L. Viner
Lighting: Robert Wierzel
First performed:
Triplex Theater
Borough of Manhattan
Community College
New York City
Commissioned by the St. Luke's
Chamber Ensemble

RED ROOM
Music: Stuart Argabright and
Robert Longo
First performed:
Rockwell Hall
Buffalo, New York
Commissioned for Robert
Longo's performance epic,
Killing Angels

1988 THE HISTORY OF COLLAGE
(in collaboration with Arnie
Zane)
Music: Charles R. Amirkhanian
and "Blue" Gene Tyranny
Lighting: Robert Wierzel
First performed:
The Ohio Theatre
Cleveland, Ohio

CHATTER
Music: Paul Lansky
Lighting: Robert Wierzel
First performed:
American Dance Festival
Durham, North Caolina

SOON
Music: Kurt Weill, Bessie Smith
First performed:
Celebrate Brooklyn Festival,
Prospect Park
Brooklyn, New York

1989 DON'T LOSE YOUR EYE
Music: Sonny Boy Williamson
and Paul Lansky
First performed:
Commissioned for Path
Dance Company
Baltimore, Maryland

FORSYTHIA
a duet with Arthur Aviles
Music: Dufay
Recorded dreamtext: Arnie
Zane
Lighting: Robert Wierzel
First performed:
Joyce Theater
New York City

LA GRANDE FETE
Music: Paul Lansky
Costumes and masks: Dain
Marcus
Lighting: Robert Wierzel
First performed:
Joyce Theater
New York City

IT TAKES TWO
Music: Ray Charles, Betty
Carter
Lighting: Raymond Dooley
First performed:
Commissioned by Terry Creach
and Stephen Koester
Dance Theater Workshop
New York City

ABSENCE
Music: Kryzysztof Penderecki,
Hector Berlioz
Costumes: Marina Harris
Lighting and decor: Robert
Wierzel
First performed:
Joyce Theater
New York City

D-MAN IN THE WATERS
Music: Felix Mendelsohn
Costumes: Damian Acquavella
and company
Lighting: Robert Wierzel
First performed:
Commissoned in part by
St. Luke's Chamber Orchestra
New York City

1990 LAST SUPPER AT UNCLE TOM'S
CABIN/THE PROMISED LAND
Music: Julius Hemphill
Text: R. Justice Allen, Ann T.
Greene, Bill T. Jones, Estella
Jones, Heidi Latsky, Sojourner
Truth
Sets and costumes: Huck Snyder
Lighting: Robert Wierzel
First performed:
Next Wave Festival
Brooklyn Academy of Music
Brooklyn, New York

HISTORY OF COLLAGE REVISITED
Music: Charles R. Amirkhanian
and "Blue" Gene Tyranny
Lighting: Robert Wierzel
First performed:
Divisions Dance Company
Cardiff, Wales

1991 HAVOC IN HEAVEN
Music: John Bergamo
Costumes: Liz Prince
Lighting: Robert Wierzel
First performed:
Berkshire Ballet
Albany, New York

1992 BROKEN WEDDING
Commissioned and first
performed by the Boston Ballet
Music: Klezmer Conservatory
Band
Costumes and set: Liz Prince
Lighting: Robert Wierzel
First Performed:
The Wang Center
Boston, Massachussets

DIE OFFNUNG
Commissioned and first
performed by the Berlin Opera
Ballet
Music: John Oswald
Costumes: Liz Prince
Lighting: Robert Wierzel
First performed:
Deutsche Opera Berlin
Berlin, Germany

LOVE DEFINED
Commissioned and first
performed by the Lyon Opera
Ballet
Music: Daniel Johnston
Set: Donald Baechler
Costumes: Bill Katz
Lighting: Robert Wierzel
First performed:
Maison de la Danse
Lyon, France

OUR RESPECTED DEAD
Music: Daniel Johnston
Set: Donald Baechler
Costumes: Bill Katz
Lighting: Robert Wierzel
First performed:
Joyce Theater
New York City

FETE
Music: Paul Lansky
Costumes: Liz Prince
Lighting: Robert Wierzel
First performed:
Joyce Theater
New York City

LAST NIGHT ON EARTH
Music: Kurt Weill, Bessie Smith,
traditional sung by Bill T. Jones
Costume: Rifat Ozbeck
Lighting: Robert Wierzel
First performed:
Joyce Theater
New York City

1993 AFTER BLACK ROOM
by Arnie Zane, restaged by Bill
T. Jones
Set: Robert Wierzel after Arnie
Zane
Lighting: Robert Wierzel
First performed:
Cannes Festivale Internationale
de la Danse
Cannes, France

ACHILLES LOVED PATROCLUS
Music: John Oswald
Audiotaped narrative: Derek
Jacobi reading *The Iliad*
Costumes: Liz Prince
Set: Robert Wierzel
Lighting Design:
Robert Wierzel
First performed:
Joyce Theater
New York City

WAR BETWEEN THE STATES
Music: Charles Ives
Costumes: Isaac Mizrahi
Lighting: Robert Wierzel
First performed:
Joyce Theater
New York City

THERE WERE SO MANY . . .
Music: John Cage
Costumes: Linda Pratt and Jean
Claude Mastroianni
Lighting: Robert Wierzel
First performed:
Joyce Theater
New York City

AND THE MAIDEN
Music: Bessie Jones and Group
from "Georgia Sea Island
Songs"
Costumes: Liz Prince
Set: Bill T. Jones
Lighting: Robert Wierzel
First performed:
Joyce Theater
New York City

JUST YOU
Music: Frank Loesser, Harry
Woods, Coslow Johnston,
Klages-Greer, Cole Porter, and
Hoffman-Manning
Lighting: Robert Wierzel
First performed:
Joyce Theater
New York City

STILL/HERE
Music: *Still:* Kenneth Fragelle,
Traditional sung by Odetta, the
Lark String Quartet and Bill
Finizio; *Here:* Vernon Reid
Video art: Gretchen Bender
Spoken text: participants of
Survival Workshops and
Lawrence Goldhuber
Costumes: Liz Prince
Lighting: Robert Wierzel
First performed:
Biennale Internationale
de la Danse
Lyon, France

ABOUT THE AUTHORS

BILL T. JONES began his dance training at the State University of New York at Binghamton, where he was co-founder of the American Dance Asylum in 1974. Prior to founding the Bill T. Jones/Arnie Zane Dance Company in 1982, Mr. Jones choreographed and performed nationally and internationally as a soloist and as a duet company with his late partner, Arnie Zane. In addition to creating over forty works for his own company, Mr. Jones has been commissioned to create dances for a number of modern and ballet companies, including the Alvin Ailey American Dance Theater, the Boston Ballet, and the Lyon Opera Ballet (where he was appointed resident choreographer in 1993). Mr. Jones has also directed a number of operatic and theatrical works for the Guthrie Theater, the Houston Grand Opera, the Glynbourne Festival Opera, the Munich Biennale, and the BBC. He has been the subject of a number of documentary films, including "The Making of *Last Supper at Uncle Tom's Cabin/The Promised Land*," which was featured on Great Performances, and a forthcoming PBS special on the making of *Still/Here* produced by Bill Moyers. Mr. Jones and media artist Gretchen Bender are currently directing a television version of *Still/Here* that is scheduled to air in the winter of 1995–96.

Mr. Jones has been the recipient of two New York Dance and Performance (Bessie) Awards, a Dorothy B. Chandler Performing Arts Award, the *Dance Magazine* Award, and, in 1994, a MacArthur Fellowship. He lives in a small town outside of New York City.

PEGGY GILLESPIE is a freelance writer whose work has appeared in such publications as *Movement Research*, *The Boston Globe Sunday Magazine*, and *Redbook*. With Lynn Bechtel, she is the co-author of *Less Stress*, a book based on her work at the University of Massachusetts Stress Reduction Clinic. She is also one of the writers and organizers of two touring photo/text exhibits—one on multiracial families, the other on lesbian and gay families. She lives in western Massachusetts with her husband, artist Gregory Gillespie, and their seven-year-old daughter.